KAPWANI KIWANGA

KAPWANI KIWANGA

Off-Grid

Edited by Massimiliano Gioni and Madeline Weisburg

NEW MUSEUM

Contents

Foreword

—

Lisa Phillips

Kapwani Kiwanga's evocative, research-based artworks, which span film, sculpture, performance, and installation, deftly reflect upon some of the most pressing concerns of the contemporary era. Engaging with issues including marginalized histories, the global impact of imperialism, and the surveillance state, Kiwanga's works are notable for both their sociological depth as well as their spatial originality. Her projects maintain an extraordinary physical presence, conceptual dynamism, and sense of formal refinement, and with materials as diverse as sisal, aluminum, live plants, and sand, they become vessels through which history and systems of power intermingle with human desire and bodily experience.

"Off-Grid" demonstrates the New Museum's long-standing commitment to debuting some of the most rigorous and exciting artists from around the world to a New York audience. Installed in the New Museum's Fourth Floor gallery, this exhibition premieres a new commission by Kiwanga through which she bridges historical research with a site-specific spatial intervention. Kiwanga's work is very much of this moment but resonates across multiple histories, and we are confident it will remain compelling and challenging for years to come.

I would like to thank the curators of the exhibition, Massimiliano Gioni, *Edlis Neeson Artistic Director*, and Madeline Weisburg, Curatorial Assistant, for their work in bringing this exciting exhibition to the New Museum. I would also like to thank David Hollely, Director of Exhibitions Management, and his entire team for their work in realizing such a complex installation; in particular: Abby Lepold, Senior Registrar; Carlos Yepes, Registrar; Patrick Foran, Chief Preparator; Arkadiy Ryabin, Audio Visual Preparator; and Olivia Biggs, Production Preparator. I would also like to thank Isolde Brielmaier, Deputy Director; Diane Vivona, Vice President, Advancement; Dennis Szakacs, Chief Operating Officer; and their teams for their support in making this exhibition possible.

This catalogue is the result of a collaborative effort taken on by the exhibition curators, designer Nicholas Weltyk, and editor Sarah Stephenson. I am grateful for their hard work and coordination throughout the book production process. It includes insightful new essays that survey Kiwanga's ambitious installations and sculptures by Glenn Adamson, Rashid Johnson, Kathleen Ritter, and Yesomi Umolu, an interview between Weisburg and surveillance studies scholar Simone Browne, and an extensive interview between Gioni and the artist. I am thankful to these writers for their brilliant texts and reflections.

I'd like to gratefully acknowledge our Board of Trustees and generous sponsors for their support. This exhibition is part of a three-year initiative, launched in collaboration with Kvadrat, to premiere ambitious new productions by emerging artists. Major support for this exhibition is provided by the International Leadership Council of the New Museum. Support is provided by the Toby Devan Lewis Emerging Artists Exhibitions Fund. Artist commissions are generously supported by the Neeson/Edlis Artist Commissions Fund. Additional support is provided by Shelley Fox Aarons and Phil Aarons, and the Kaleta A. Doolin Foundation. I also extend my special thanks to the Artemis Council of the New Museum as well as to Liza Mauer and Andrew Sheiner, and Nicoletta Fiorucci. Education and community programs are supported, in part by the American Chai Trust. This publication is made possible by the J. McSweeney and G. Mills Publications Fund at the New Museum.

"Off-Grid" also owes its success to the generosity of Kvadrat. I extend my sincere gratitude to Anders Byriel, CEO, Njusja de Gier, Senior Vice President of Marketing, and Julia Rodrigues, Advisor, for their steadfast commitment that, throughout the years, has allowed us to produce many ambitious new commissions at the New Museum. These include projects by Daiga Grantina, Petrit Halilaj, Adelita Husni-Bey, Pipilotti Rist, and Cally Spooner. We are thankful for their continued partnership.

This exhibition would not have been possible without the support of Kiwanga's galleries: Galerie Poggi in Paris; Goodman Gallery in Johannesburg, Cape Town, and London; and Galerie Tanja Wagner in Berlin. In particular, I would like to acknowledge Jo Stella-Sawicka from Goodman Gallery for her guidance and advocacy for Kiwanga's work. Ylinka Barotta and the staff of the Moody Center for the Arts at Rice University in Houston provided helpful insight into the production of this exhibition. I would also like to extend my sincere thanks to Loïc Chambon of Studio Kapwani Kiwanga.

Finally, I would like to thank Kapwani Kiwanga for her brilliant installations, which mix elements of the past, present, and future to chart a vision of possibility from within this complex world.

Lisa Phillips
Toby Devan Lewis Director, New Museum

Preface

—

Anders Byriel

Through its unique power of transforming what exists into magical assemblages of new possibilities, art has always been a fundamental way for me to explore and more deeply understand my experience of the world. In this time marked by troubling uncertainties and the looming threat of environmental disaster, I am convinced that, more urgently than ever, we need artists to help us untangle the complexities of our reality and plot images for the future.

The seductive presence of Kapwani Kiwanga's works is only the first layer of a rigorous practice that I see as precise in her use of materials, colors, and scale as it is in terms of a structural critique of our present. The sensorial encounter with her pieces produces poetic yet sharply clear images of our shared troubles but is also generous in sketching fluid routes to move forward. In the completeness of this aesthetic experience, I am reminded again and again of the fundamental power that beauty holds in sustaining hope and joy and of the essential role that they play, in turn, in the daring practice of weaving new visions.

Cross Currents

—

Kapwani Kiwanga in Conversation with Massimiliano Gioni

Massimiliano Gioni: I would like to start by asking how you came to create the type of work you make. We are in a moment in which definitions of art are becoming narrower, particularly when it comes to what is shown in galleries, auction houses, and even museums, with painting being the typically accepted definition of what art is meant to be. It must be particularly difficult for a young artist today to preserve the freedom of making works that are expansive and complex. Do you think your approach was influenced by the fact that you were not initially trained as an artist?

Kapwani Kiwanga: The way I work is mainly responsive. That might have to do with the fact that I didn't have formal training. I didn't go to an undergraduate art program, and I never had aspirations to be an artist. Life brought me to this way of expressing myself. In the past, I tried other ways of communicating, and in the end, I felt that the best fit for me was this particular artistic language, which I had to shape for myself.

The work that I do comes out of close observation of the world and from sitting and wrestling with different questions and concerns that I find of interest. What I am trying to do is find forms that will allow me to share that kind of thinking with other people. I am trying to avoid a closed narrative or an explicit definition of my position, which, of course, is very clear to me, but it's not the aim of my work. My work is an invitation to open up a space of reflection and contemplation, a space that transmits what I may have come across through research and questioning a particular subject matter, feeling, or situation.

The work is born from this individual questioning and then, from a desire to share these questions with other people, to involve them in a conversation. I haven't really defined, formally, what my work is and what it is based on because that changes all the time. My work is often responsive to the place I'm invited to exhibit in, not only the architectural space but also the historical, political, and cultural spaces that envelop them.

I work in a variety of forms—installation, sculpture, performance, video—and I allow myself the flexibility to respond to a specific place. The form I choose for a specific work ends up being the tone in which one addresses a public. The work can feel more intimate at times, or more spatial or more culturally oriented.

MG: Have there been specific examples of artists or artworks that were foundational to you or gave you license to do what you wanted to do?

KK: I wouldn't say there were specific artists or artworks. In a sense, it was much bigger. I always go back to concepts and questions. Concepts are really what inspire me, more than anything else. And by that, I mean thinkers, writers, but also everyday life.

When it comes to artists, I was interested in the Black Audio Film Collective in terms of their structure and working methods. They were working in television, in the art space, and also in cinema.

Before coming to art, I was working in documentary television. The Black Audio Film Collective was quite inspiring in their mobility between different audiences and mediums. Their combination of the political and the aesthetic interested me.

MG: I didn't know you started working in television. Was it in Canada? Was it state TV? There is a whole tradition of experimental television in Canada . . .

KK: At that time, I was living in Scotland, so I was working for British television: Channel 4 and BBC affiliates. I was a freelance director, but I quickly realized that television was not the best place for me. It's a platform I found very interesting initially because it was accessible. You didn't have to go through the doors of a museum or a university. You could just turn on your television and stumble across ideas. But I realized that I wasn't going to be able to express myself in the complexity I felt was necessary for the ideas I wanted to explore. I didn't want to have to fit into the television format, with its specific restrictions. That's how I stumbled into art.

MG: You didn't study art. You studied humanities. How did your education impact your work as an artist?

KK: I studied anthropology and comparative religion. Originally, I was accepted into English literature, but I found the course offerings were not diverse enough.

MG: Where did you study?

KK: In Montreal. The way literature was taught was too limited for me. There was just not enough curiosity for different forms of literature and for the different ways in which humans live and think about the world. Anthropology seemed a bit broader to me. It had its own limitations, but it seemed more open. That was my first training, but I realized that academia wasn't the right place for me. I love the rigor of research in academia—I hold onto the inquisitive approach of academia in my own artistic work. The research approach I bring to my work comes from both natural skills and those I learned in academia. In anthropology and the humanities, you learn to use observation and research to question different social structures and cultural models, which I do in my artistic practice.

MG: I want to ask you about growing up in Canada. My impression—from having lived there for a couple of years as a teenager in the early 1990s—was that conversations around identity and difference were somewhat more sophisticated there than in the United States.

KK: I don't know. I've been living in Europe for most of my adult life, so my perspectives might be quite different now. The Canadian ideal of multiculturalism is probably something I took for granted while growing up. And, to me, it was always clear that within the notion of multiculturalism, there were still different tensions, hierarchies, and power struggles, all of which are still present in Canada.

My upbringing was mostly also very working class, which has made my experience quite naturally open to different cultures and less worried about any presumed construction of a Canadian identity. Actually, the very notion of identity is a concept I always find quite difficult; I am more interested in fluidity and in change if one speaks of identity. The idea that there is always a multiplicity of ways of doing things—whether baking bread or understanding the world—was always very central to my upbringing. I think it probably had more to do with the immediate environment in which I was growing up rather than the nation I was living in.

MG: I don't want to focus excessively on geography, even though it does play an important role in your work, but why did you decide to move to Europe?

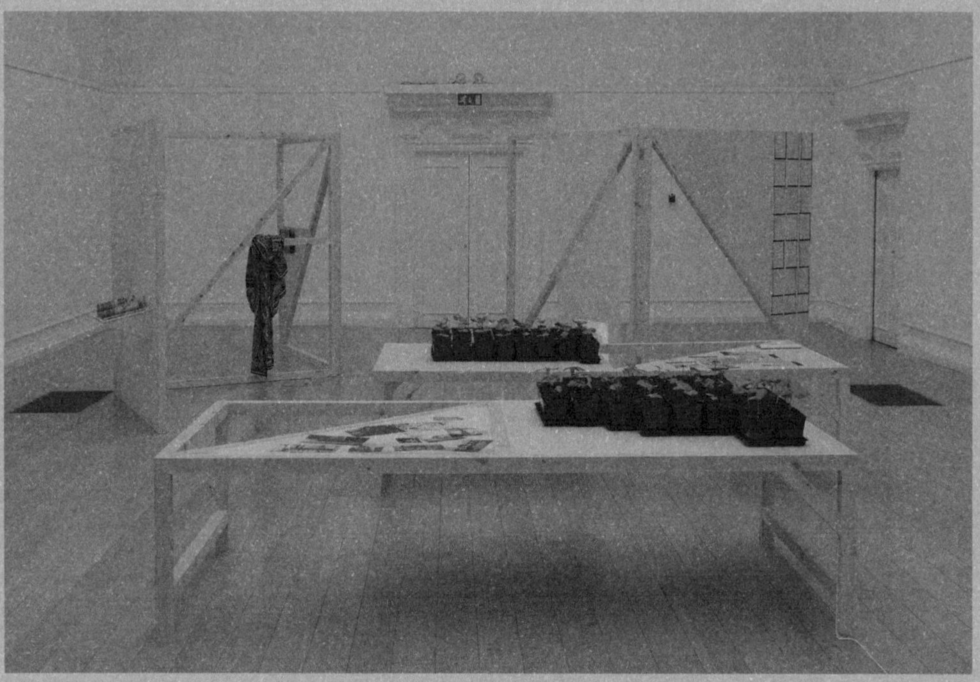

Kapwani Kiwanga, *Kinjeketile Suite*, 2015. Mixed media installation, dimensions variable

KK: I came to Europe wanting to work in cinema since I was drawn to European cinema more than North American cinema. So, I came to Europe wanting to make films. I ended up going to France, more for economic reasons, really. I got a small scholarship to study in Paris.

MG: Some of your earliest works are mixtures of lectures and moving images. How did those early pieces relate to what you were doing in the space of cinema?

KK: The lecture performances were more directly linked to my academic training. They explore discursive space and are about analyzing and critiquing the tools and strategies of knowledge production.

On the other hand, my familiarity with moving images allowed me to weave this material into the performances, and the images, in turn, allowed me to ask questions about truth and fiction, about how facts and truths are constructed. In the lectures, I appear as alter egos. I take on the role of an anthropologist from the future or a conservator of an imaginary museum. In these performances, I am playing with the idea of authority and testing the audience's comfort around truth. This was before "fake news" became a common expression. I was interested in the ways language and text build a certain reality and support a status quo.

I suppose this is how the performances are connected to my experiences in documentary filmmaking. They both deal with the ways in which reality is constructed and revealed through narration. The lecture and the editing room are comparable—they are places where reality is constructed.

MG: Do you think your installations also follow a similar logic of montage?

KK: They are more about layering, which also exists in the realm of cinema. I guess you could say some of my early installations were exploded narratives. Works like *Kinjeketile Suite* from 2015 are research projects that become a type of exploded documentary with my voice in the space and different documents and objects presented in a disassembled narrative. When it came to cinema and the documentary, I was frustrated by the convention of the single screen, which privileges a specific linear narrative. So, for me, working in space became a way of allowing for a multiplicity of perspectives to be embodied by the viewers.

MG: The lecture that became more visible and popular was your *Afrogalactica* piece.

KK: The *Afrogalactica* series is composed as three different lecture performances that are all about forty-five minutes long. They are rarely performed together. That series grew out of an earlier work, from 2009, *The Sun Ra Repatriation Project*, which I call a "video document." I was looking at different people who had known Sun Ra, and then I created an interplanetary communication system, which eventually led me to send a composite sketch of Sun Ra toward Saturn via a radio telescope. The idea was to perform a ritual gesture as a way to return Sun Ra to his origin, as he claimed he was—or had come—from Saturn.

As I was working on this project, I accumulated a lot of other research materials. I had all this extra information and documentation and decided to turn it into a performance. It was my first performance, and it grew out of my research around Afrofuturism.

MG: Would you say these works are the first in which you started your interrogation of African culture? Many of these pieces examine various origin myths and notions of repatriation and return to either native or imaginary lands—I'm curious about how these projects developed and if you see them as autobiographical.

KK: I think my interest in Africa comes from two main considerations. First, there is the continual and deliberate erasure of Africa in every field of knowledge. There is also its omission from most definitions of the future. It is as though a vast majority of the planet cannot imagine a future of which Africa will be part. And then, of course, my interest in Africa also comes from personal interests.

I should say that, even before I started the *Afrogalactica* series, there has rarely been just one geographical or temporal preoccupation in my work. Even the pieces that are very much rooted in Africa, like the series of works around the Maji Maji Rebellion of the early twentieth century, inevitably connect to Europe through its history of colonization and scientific expeditions. My work is interested in weaving these histories together and showing how they are deeply connected.

MG: How did your project *Flowers for Africa* develop?

KK: The *Flowers for Africa* project began in 2012. I was invited to a residency in Dakar, Senegal, where I was thinking about the history of African independence. In Dakar, I started conducting research in the National Archives, alongside other institutions. It was important for me to work with public archives because I was interested in the idea of democratically accessible history.

I was looking through different still and moving images that related to that moment when Senegal—which, at the time, was called the Federation of Mali—separated from France. I wasn't really sure how to use those images, and I was also somewhat uncomfortable about reproducing pictures of politicians—exclusively men—in situations of power. There was also a kind of immediate, seductive quality to those images because they date to the 1960s. They can feel quite nostalgic.

As I was trying to find a way to use these images and make them come alive without succumbing to their nostalgic beauty, I started noticing some floral arrangements in them. It occurred to me that those flowers had been witnesses to history, and I was fascinated by the idea that the transition from one power to another was sanctioned with flowers. To me, the floral arrangements also pointed to all those individuals who had been left out of the frame, out of the picture. The flowers were also connecting history to nature and the nonhuman, putting political and social struggles in relation to the cycles of nature.

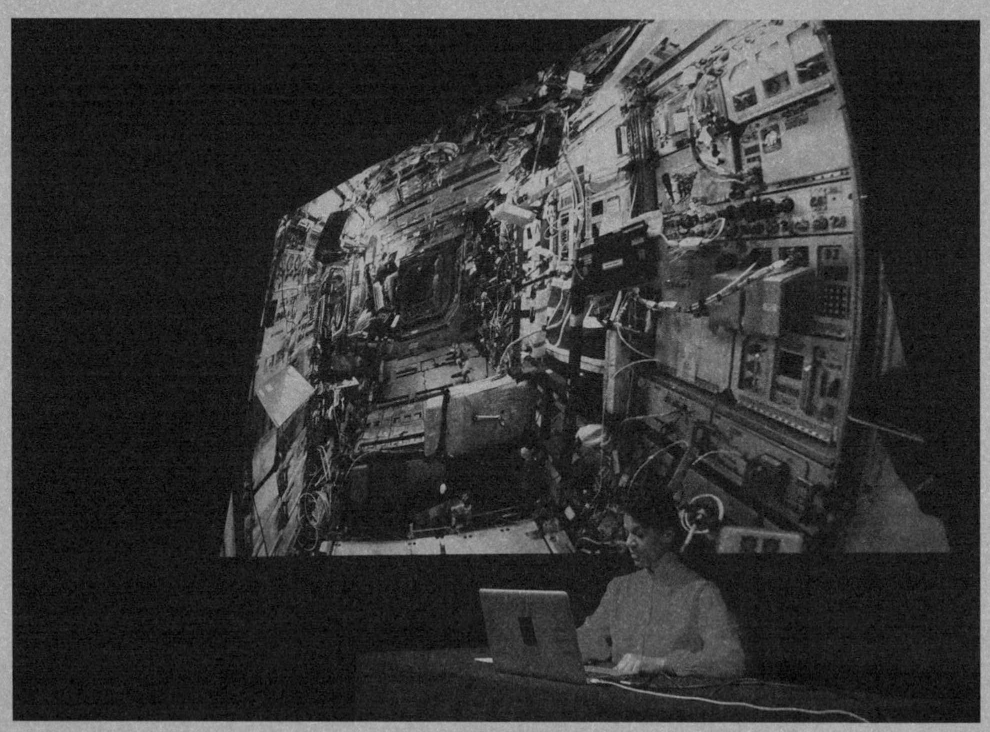

Performance view: Kapwani Kiwanga, *Afrogalactica: A Brief History of the Future*, EMPAC/Curtis R. Priem Experimental Media and Performing Art Center, Troy, NY, 2018

As I started thinking about the flowers, I needed to decide what to do with them. I knew that photos or sculptures were not going to work because they were so definitive and heavy. A performative approach seemed much more appropriate and in line with my interest in change, mutability, and flux. And that's when I realized that, in order to keep things open, embrace change, and accept decay, I needed to work with cut flowers. It was also a kind of antidote to the decorative and the celebratory. You have the flowers in all their beauty, but you also see them decaying, fading, drying away. It recalls the past but is not weighed down by it. The flowers exist in our present and are ephemeral, so there is an interplay between past, present, and future.

As a viewer, you know perfectly well that these compositions are reconstructions, so they immediately make apparent the fact that historical research is always a form of interpretation. And when it comes to the floral arrangements, the interpretations can be very personal, even sentimental. They are not necessarily factual. In a sense, this approach connects all the way back to my *Afrogalactica* research, as it asks: What is fact? What is fiction? *Flowers for Africa* speaks to my distrust of the authority of the documentary image.

MG: How are the floral arrangements made? Do you work with a florist?

KK: I work with florists who live in the cities where I'm showing the pieces. I start a conversation with them, show them the image, and choose the person I want to collaborate with. That person must reproduce the images to the best of their ability. I discuss the historical context with them, and together, we look at the images and discuss the size of the bouquet based on the photographic prints and the spaces where I am showing the work. Pretty much everything else is left to the florist to interpret. Most of the photographs I use as source material are black and white, so the colors are not represented, and the flowers are often out of focus because they are not the focal point; they are usually in the background and, as such, not perfectly reproduced, which leaves room for interpretation. These are very important elements for me—both the question of interpretation and the idea of reappropriating a historic event. History is processed through a body and comes out transformed as an ephemeral sculpture. There is the basic information, which, in itself, is clear enough to be reconstructed and re-created, but I like the fact that the forensics of the whole procedure are quite fluid and open to interpretation, like the images themselves. The flower arrangements can be quite different each time, but that's part of the process: I am not interested in the piece being an exact replica. So that's pretty much what happens. The arrangements are then displayed and left to run their course.

MG: So you leave them to decay?

KK: Yes, that's the protocol. They are meant to stay on view until the end of the show, and then they get composted. If they are part of a permanent collection or a particularly long display, they can be kept on view for up to twelve months; after that, they have to be reactivated, so they don't become a kind of relic, a dried bouquet—that would be too static.

MG: I am curious about your choice to describe some of your works as "protocols." Is the "protocol"—which I am assuming is a set of instructions—an actual physical object, something like a certificate? Does it actually exist?

KK: Yes, it physically exists. Not all my work is based on protocols, but a large part of it is. Some of my installations are based on protocols that describe the light and color conditions and measurements, all the data needed to re-create a piece. For *Flowers for Africa*, the protocol is a document that states the instructions and conditions for the creation of the artworks. The protocol includes the source image used to create the floral arrangement and all the information about how to present the work.

My *Linear* painting series and *pink-blue* and *Patchwork* are also protocol works. These are pieces based on historic research I have made into colors used in different institutions, so the protocol explains how the pieces should be made for each new presentation. Other protocol works include directions on how to interact with the land in a certain way. In the case of *Positive-Negative (morphology)*, the protocol describes how to, for example, extract land from a site and bring it into the exhibition space and how to return it to the site after the exhibition is over.

MG: The word "protocol" immediately connects to the language of bureaucracy and state ceremonial events. It is very loaded but also somewhat parodic, almost a pantomime of the pomposity of official events. The connection between Conceptual art and bureaucracy has been widely discussed in academia. Were you thinking about the whole tradition of Conceptual art and instruction pieces when you conceived of these protocol works? Were precedents such as Seth Siegelaub's artist contract important to you?

KK: I don't consider my use of protocol as a pantomime but rather a care guide. It was the material itself that necessitated this approach, particularly *Flowers for Africa*, which was my first "protocol work." There are very specific, practical questions that the protocol addresses. I needed to find a way to explain under which conditions the work should exist. I am interested in the openness of interpretation, but I also need to provide a set of instructions and boundaries within which that interpretation could take place.

MG: One could say that the other side of the protocol is the studio, the space where the artist works. Does an immaterial artwork require a specific space for its production and conception? These, again, are questions that have been quite crucial in the history of Conceptual art. Is the "protocol" the result of specific needs in your life and in the way you organize your workspace? Do you have a studio?

KK: These works first developed in the continuous back-and-forth between the conditions of production and the ways in which the works are distributed and experienced. My performances, for example, were born out of a very specific economy and the total lack of studio space. I had never studied art, so I had never been trained to think that you needed a studio to make work. And, of course, there was also the fact that I couldn't afford a space of my own. I had myself, my body, a computer. I had access to archives, documents, libraries. That's how the performances were born: out of a specific economy and the tools I knew how to use and had access to.

Now I do have something that resembles a studio, but it is a place where I can assemble some objects and test things out. The actual physical objects are mainly made elsewhere and then brought into the studio to be assembled and looked at or thought about. There is so much work that happens on the computer and in discussions with others, both in the planning and the execution of the shows, so the studio is less about production and more a kind of testing site for compositions. For me, the exhibition space often functions like a studio.

I think, in the end, the studio is a mobile and constantly evolving situation in which each element of a work connects to the other. The space of the studio exists in my head and also wherever I'm collaborating at the moment.

MG: You just said something quite important about your site-specific environmental pieces. You often only see them when they are exhibited. How do you set out to build such works? How do you conceive them and develop them?

KK: It is important to visit the space where I am meant to work. So, usually, it's my body that's first attending to the space and thinking about how to make spaces and experiences within a designated location, or how to make trajectories within a space. And then there is a mental projection and, of course, sketches and tests, but also simple intuition. Some of the spaces I am asked to work in are vast; I can't set up a scale simulation or a model; in that way, the exhibition becomes a test site in itself.

MG: Is there a piece you consider paradigmatic of the way you approach your environmental works? Your 2020 installation *Plot* at the Haus der Kunst in Munich has become an important reference point in your work.

KK: I think it goes back to a more general approach to responding physically to a space. Obviously, the Haus der Kunst is not the easiest of spaces. It was built as part of a very specific strategy: it was commissioned by Adolf Hitler and was meant to make bodies feel a particular way in that space. Working on that project and in the main hall of that building meant trying to propose another position or another way of being in that space. The expression might be a bit overused, but I thought about "soft power." I thought of alternative worldviews to those proposed by the building. I worked with an idea of lightness and transparency, and I tried to create an environment that was enveloping, that held the space in a way that was soft and fluid. It was a way to translate into space a view of the world that could be hospitable and permeable.

MG: The Haus der Kunst was also conceived to promote very specific ideas about race. I am wondering if, in that installation and other works, you think about how spaces are racialized?

KK: I'm always interested in how structures exist, how they are put into place, and how they affect how we move in the world. Those questions can also be "racial," if we want to use that terminology. Personally, I see it more as a question of power. So, with my work, I am trying to understand how power structures are created, through legislation, through urban planning, even through the use of color. Cities and architecture rely on structures that shape space, time, language, and color. How does that serve different power agendas? And how do those structures keep some people in comfortable positions and others in a state of over-alertness and fear? That's what interests me, more than just one specific way of enforcing power.

There are some projects that might appear to be more openly about race or visibility, like my project at MIT List Visual Arts Center, "Safe Passage," but the central question, for me, is to reflect on how the body might understand questions of power imbalances, and either acquiesce or find ways around them. Ultimately, it is about trying to make bodies understand that there might be alternative ways of being in the world, ways that might be more generative. I want these discussions to be felt and experienced in the bodies of the viewers. The politics are embodied. To me, it is a political proposition that is physically rooted: it's about trying to understand how we can change the way we relate to each other and the world. That's how I see spaces and bodies intersecting with each other.

MG: Can you talk about how the project for the New Museum developed?

KK: For the New Museum, I have been thinking about light as a kind of raw material that can be instrumentalized, harnessed, or even weaponized to different ends. In part, the project connects with my exhibition at MIT in 2019. Both shows deal with ideas around surveillance and obscurity, for which the writing of Simone Browne has been important; in particular, in relation to the so-called "lantern laws," which were effective in New York and Boston in the eighteenth century and prohibited enslaved Black and Indigenous people from walking around at night unless they were accompanied by a white person or carrying a lantern.

At the New Museum, in the tall galleries on the fourth floor, I started thinking about creating a space in which the natural light could be refracted and rebounded, subtly diffused. I have been thinking about making objects and sculptures that reflect and obscure light, creating a sense of movement, a space in which light and energy are constantly moving, albeit slowly. This sense of things being in flux is always important in my work.

MG: The use of solar light also immediately alludes to ecological questions . . .

KK: Yes. I have been thinking about what it might mean for a show or a museum to exist off the grid, unplugged, in a sense. So, there is also this proposal inscribed in the show—a kind of alternative imagination of the future.

MG: When thinking about light, geometry, and installation art in New York, one cannot avoid thinking about the legacy of Minimalism and the whole debate around art and objecthood. Do any of these ideas play a role in your work?

KK: In the white cube of the New Museum, it is hard not to be reminded of that tradition, but I have to say that I have never consciously thought of my work in relation to Minimalism. Those conversations come into my work more intuitively. Or you could say that, ultimately, my work shares with those precedents an interest in phenomenology, in the idea of an embodied experience of the self through the spaces around us. I guess one can read my work from that perspective, but there isn't any kind of intentional reverence or reference to that tradition.

I am more interested in how the use of a particular material connects to traditions and cultures outside of the frame of "art." And then there are questions around visibility and opacity, which, to me, are more relevant for this exhibition—this idea of both hiding and affirming one's presence in darkness. This has a particular form when considered in relation to racialized subjects. The show is fundamentally about light, as it exists along a spectrum of visibility. A lot of what interests me about this idea is how light is a type of energy that can be put to use. For example, if one considers surveillance, one sees how lights can be weaponized. This can be seen across a broad range of examples in culture and history—from lantern laws and identity photographs to floodlights used to facilitate the monitoring of civilians.

MG: Is this installation also a reflection on the role museums play in establishing certain regimes of visibility?

KK: I think of the museum as a stage or frame in which people circulate and see each other as they observe artworks. I understand the importance of institutional critique, but I don't approach my work that way. I have created installations that have dealt explicitly with the role museums have played in building certain notions of culture and ownership, particularly through ethnographic displays and collections, but those were interventions within specific museums.

MG: Can you speak more about your show at the MIT List Visual Arts Center in Boston?

KK: The show was entitled "Safe Passage" and was the first time I started thinking about light in relation to the history of colonial North America and particularly the so-called "lantern laws" and their connections with definitions of visibility and opacity.

I developed a series of sculptures that incorporated light. They were generally life-size, as tall as a person, but they were rather futuristic in their design. The sharp lines also contributed to a sense of forms being somewhat fugitive; they were fleeting, escaping. The surfaces of the sculptures were dark, so they absorbed or reflected lights in ways that were different from the surfaces of the white walls surrounding them. The MIT show was very much about artificial light, while the New Museum focuses on natural light.

MG: Speaking of filters, in your most recent show in the US, at the Moody Center for the Arts in Houston, you have used glasses and lenses to capture and refract light. Do you see any direct connection between this show and the exhibitions at MIT and the New Museum?

KK: In the show in Houston, sand plays an important role. I was thinking about how materials can find radically different functions. Sand is used in the fracking process, as well as for making glass. For the New Museum, I am thinking about light as a material as it can be employed in different ways—whether harnessed, refracted, or weaponized. I am fascinated by the idea that even the most solid, inert materials are always in a state of fluctuation. The other central piece at the Moody, the 2021 installation *Maya-Bantu*, also engages with the idea of an unfixed form.

MG: Pieces like *Maya-Bantu*, which uses this peculiar fiber called sisal, have always made me think of forms, commodities, and species migrating across different cultural and economic environments. Just like your *Flowers for Africa* project, your fiber sculptures trace the trajectory of resources that expose a complex network of forces at work on a global scale. With the sisal pieces, you have often emphasized how this fiber was native to Central America, then exported to Tanzania, and became essential for the German economy.

KK: Yes. I think that my work explores how cultures, people, and materials travel and cast roots in different places, mutating and changing. Definitions are built over time. What I try to do with my work is show that these definitions are never final or static. As much as my aesthetic may appear to be pared down, I am interested in multiplicity and complexity.

Escape Velocity

—

Glenn Adamson

"I'm very reluctant to talk about what's happening now. The hot topic; the outrage of the moment. It seems necessary to ask: How did we get here?" Kapwani Kiwanga is in Paris; I am in New York. It's our first conversation, and the date is May 2020. I'm meant to be writing an article about her for *Art in America*, but at that hyperventilated mid-election moment, it seems natural to bring up the latest news. Kiwanga gently deflects me. It becomes immediately clear that she wants to take a wider view. Her art is not a hair-trigger registration of the now but a complex and layered affair, sitting within multiple frameworks of reference. Her thinking is whatever the opposite of instrumental is. All this said, for anyone wanting to understand the present moment, Kiwanga's art offers a way in, and maybe even out.

Kiwanga was born and raised in Canada, and these days is based primarily in Paris. Pandemic lockdowns aside, she has long maintained a peripatetic lifestyle, like so many contemporary artists. She maintains an intensive exhibition schedule in Europe, South Africa, and North America, and when she can, travels to locales that "could be seen to be on the periphery," like Haiti and Morocco. Canada has remained an important reference for her, though, and also a theater of operation. "It's when you're not in a place," she says, "that you realize how much that place is in you." In writing the story of her work, it makes sense to begin where she did.

That was Hamilton, a midsize city in Ontario that used to be surrounded by tobacco farms. These days, much of the land has been converted to ginseng cultivation, and it is common to see greenhouses fitted with a polypropylene fabric called "shade cloth." The canopies diffuse sunlight while permitting air to pass through. Kiwanga brings multiple associations to this utilitarian material. The fabric's bold color and canvas-like texture are reminiscent of modernist abstraction, while its name evokes the slang expression "throwing shade," memorably defined by journalist Anna Holmes as "the art of the sidelong insult . . . a compliment that could be interpreted as the opposite of one."[1]

The plant shelters also reminded Kiwanga of Wardian cases, small glass enclosures used in the Victorian era to protect "exotic" botanical specimens, such as orchids and ferns, outside their home habitats. Shade cloth is a similar technology of displacement and, in this sense, a political material, recalling histories of colonialism. Yet, it is also perforated and easily torn. It's just an agricultural textile, but it seems to Kiwanga to symbolize what she's always seeking: an "exit strategy," which acknowledges the conditions of cultural impasse while also indicating a path forward: "A calling to go around or through."

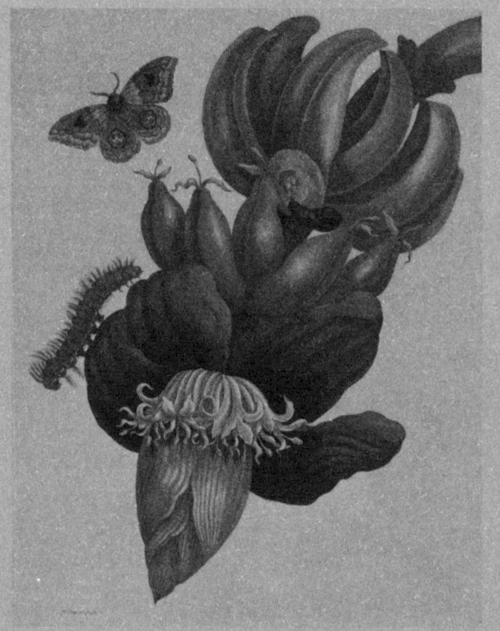

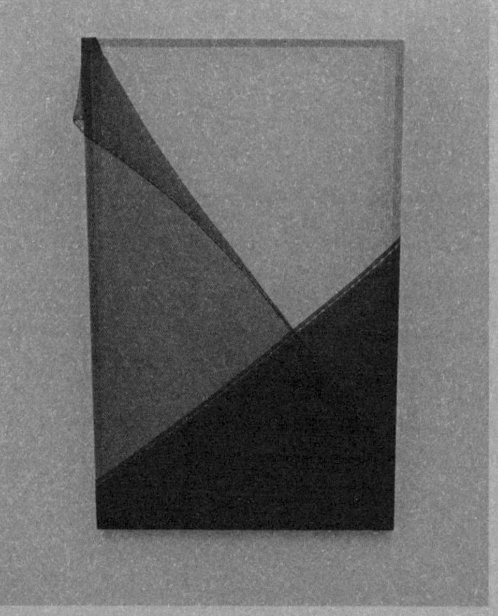

Left: Maria Sibylla Merian, *Banana Tree Flower with Io Moth*, 1702–03. Watercolor with gum arabic over lightly etched outlines on vellum, 15 1/5 × 12 1/5 in. (39.5 × 31 cm)
Right: Kapwani Kiwanga, *Three Shades*, 2018. Steel, wood, shade cloth, epoxy paint, 82 7/10 × 47 1/5 × 15 7/10 in. (210 × 120 × 40 cm)

Kiwanga has used shade cloth in various configurations, including an outdoor sculpture called *Shady* (2018; pp. 190–93), which somewhat resembles a buttressed room divider or a Japanese folding screen that just kept on unfolding, as well as a series of smaller wall-hung works that look like twisted and tilted paintings. These compositions present an experience of visual interference, moiré patterns emphasizing the material's function as a filtering screen. This is an apt metaphor for one of Kiwanga's presiding concerns: the linkage between acts of looking and acts of power. On the one hand, being seen in public is a prerequisite for political agency. On the other, visibility has often meant being a target. This confounding contradiction lies at the heart of Kiwanga's practice and her current presentation at the New Museum.

Before we get to that, though, it's worth considering a further project that Kiwanga staged in her homeland, at the Musée d'art de Joliette in Quebec, in 2018. Titled "Sunlight by Fireside," that exhibition materialized another central theme of her work—the dialectic of place and displacement—in no uncertain terms. Kiwanga had a trench dug outside the museum and the dirt moved into the gallery, an act intended to draw attention to the seizure of land from its Indigenous inhabitants. (It hardly needs emphasizing that, as a Canadian of non-Native heritage, Kiwanga is implicated in that history.) Prior to her physical removal of the earth, she hosted a sort of ritual: an open conversation by a bonfire, in which she and members of the museum staff and the public discussed the issue of decolonization; she remembers the event as "sometimes convivial, sometimes heated." She then had local potters take ashes from the fire, combine them with clay sourced from the region, and make a wall of ceramic tile, formed and fired in such a way as to encourage warping, as if the material itself were expressing the stress and trauma of cultural dislocation.

The method that Kiwanga used here, in which her own authorship is strategically distributed in a community, also informed *Nations*, a series of sewn and sequined wall sculptures made for her in a textile workshop outside Port-au-Prince beginning in 2009. Each includes an image from Haiti's troubled past. *Nations: Ogé's Uprising, 1790* (2020), for example, refers to an insurrection by freemen of color—ultimately unsuccessful—that presaged the Haitian Revolution soon to come and its eventual establishment of a free Black republic. The central image, based on a period print, shows five hands in various attitudes of attack and outreach, prefiguring later gestures of protest and rebellion. Recognition is at issue once again, this time at the scale of the state. Nations, like individuals, may be more or less visible. Kiwanga has provided emblems for a liminal condition, in which a people struggles to be seen as an entity at all.

Kiwanga's recourse to the hands of skilled textile workers in the *Nations* series positions the works in a vernacular context. Materially, they are very close to actual flags, including ceremonial *loa* ("spirit") banners customarily used in Haitian Vodou (important during the Haitian Revolution as a "galvanizing force," as Kiwanga points out). Having provided her artisan collaborators with a basic design and image, the artist intervened as little as possible in their formal choices, even leaving key matters like color selection up to them. There are certainly precedents for this. Alighiero e Boetti springs to mind. Kiwanga rejects such comparisons, though, at least to the extent that they become a rubber-stamping exercise. She has no interest in "circling back to what has already been validated. . . . I have affinity and respect for those that came before, but so much more interest in social science. Theory comes first, and then I navigate it through the body."

In 2020, Kiwanga staged an exhibition animated by exactly that principle at Kunstinstituut Melly (formerly Witte de With) in Rotterdam. It showcased another area of her research interests, the history of vernacular botany as a technique of resistance—part of her ongoing interest in the idea of nature as an archive in its own right. Particularly arresting, to her, was the propagation of plant-based knowledge among "maroon" communities, made up of self-liberated, formerly enslaved people and their descendants, who lived secretively on the periphery of colonized societies. Kiwanga was struck by the strategies they used, the way they would "meld with their environment in order to survive. They cleared land, but did not impose rigid structures on it, extracting in a more or less gentle way from the earth, leaning into what already exists."

There is clearly a model here for how we might all live differently, lighter on the land. The idea of rural refuge also took on unexpected associations with the onset of the pandemic; even as Kiwanga's show was opening, flight from the cities was at its peak. But true to form, her explorations of marronage are specific and subtle, rather than programmatic. Two stories from Suriname, on the northeastern coast of South America, had particularly captured her attention. One describes the use of plant-based toxins among enslaved people, either to assassinate plantation holders or perform self-abortions, so that a child would not be born into slavery. Another tells of women who, fearing capture or forced displacement, braided rice into their own or others' hair, carrying that seed bank with them to their uncertain future.

Kiwanga gave literal shape to these motifs in Rotterdam. Her work *Semence* (2021) consists of grains of African rice (*Oryza glaberrima*) rendered hyper-realistically in ceramic, a gesture that immediately called to mind Ai Weiwei's porcelain sunflower seeds, but to approximately opposite effect. Ai's innumerable fabricated seeds have a deathly effect of crushing sameness and could be read as a critique of political conformity in contemporary China. Each of Kiwanga's grains feels like a little package of life, a tribute to individual resilience. The exhibition also included blossoms made of paper, springing up from yellow platforms like so many magic tricks, based on the peacock flower (*Caesalpinia pulcherrima*), which can be used as a natural abortive. She titled these *The Marias* (2020; pp. 117–19), a name redolent of Christianity, of course, and also a somewhat arcane reference to Maria Sibylla Merian, a pioneering naturalist who worked briefly in Dutch Surinam centuries ago. (Merian's illustrated *Metamorphosis insectorum Surinamensium*, published in 1705, broke new ground by depicting butterflies, caterpillars, and beetles in their natural habitats, crawling along the very plants that they did in nature—an early step toward the understanding of ecological interdependency.) Primarily, though, Kiwanga's elegant bouquets are objective correlates for the women of the African diaspora. All those Marias: strategic poisoners, women transporting in their hair the means of their own self-preservation, whose stories are all but lost to us. They are conjured here as figures of inventive disruption, who lived in a world of horror and found a way to outwit its rules. If they could manage that, her work implicitly asks, what might we be able to do?

Kiwanga's exhibition at the New Museum extends this thinking into a more obviously contemporary framework. The title, "Off-Grid," certainly resonates with the idea of marronage—of life grown in the interstices of power—and also glances sidelong (throwing shade, as it were) at the grid's central place in art history, famously theorized by Rosalind Krauss as embodying "modern art's will to silence, its hostility to literature, to narrative, to discourse."[2] Most explicitly, though, "Off-Grid" is a reference to the technological infrastructures that undergird our lives and the persistent utopian impulse to evade them, picking out a new pattern in the shadows.

This is a topic she first investigated in her series *Glow* (2019), initially shown at the MIT List Visual Arts Center in her 2019 exhibition "Safe Passage." These are black, human-size geometric monoliths, each with a single embedded LED light. The sculptures call twenty-first-century police floodlights to mind, but for Kiwanga, the more important allusion is to eighteenth-century lantern laws, as described in Simone Browne's scholarly study *Dark Matters: On the Surveillance of Blackness*. These ordinances required enslaved people to carry lit candles with them by night if they were not accompanied by a white person—a disturbing legal precedent for Jim Crow sundown laws and contemporary racial profiling. Kiwanga's forms recall commercial lighting fixtures, but their scale and silhouette make them something far less familiar. Like her works in shade cloth, the *Glow* sculptures make reference to the unstable power dynamics of visibility. They could be read as stand-ins for Black bodies under scrutiny, but also as watchful sentinels, the ones doing the scrutinizing.

There's a reference here to Foucault's famous argument about the panoptic disciplinary regime: when surveillance is internalized, subjectivity does its own self-policing. That key insight has new force these days, given the new watchers that tech companies have inveigled into our homes and pockets. It's no coincidence that

Kiwanga's monoliths have the sleek design of a lately launched smartphone. Yet, as ever in her work, there's also a sense that power can, in fact, be eluded. The implied incipient movement of the *Glow* sculptures—they seem like they might start up under their own power, gliding right out of the gallery in eerie silence—embodies the principle of fugitivity that Kiwanga sees as essential to her work.

In "Off-Grid," these themes are applied to the scale of the whole exhibition. As a starting premise for the project, Kiwanga determined that she would use only natural light to illuminate the space—not as easy as it sounds, as the gallery in question, on the New Museum's Fourth Floor, contains only a modest skylight and few windows. In this sense, the exhibition's title is quite literal. It denotes a splendid isolation from the energy economy that we operate, all day, every day, at such high cost. Likewise, light is liberated from its prevalent instrumentality. We may not notice because the phenomenon is so pervasive—just as fish don't realize they are in water—but light has become an unprecedentedly powerful material of social control. It is almost entirely through its manipulation that we distribute information (through our innumerable screens) and gather it (through our equally legion technologies of surveillance).

In a single stroke, by enacting her own independent light system, Kiwanga severs herself from these unwelcome contingencies. (Here, one might think again of Merian and her miniature ecosystems.) Within this carefully engineered pocket of space, light runs free. It is, to use another overdetermined term of art theory, "autonomous"—an idea strongly associated with abstraction and the ideal of a pure act of looking. Kiwanga strategically displaces this value from formalist aesthetics to functionalist ethics. "I wanted to show how light can not be weaponized," she says, "but remain generative."

The word "remain" there is important. As noted, she has never been one for chasing the latest thing, but in "Off-Grid," she is tapping into something beyond ancientness itself. The age of light is another we tend to lose track of, perhaps because it's so difficult to wrap our little human minds around it. Moonlight, by the time we see it, is a little more than a second old; sunlight, 8 and 1/3 minutes. Alpha Centauri, the star closest to our solar system, is more than four light-years away; the light from the most distant stars we can see with the naked eye has been coming toward us for about four thousand years. Thus, we are bathed in temporal differentiation all day, every day, our whole lives through. When we choose to harness this energy—by growing crops, using solar panels, or manufacturing hormones within our own bodies—it may appear to us reborn. But as a simple matter of physics, we are only redirecting it. As Kiwanga puts it, "Light is continually rebounding, refracting. It is unfixed, in continual flux."

Viewed from this cosmic perspective, "Off-Grid" has unexpected connections to Afrofuturism, a worldview that she has investigated in earlier projects—notably, her performance lecture *Afrogalactica,* first realized in 2012. Here, she assumes the role of a future anthropologist, looking back at the formation of a pan-African state and its space exploration efforts. The script is littered with sly allusions—like that to the lead vessel in the interstellar fleet, "*Black Star*, the mothership," a nod to both Marcus Garvey and George Clinton. The pose that Kiwanga adopts in this piece, that of a coolly disinterested scientist, is as far as possible from the Napoleonic stylings of Garvey or Clinton's ludic funk jams, including, let's definitely not forget, the five minutes and forty-six seconds worth of disco-inflected perfection that is Parliament's "Flashlight." But Kiwanga has placed herself, thoughtfully and precisely, in that Black intellectual lineage, which, as Mark Dery has written, "offers a mythology of the future present, an explanatory narrative that recovers the lost data of historical memory, confronts the dystopian reality of black life in America, demands a place for people of color among the monorails and the Hugh Ferriss monoliths of our tomorrows."[3]

There is also another, less hopeful, sort of future implied in "Off-Grid"—that of imminent social collapse. We've all seen that movie, the one where characters stumble through a postapocalyptic scenario, the lights guttering, powering down, and never coming back on again. Not that we need to imagine what it would be like if museums went dark. For that is exactly what happened during the worst of the Covid-19 pandemic. It remains to be seen whether that was a once-in-an-institutional-lifetime anomaly or a glimpse of things to come.

Kiwanga encourages us to stare directly into this bleak prospect, allotting just enough blank space in the installation for us to fill it with our free-floating anxieties about climate change and political conflagration. This is well and truly the void, and not in the transcendent manner of, say, Yves Klein, or for that matter, the harmless banality of Martin Creed's 2000 *Work No. 227: The Lights Going On and Off* (which is just what it sounds like). Nor, however, does Kiwanga give us simply a howling emptiness. She can't pretend to give us a map, but she has populated the exhibition with navigation tools.

This is one of the most interesting aspects of her work in general, and "Off-Grid" in particular—and here I use the term "interesting," as Sianne Ngai has proposed, as a means to "facilitate our return to the object for judging at a later moment, like sticking a Post-It in a book."[4] Kiwanga stages just such a deferral, in which both utopian and dystopian potentialities remain active. Step on in, adjust yourself to the tiny extra-territorial space she has provided, and you may well feel a sense of release, even the stirrings of hope. Maybe that's all we need. For, as a wise man once said, everybody's got a little light under the sun.

This essay is adapted from an article that originally appeared in Art in America, *July 30, 2020.*

1 Anna Holmes, “The Underground Art of the Insult,” *New York Times*, May 14, 2015, https://www.nytimes.com/2015/05/17/magazine/the-underground-art-of-the-insult.html.
2 Rosalind Krauss, “Grids,” *October* 9 (Summer 1979): 50.
3 Mark Dery, “Afrofuturism Reloaded: 15 Theses in 15 Minutes,” *Fabrikzeitung*, February 1, 2016.
4 Sianne Ngai, “Merely Interesting,” *Critical Inquiry* 34, no. 4 (Summer 2008): 784.

Weaving Fabrics

—

Yesomi Umolu

"Opacities can coexist and converge, weaving fabrics. To understand these truly one must focus on the texture of the weave and not the nature of its components."
—Édouard Glissant, *Poetics of Relation*, 1990[1]

The late Martinican poet, novelist, and theorist Édouard Glissant conceived of opacity as an unquantifiable difference. A key concept within his pivotal 1990 book *Poetics of Relation* is that opacity exposes transparency. For Glissant, transparency is a building block of Western thinking and, by extension, the colonial project. Transparency seeks to make things understandable and known within the confines of Western epistemology. This creates a context wherein non-Western knowledge, identities, and cultures are encapsulated through the Western gaze—where difference is identifiable and serves to keep things apart. Conversely, opacity is difference that is expansive; it is that which establishes relations between things.

Reflecting on Glissant's work, American poet Fred Moten explains:

> Opacity implies a sort of blurring or obscuring, a complication, but it also still implies the capacity to see through, to see through that complication, and to see through it even if that seeing through produces something that others might want to think of as a kind of distortion or a lack of clarity. . . . What opacity implies is a kind of ongoing devoted thinking. . . . Not just seeing something, but also seeing through something. And within that context, knowing is a project, is an activity, that doesn't come to an end.[2]

When I probed Kapwani Kiwanga during a recent conversation initiated in preparation for this text on the theories that influence her practice, she remarked upon Glissant's and Moten's writings. Although she makes the distinction that her artworks are not derivative of existing concepts from the likes of these two thinkers, she noted that they are in affinity with them. To this end, I would like to reflect on the idea of opacity—as an unquantifiable difference and complication of things—when thinking through Kiwanga's work. I use "things" here as a general category—the term describes myriad subjects, materials, methodologies, narratives, and so forth that traffic through the work. This is by no means an exhaustive account, however, but a sketch of her practice.

Knowing

It is an oft-cited fact that Kiwanga studied comparative religion, anthropology, and documentary film en route to developing her artistic career. The research-based study and investigative fact-finding underscoring the artist's practice are certainly testaments to her earlier training. Like many of her contemporaries, Kiwanga starts with a question and then draws on research from various sources, including archives, books, and articles, to inform her artworks. Sometimes these pieces incorporate found texts and documents synonymous with the findings of an inquiry, while others translate and transmute research into blocks of bright color on canvas, natural fibers fashioned into sculptures, or light-filled environments.

Much has been written about the anthropological turn in contemporary art,[3] where artists take on the role of researchers, parsing through archives and material culture to create pieces that produce or reveal associations between things.[4] Kiwanga's work certainly has affinities to such practices, not least expressing a shared interest in critiquing normative ways of organizing knowledge within the Western paradigm. For instance, in her early lecture performances and video works, such as *The Conservator's Tale* (2015) and *Afrogalactica: A Brief History of the Future* (2012), Kiwanga assumes the role of a conservator/archivist and an anthropologist from the future, respectively, enacting how people in these professions engage with material culture and histories. Both works reflect on different forms of world-building. In the former, Kiwanga considers the construction of Western subjectivity through an accumulation of things from other places; in the latter, she explores futurity and the possibility of the post-colony through popular culture archives. The characters the artist inhabits are, of course, stand-ins for Kiwanga herself, mirroring her own process of researching a multitude of topics, from science fiction to museology, space travel to Afrofuturism.

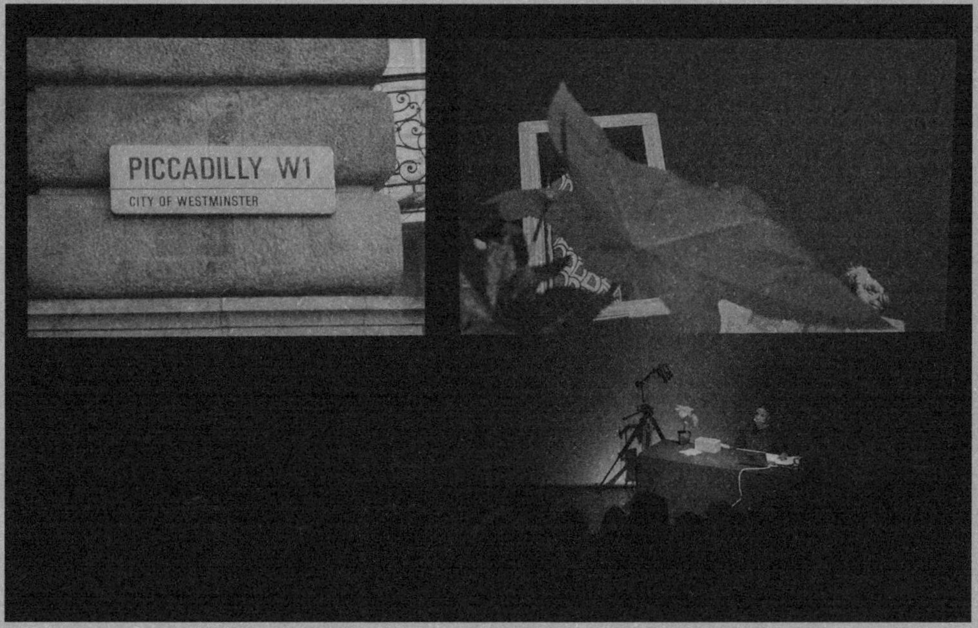

Performance view: Kapwani Kiwanga, *A Conservator's Tale*, La Ferme du Buisson, Noisiel, France, 2017

Through opening her artistic research to performative reconstruction, in these works, Kiwanga brings to the fore the subjective, speculative, and fictional dimensions of any given conception of the world—whether rendered through scientific fieldwork, formal and informal belief systems, cinematic rendition, or artistic representation. This approach connects directly to Glissant's project and his deployment of opacity as a means of making a different world—beyond the colonial—with political intent. In Kiwanga's work, we often see a privileging of the unquantifiable difference of Afro-diasporic and transnational perspectives, one that attempts to see and see through the complication of slavery, colonialism, and racial capitalism to image and imagine a different world.

What does imaging and imagining a different world imply for the artist? During our conversation, Kiwanga gave me pause for thought when remarking that she resists creating images despite her image-making background. If images are considered singularities (fixed points in time) and, by extension, are the very evidence of transparency (all that is known or perceivable sits within the frame), then Kiwanga resists making them by working with and through fragments and details. In this way, her work subverts learned approaches to analyzing, organizing, and constructing knowledge or images and evades fixed or totalizing forms to arrive at a practice of knowing that ostensibly aligns with Glissant's and Moten's words above.

By way of illustration, an early video piece, *Vumbi* (2012; pp. 210–11), depicts the artist on a rural roadside in Tanzania tending to a wall of vegetation covered in red dust. Kiwanga carefully selects individual leaves and wipes away the dust from their surfaces to reveal a lush green color. The newly green leaves create interruptions in the otherwise monolithic form, introducing difference into the whole. Here, we see the artist engaged in a persistent act of care, undeterred even when passing cars cause more dust to inevitably resettle on the leaves. It is perhaps not a stretch to suggest that *Vumbi* is demonstrative of the devoted thinking *and doing* that run throughout Kiwanga's practice—one that takes care to reveal what lies beneath and beyond the surface. Moreover, when we pay close attention to the moments when dust hangs in the air—when the artist is partially engulfed in a hazy plume of red and the moving image hovers at the threshold of legibility and illegibility—we come to further understand the complication at the heart of Kiwanga's practice. It is invested in simultaneously revealing and obscuring things.

Blurring

Throughout Kiwanga's oeuvre, we encounter different screens, blinds, curtains, and architectural enclosures that simultaneously shield and expose. We see this in works such as *Shady* (2018; pp. 190–93), the artist's large-scale sculpture featuring shade cloth, an agricultural fabric of different colors, which is shown stretched and layered across a large steel frame. Taking advantage of the cloth's ability to moderate light and, consequently, evoke different degrees of visibility, the sculpture offers a range of transparencies or opacities. *Jalousie* (2018; pp. 166–67) achieves a similar effect by using a series of louvered and vertical two-way mirrors to permit, obstruct, or reflect views as people move around it. In both these works and others, Kiwanga intentionally distorts the viewer's field of vision, altering their senses and perception.

While these artworks physically embody processes of revealing and obscuring (present throughout her practice), it is important to note that they should not be reduced to solely inducing a phenomenological effect. Rather, as they align with Moten's reading of opacity as a blurring, they create a space where the very nature of knowing—whether in relation to acquired knowledge, our physical understanding of an object, or our bodies in space—is brought into question. As Kiwanga remarks:

> I'm not trying to restate what one knows. I'm . . . trying to see what ways to get past what we know. To do that requires very simple things like just looking at it differently, or just even looking at it for the first time. And it's about being able to sit with it long enough that you can allow yourself different ways beyond it. These "exit strategies" are very personal but they can be collectively experienced as well. It's not completely revolutionary, but being aware of one's body in relation to power and to space, that can be an invitation to think of an exit strategy.[5]

Another crucial complication in Kiwanga's work is how it converges Western and non-Western epistemologies, which the artist derives from her anthropological studies and transnational background. Kiwanga admits that despite being a "forerunner and enabler of colonialism," anthropology was also a primary meeting point for Western and non-Western knowledge.[6] This criticism, which continues to be leveraged at anthropology today, is due to the fixity of its occidental approach to knowledge and its rendering of global cultures through the limited prism of Western academia. Consequently, as a field that has been deeply invested in being the repository for knowledge about all humanity, anthropology is de facto an encapsulation of Glissant's conception of transparency.

Kiwanga, however, has remarked that "one of the constructive things that anthropology created—and that I've found feeds into my practice—is the reflexive opening up of a text."[7] Here, the artist refers to the recasting of the anthropological paradigm in the 1970s to consider it a subjective medium. This led to an evolution in the discipline's methodologies that redefined the anthropologist's authority and the authenticity of their work, especially as it relates to fieldwork and its attendant documents. If an earlier tradition, predicated on transparency, posited fieldwork as a site of one-directional extraction and located the knowledge derived therein as objective truth, then reflexivity considers it an encounter between subjectivities and knowledge as unfixed.

For Kiwanga, reflexivity offers the possibility of playing with different codes, switching subjects, and articulating power dynamics (both within and beyond the colonial sphere), while acknowledging her own position.[8] She has said that her work "often [deals] with questions of power imbalances, but it's never as if there are two poles that are fixed. They are always positions that slide between the extremes on various spectrums."[9]

Weaving

In 2015, Kiwanga presented her first solo exhibition in the United Kingdom at the South London Gallery. Here, she explored the story of the Maji Maji uprising—a major rebellion and resistance movement in colonial East Africa that took place in present-day Tanzania between 1905 and 1907. The installation comprised of fabrics draped and stretched, fibers loosely gathered and woven, documents laid and pasted, screens blocking and revealing, plants growing and withering, spoken words, and moving images. A veritable confluence of things, the exhibition recounted the tale of the spiritual medium Kinjeketile, who inspired an indigenous population to fight their German colonizers without fear of death thanks to *maji maji* (sacred water), which gave powers of immortality to those who consumed it.

The components that made up the installation, including fabric, rope, documents, screens, plants, words, and images, articulated different threads in this story. The traditional *kanga* fabric bearing inscriptions alluded to the "all-seeing eye" of Kinjeketile; the sisal rope represented the extractive economy of the colony; the documents offered an abridged archive; the screens staged the research site; the castor plants suggested nature's healing qualities; the recorded words and images offered contemporary evocations of events past.

The exhibition was emblematic of Kiwanga's approach to staging meeting points in time, wherein she illuminates overlooked histories or perspectives in order to challenge systems of domination. By placing different objects, materials, and narratives in relation—oscillating between what is known and unknown—Kiwanga makes visible things that have been obscured, inaccessible, or rendered invisible. This is the same care she expresses in *Vumbi* as she attends to seemingly inconsequential things that go unnoticed or are otherwise ignored. Indeed, with the story of the Maji Maji, Kiwanga brings to the fore the convergence of colonial subjugation with African liberatory movements, training her lens on the agency of African knowledge systems (represented here by Kinjeketile) in the face of colonial power. Moreover, the artist reveals the relationship between raw materials, land, and extractive economies in the colony to the contemporary nation-state, with the sisal pointing to the continued relevance of this imported cash crop to Tanzania.

Elsewhere, the artist has worked with other raw materials and commodities such as rice, sand, and ash to illustrate their sociopolitical and economic impacts. Kiwanga's weaving of historical events with material histories and contemporary conditions extends to the artist's recent explorations of race, the surveillance state, and technologies of visibility. This is through her research into contemporary policing tactics and historic legal ordinances in the United States, which have engendered the forced visibility of Black Americans through the weaponization of light. In these works, Kiwanga meditates on Blackness being imbued with the ability to moderate and even evade light, like the shade cloth, or, indeed, to engage in fugitive acts of defiance, like the Maji Maji. Her continued adeptness at deploying opacity—as a material condition and an exit strategy—to expose the limits of prevailing regimes of visibility and representation is compelling.

Returning to Glissant's metaphor of weaving, it indicates that there is abundant, even radical potential in opacities coexisting and converging to create new fabrics, new realities. By focusing on the texture of the weave—the forms crafted when differences coalesce and evade illumination—Kiwanga arrives at an expansive understanding of things.

1 Édouard Glissant, *Poetics of Relation*, trans. Betsy Wing (Ann Arbor: University of Michigan Press, 1997), 190.

2 Nehal El-Hadi, "Ensemble: An Interview with Dr. Fred Moten," *MICE Magazine: Opacities*, no. 4 (June 2018).

3 Kaelen Wilson-Goldie, "The Stories They Need," *Frieze*, September 25, 2014, https://www.frieze.com/article/stories-they-need.

4 I am thinking here of the work of Gala Porras-Kim, Candice Lin, and others, which expressly deals with the vestiges of anthropology and its impact on the status of cultural objects, especially those relating to Western collecting and museological practices from the colonial era to the present day.

5 Kate Brown and Kapwani Kiwanga, "I'm Proposing Many Ways of Seeing: Artist Kapwani Kiwanga on Unearthing Buried Histories to Imagine the World Anew," *Artnet*, August 20, 2020, https://news.artnet.com/art-world/kapwani-kiwanga-interview-1901953.

6 Adrienne Edwards and Kapwani Kiwanga, "Those Cracks Which Allow Things to Grow Out of Them Are Interesting to Me," *Frieze*, May 10, 2018, https://www.frieze.com/article/those-cracks-which-allow-things-grow-out-them-are-interesting-me.

7 Edwards and Kiwanga, "Those Cracks."

8 This is, of course, a position affected by the artist's training as well as her trans-national heritage.

9 Ella de Elzen, "Present Futures: In Conversation with Kapwani Kiwanga on Power, Archival Research and Plants," *Public Parking*, February 5, 2021, http://thisispublicparking.com/posts/present-futures-in-conversation-with-kapwani-kiwanga-on-power-archival-research-and-plants7.

Sodade

—

Rashid Johnson

"Who showed you . . .
this distant way?
Who showed you . . .
this distant way?
This way . . ."
—Cesária Évora, "Sodade," 1992

sau·da·de
/sou'dädə/
n. a feeling of longing, melancholy, or nostalgia that is supposedly characteristic of the Portuguese or Brazilian temperament.[1]

As of late, I've found that this cold, wet winter has taken a toll on me. I feel a longing for warmth and the peace that comes from exposed toes and uncovered fingers. The beautiful voice that belongs to the Cape Verdian singer Cesária Évora is the thing that is keeping me most sane. It is her song "Sodade," in particular, that has drawn most of my attention. In this song, performed in Cape Verdean Creole, I find a spirit that both uplifts and makes conscious the struggles, sadness, and longing that often accompany peoples who have been subject to colonial structures of oppression. This term, *sodade*, as understood in Évora's native language, exercises a nimbleness that few words are able to accomplish. Its ability to speak with a sense of nostalgia while keeping us in the present leads me to the work of the artist Kapwani Kiwanga.

Kiwanga employs a set of tools and a delivery system that produce radical opportunities for interpretation. The work is at once an homage to its art-historical antecedents and a stark rebuke of the structures that fostered these ideas. It is this duality that draws me closer to her project. There is a rigor and research in Kiwanga's work that forces us to listen and respect its seriousness. At the same time, there's a poetry that spirals us into the potential to dream. These are the dichotomies that often find themselves present in the most successful artistic projects. Kiwanga offers us the opportunity to be taught, embraced, scolded, and soothed simultaneously. Can something be the father, the mother, the foe, and the friend? I've often found that the best artworks manifest these goals. All of this said, the power that exists in beauty is never lost on Kiwanga. For all of the work's attempts to unpack its unruly subjects, it continues to commute and carry beauty as its most humble passenger. It is these things that lead me back to the hauntingly beautiful words of Évora: "Who showed you . . . this distant way?" It appears Kapwani Kiwanga is one of our guides.

1 *Oxford Dictionary of Difficult Words*, comp. Archie Hobson (Oxford: Oxford University Press, 2004), s.v. “saudade.”

Surveillance Studies

—

Simone Brown in Conversation with Madeline Weisburg

Madeline Weisburg: Some people think of mass surveillance as a relatively new phenomenon—a byproduct of digital technology. I am thinking of the NSA, data collection in the service of targeted advertising, the theater of security at airports. But in your book *Dark Matters: On the Surveillance of Blackness*, you also frame surveillance in relation to much older technologies—including artificial light and printed text—that continue to have analogues in the rubric of mass-surveillance practices today. Specifically, these are informed by methods of policing Black life that date back to slavery. In other words, technology has been used for a very long time as a tool of observation and control that is modulated based on who you are.

Simone Browne: When I first started thinking about surveillance and the study of it proper, I found that histories and accounts regarding the way Black people cope with, deal with, undergo, and also resist surveillance were never really part of the conversation. In all of the examples you lay out in your question, around the theater of security at the airport, for instance, or maybe even the impression of security established around Covid now—like temperature checks when we enter places and so on—and the post-Snowden data collection we know about, there are still ways in which race is fundamentally embedded. Surveillance can be seen as the operating system of race and racism.

MW: Essential to your work is the concept of "racializing surveillance." I'm wondering if you could talk about your choice of presenting this idea as an operative "-ing" phrase.

SB: I see it as active. Through surveillance practices, race gets reified—that is what I meant by racializing surveillance. Historically and presently, surveillance is a way of reifying borders, bodies, performances, and acts. For example, you can think of the census and the shifting ways race has been defined and then indexed through that practice in the US. Or you have the redefinition of voter ID laws across the country now, which is an ongoing strategy to roll back decades of progress on voting rights. The process of reification is very pervasive, and it's at work even in popular culture and entertainment.

In the NFL, for example, they invented the notion of "race-norming"—a concept utilized until last year or so where Black football players were assumed to have a lower baseline cognitive function, and therefore, the NFL would make it harder for those players to say they have cognitive impairment due to head injuries caused during football games. All of this is, of course, a disturbing example of an inherently anti-Black form of scientific racism.

The same goes for when we think about kidney disease. There is another kind of "race-norming" practice in how measurements are taken. When doctors estimate how a body filters creatinine, they add a caveat for those that are African American, which makes it much harder for people to receive accurate results or gain access to the healthcare they need—such as kidney transplants or other imperative medical procedures.

Racializing technologies are also very much present in the ways in which the Covid emergency is being handled right now. For example, pulse oximeters measure blood oxygen levels, but if you have darker nail beds, the readings might not be as accurate. Technologies like these are designed for a prototypically light or white body, and the racial implications of such technologies can have really negative health effects.

I wanted to think about surveillance within operating systems of our world—schooling, health, gender, sexuality—but also how race is augmented, and how, in turn, we can think through how surveillance gets augmented when we think about race.

MW: In this sense, surveillance practices have punitive effects that are all-encompassing—in the legal system, healthcare, sports, education, and in so many other fields. An important part of your study is that even though there's a rich body of literature on surveillance, power, discipline, and so forth, many of the twentieth century's most cited writers and thinkers on the subject did not factor race into their analyses. They assumed the subject to be white.

SB: In my work on racializing surveillance, I often refer to the writings of John Fiske, who has frequently emphasized how many authors and thinkers—whether it was George Orwell or Michel Foucault—did not factor in how race functioned when it came to surveillance. One of Fiske's key observations is that those writers underestimated the fact that, in their work, the seeing eye is always systematically assumed to be white. This is probably pretty obvious to a lot of other people—particularly Black folks and other racialized folks in the US—but even the presumedly most brilliant philosophers did not factor in how the white gaze operates as the primary, disciplinary gaze when it comes to the surveillance of Blackness and surveillance in general.

MW: You say it quite beautifully in your book when you quote the theorist Rob Boyne and his invitation to "draw a black line through Foucault's idea of the panopticon."

SB: In my work as an educator, of course, I continue to teach and also learn from the writings of Foucault. Boyne has spoken about the need to draw a black line through discussions around visibility and the panopticon, panopticism, and all the other derivatives associated with those concepts. It actually reconnects to Heidegger and then Derrida—this idea of *sous rature*. You draw a line through it, but you can still see what's underneath. It is not a complete erasure but a way to emphasize that, when thinking of certain definitions, the common understanding and framing of surveillance are incomplete.

Personally, I have tried to draw that black line by examining another architecture of surveillance and oppression: the slave ship. Both the panopticon as imagined by social theorist Jeremy Bentham and the description of the Brooks slave ship were produced as diagrams around the same time, in the late 1700s. For Bentham and his brother Samuel, their diagram was made in an effort to create a better model for prison management and the management of factories. The other diagram was conceived as a tool in the promotion of abolition and to understand the floating prison of the slave ship.
I have tried to see the panopticon in relation to the slave ship and to

understand the architecture as connecting to that of prisons imagined in pretty much the same years. I wanted to think about another way of understanding and experiencing the panopticon.

As you know, the panopticon is based on the idea that those who are incarcerated are looked at but cannot see who is looking at them. In my writing, I wanted to think about the ways in which Black women's practices of looking—like returning that gaze—act as forms of resistance and help reshape our own understandings of surveillance.

MW: Right, one of the most evocative approaches in *Dark Matters* is your focus on Black communities and individuals that have not only been disproportionately targeted by surveillance practices but have also historically resisted them or purposefully intervened in or subverted those practices.

SB: In my book, I write about and use "dark sousveillance"—a kind of countersurveillance—to describe scenarios that are both oppositional and hopeful. Within this mode of operating in the world, tools of social control, whether on the plantation or in city spaces, can be co-opted, repurposed, and challenged.

Maybe one way to think about how racializing surveillance operates and how artists, specifically, have come to critique it, as I have just described, is the net art piece from 2001 *Blackness for Sale* from *Black Net.Art Actions* by Mendi and Keith Obadike. For this piece, Obadike put his Blackness up for sale on eBay as a critique of the auction system, with all its specific implications for Black folks in the history of US slavery. He didn't put *himself* up for sale but included descriptors such as, "This heirloom has been in the possession of the seller for twenty-eight years, and it comes with a list of benefits and a list of warnings." Some of the warnings are: "The seller does not recommend that this Blackness be used in the process of making or selling 'serious' art"; and, "The seller does not recommend that this Blackness be used while making intellectual claims." It goes on and on, providing warnings regarding voting, shopping, and access to spaces. *Blackness for Sale* exposes how racialized surveillance works in practice, having a tremendous impact on every aspect of one's life.

MW: I'm glad you brought up this piece. So much of your scholarship underscores the intricacies of being monitored, both online and off.

SB: There was a time, of course, when people didn't have cameras, cell phones, or these kinds of things. It was just one-on-one, looking and looking back. Unfortunately, there aren't many accounts of what looking back or returning the gaze was like for Black folks under slavery, but we do know it was heavily regulated and continued to be so even post-emancipation. To look back could mean to die, or to be killed. I wanted to insert that history into the conversation within surveillance studies. Looking back was dangerous and regulated, and there were specific rules around reckless eyeballing or against staring at a white person for too long and what implication it could have.

I'm interested in what it means to have a knowing understanding of surveillance under white supremacy, under slavery, and how that understanding allows for a knowledge that could lead to resistance, rebellion, and refusal. I have just started reading Tina Campt's *A Black Gaze*. I like that it's not titled *The Black Gaze*, but *A Black Gaze*. There is a multiplicity in it. She says, "A Black gaze is a structure, a visual engagement that implicitly and explicitly understands Blackness as neither singular nor a singularity. It embraces instead the multiplicity of Blackness these artists simultaneously grapple with and personify." For Campt, it's a provocation to see Blackness differently. This is so much more liberatory than, say, John Fiske and his understanding of the absences that Foucault and Orwell didn't see. This is what Black feminist theorizing allows us to think with.

MW: On the cover of *Dark Matters*, there is a 2008 work by the South African artist Robin Rhode, in which a figure intentionally gazes into a corner. It brings in this type of thinking about a more physical or sensory response to the constraints of surveillance, based on sight and movement. I wonder if you could talk about that piece or what made you want to put it on the cover.

SB: The piece is called *Pan's opticon*. When I first saw it, I liked that you think of "Pan" as a multiplicity and "opticon" as having to do with seeing and vision. The optics here—the Black gaze, the African, South African gaze—take hold of and possess that structure. There is this "seeing–being seen" dyad that was extraordinarily powerful to me. Rhode has his doppelganger in these images, and jutting out of what I imagine are the figure's eyeballs are inside calipers.

I was also taken by the fact that his back is turned to us, the viewer. Nonetheless, there is that moment of returning the gaze, looking back, and challenging the various stereotypes projected—particularly in apartheid South Africa—onto the Black male body. This piece spoke to all these various subjects and tensions. His work is foundational to how I think about artists as theorists who articulate and critique surveillance practices.

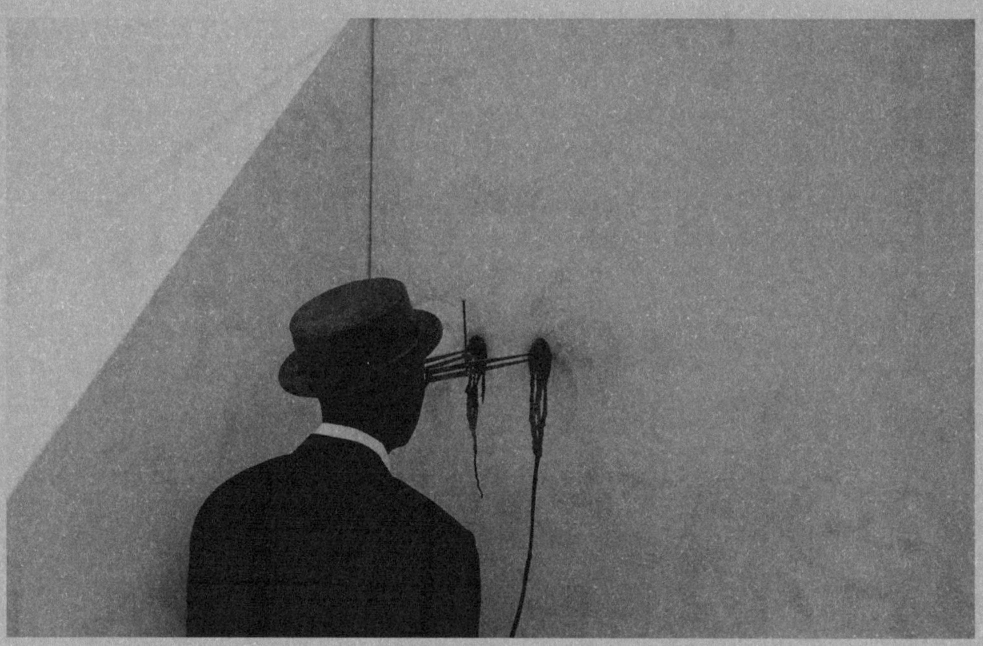

Robin Rhode, *Pan's opticon*, 2008 (detail). Digital pigment print mounted on four-ply museum board, 17 7/10 × 27 8/10 in. (45 × 70.5 cm)

MW: In addition to the act of seeing, you talk about the embodied effects of light itself and how they relate to ideas around visibility or the ability to be seen or perceived. Crucially, you present a study of the so-called "lantern laws," which were instituted in New York City and around British colonies in the northeast in the eighteenth century. Can you explain what these were and what was involved in the circumstances around them?

SB: These were laws popularized in the eighteenth century that regulated the movement of enslaved Black and Indigenous people in spaces in New York City and other British holdings prior to the foundation of what is now the United States. Come sunset, if any enslaved Black person or Indigenous person was found unsupervised by a white person and without a lit lantern, they could be subject to arrest and seizure. We can't really know what would happen if it was raining or the wind blew, but either way, the lit lantern became a supervisory device.

There are myriad possible readings and protocols of control and visibility activated by those historical scenarios. Whose bodies are used for the lighting infrastructure of a city or a space? How does the past allow us to think about our present? You could think of the lantern laws in relation to all the videos on social media of "Barbecue Becky," "Permit Patty," or others in which white people take it upon themselves to supervise racialized people of color having a picnic, shopping, or just being. That supervisory impulse has a long history. It's not the only genealogy, but within US history, a precise lineage connects the present to the lantern laws.

That history of surveillance, supervision, forced visibility, and control could lead to arrest, discipline, and, importantly, a type of visual terror through violent illumination. That is how I wanted to think about light. I am not thinking only about how white folks take upon themselves the roles of supervisors or use 911 like a customer service call but also of the ways in which the use of light is weaponized and instrumentalized to impart specific systems of control and visibility that extend the panopticon to the scale of a city.

MW: The embodied effects of surveillance figure into Kapwani Kiwanga's work, in part, through her use of light as a material. Like you, she is concerned with connections between illumination and surveillance that have persisted throughout history and into the present. You have discussed how colonial lantern laws have numerous contemporary analogues.

SB: Now, for example, the NYPD uses large-scale light generators to surveil certain areas, often illuminating specific residential blocks in predominantly Black neighborhoods with harsh artificial light all night long. As in the eighteenth century, when lantern laws subjected Black bodies to heightened visibility, mobility is still managed via police lights in a new but no less violent form of illumination.

When we think about the sensory impact of those machines, we must also consider that the bright artificial light can disrupt sleep patterns, and the generators produce a loud hum, making them part of a noise campaign. Furthermore, there is the issue of smell. Many inhabitants of cities like New York easily recognize the smell and look of the noxious oil that these generators constantly emit.

It is important to consider, specifically, in what places these violent artificial lights are allowed to operate under the guise of risk-management, surveillance, security, and anti-terrorism. Their placement reveals clear patterns that, I believe, draw a line—although not necessarily the only line, or a straight line—between the events and social practices of the eighteenth century and those of the twenty-first century. They say that history doesn't repeat itself, but it rhymes. The rhythm of that type of surveillance from over three hundred years ago is still with us in our contemporary moment.

A Violent Illumination (Notes)

—

Kathleen Ritter

Consider the following paragraphs as an appendix of sorts—a series of endnotes, an annotated index, or a sidebar of hyperlinks—to Kapwani Kiwanga's exhibition at the New Museum.

Kapwani has asked me to contribute a text to this publication based on our recent conversations. Kapwani is a friend—one with whom I share several commonalities. We are both living in a city that is not our own, raising young children. We navigate our daily lives in a foreign language and culture. We are both artists and researchers, with areas of overlap in our interests, aesthetics, and politics. At the time of writing, several months before the exhibition, her plans are still taking shape. Kapwani describes her intention for the installation as an embodied experience, a staging of selective visibility, and a sensation of seeing and being seen. In developing her concept, she has imposed one restriction: to use the skylights and windows of the museum as the central source of light. This parameter is not randomly chosen; it is informed by a body of research investigating light as a mechanism of control.

The following notes capture some of our exchanges, shared research between our respective art practices, and my own leaps from one thought to the next. They map historical and contemporary examples of light used in public spaces, especially where light takes a panoptic turn. While some seem neutral, others show a more disciplinary use of light as a means of exercising power. There are long-standing precedents in which light operates as a stand-in for an omnipresent authority, an invisible policing and surveillance infrastructure, with the intended effect to check behavior by internalizing the sense of being watched. Most importantly, these notes highlight how panoptic lighting is unevenly distributed and that gendered and/or racialized bodies are subjects of a more intense, even violent, illumination.

Notes

1. Early attempts to organize STREET LIGHTING were made in London and Paris in the fifteenth and sixteenth centuries. In 1417, the Mayor of London ordered citizens to hang lights outside their homes on winter nights. Paris made a similar decree in 1524: lanterns were to be hung out by ground-floor windowsills at night, placed in a prominent position so that the street receives sufficient light. These laws made landowners responsible for illuminating public space and are early examples of the conflation between light, private property, and public security.

2. "LANTERN LAWS" were enacted throughout the New England area of the United States in the 1700s, which mandated Black, mixed race, and Indigenous enslaved people to carry a light source when walking alone at night so their movements could be seen and traced. In 1737, New York City enacted an ordinance mandating, "No Negro, Mulatto or Indian slave above the Age of fourteen years" be in the streets unaccompanied "an hour after sun-set" without "a Lanthorn and lighted Candle in it, so as the Light thereof may be plainly seen."[1] Citing "lantern laws" as a precedent for racialized surveillance, Simone Browne writes, "We can think of the lantern as a prosthesis made mandatory after dark, a technology that made it possible for the black body to be constantly illuminated from dusk to dawn, made knowable, locatable, and contained within the city."[2]

3. Detailed in Jeremy Bentham's plan for the PANOPTICON are small lamps, placed on the outside of each window of the inspector's lodge, backed by a reflector to throw the light into the corresponding cells and deployed to "extend to the night the security of the day." The lights would both illuminate and effectively blind the prisoners to the guard, making their presence unknowable, even unnecessary.[3]

4. The first street illumination with GASLIGHT was demonstrated and recorded on Pall Mall, London, January 28, 1807. Organized street lighting quickly spread to other cities across Europe and

North America, with Baltimore, Maryland, an early adopter in 1817, and Paris following in 1820. The use of gaslights to illuminate public space remained prevalent well into the twentieth century and coincided with the rise of photography. The soft light of gas lamps dominates images of city spaces at night, notably in photographs of Paris's streets by Eugène Atget and Brassaï, and throughout the signature, high-contrast, black-and-white backdrops of film noir.

5. Large towers of intensely bright, carbon arc lights, called MOONLIGHT TOWERS, first appeared in the 1880s. They were designed to illuminate vast areas of a city at night. The first one was installed in 1881 in San Jose, California, and was 237 feet tall. Similar towers with carbon arc lights sprouted up in cities across the US and Europe. The towers were extremely effective, but the system was laborious to maintain, as bulbs needed changing daily. Moonlight towers were sometimes nicknamed "policemen on a pole," as many speculated that the lights would eliminate the need for police altogether.

6. A patent for the handheld FLASHLIGHT was obtained by British inventor David Misell in 1899 and assigned to American Electrical Novelty and Manufacturing Company. The device was designed by Misell with three D-cell batteries housed in a paper tube with a lightbulb and a brass reflector. Competition for the trademark ensued. American Electrical published advertisements brandishing the slogan "The 'Ever-Ready' Electric Flashlight." In an effort to promote the flashlight as a tool of security, the company donated a number to the New York City police, who apparently approved of them.[4]

7. The first patent for a RECIPROCAL MIRROR—glass that appears reflective on one side and transparent on the other—was filed in the US in 1903, under the title "transparent mirror." The mirror becomes "transparent when a strong light is dashed in the rear."[5] This allowed viewing from the darkened side but not vice versa. Reciprocal mirrors find their way into security areas in public spaces, interrogation rooms, execution chambers, and other instances requiring one-way observation.

8. *GASLIGHT* is a classic British film noir made in 1940 by Thorold Dickinson starring Anton Walbrook and Diana Wynyard. The film is based on a 1938 play by Patrick Hamilton in which a man manipulates his wife into believing that she is going insane. Images of gaslights are used throughout the film as a metaphor for truth and deception. With the film's success, the term "gaslighting" was adopted in psychology to refer to a form of abuse in which the victim is covertly manipulated into doubting their own memory, perception, judgment, and eventually their sanity.

9. The use of FLUORESCENT LIGHT spread rapidly during World War II as wartime manufacturing required twenty-four-hour factory production with more economical lighting. Fluorescent lights lasted longer than their incandescent counterparts and were significantly more energy efficient. Fluorescent lighting systems became the dominant form of lighting in factories, public buildings, schools, prisons, and hospitals. The cool, constant light is associated with high levels of productivity, the rise of capitalism, the twenty-four-hour labor force, institutional spaces, and disciplinary architecture.

10. Small pressure-activated LED flashlights were given to visitors entering David Hammons's exhibition *Concerto in Black and Blue*, at Ace Gallery, New York City, in 2002. Hammons left the twenty-thousand-square-foot space completely empty and turned out the lights. The only illumination came from the flashlights in visitors' hands, which emitted narrow beams of blue light, fleetingly capturing themselves and each other, casting shadows. As artist Glenn Ligon notes, "If blackness is a construct, then we are all construction workers, and what Hammons has done is to provide the space in which blackness can be constructed in light . . . except this time it's us with our little blue flashlights, signaling one another in the dark."[6]

11. A DAZZLER is a nonlethal, anti-optic laser weapon designed to disorient, confuse, and temporarily blind people with a pulsing green laser light. Originally created for military use, variations have been designed for domestic use. The first laser dazzler was approved in

2012 by the US Food and Drug Administration for nonmilitary use by law enforcement officers.

12. As part of a New York City Police Department strategy in 2014, called Omnipresence, 150 MOBILE FLOODLIGHTS were installed outside public-housing developments in predominantly low-income communities of color. The harsh fluorescent floodlights are powered by loud diesel generators and are extremely bright. Residents have raised concerns about noise and blinding lights that render their living spaces in a permanent state of buzzing candescence.

13. In 2018, the *Oxford English Dictionary* shortlisted "GASLIGHTING" as their word of the year. In recent years, there has been an exponential uptick in the use of the term "gaslighting" in the #metoo and #timesup movements and in relationship to our contemporary "post-truth" era—in which our understanding of facts and reality is obfuscated and frequently undermined through the deliberate use of misinformation.

1 New-York Historical Society et al., “Minutes of the Common Council of the City of New York, 1675–1776,” (New York: Dodd, Mead, 1905), 4:86.

2 Simone Browne, *Dark Matters: On the Surveillance of Blackness* (Durham, NC: Duke University Press, 2015), 79.

3 Jeremy Bentham, *The Works of Jeremy Bentham* (Edinburgh: William Tait, 1843), 4:41.

4 David Misell. 1899. Electric device. US Patent US617592A, issued January 10, 1899.

5 Emil Bloch. 1903. Transparent mirror. US Patent US720877A, filed September 26, 1902, and issued February 17, 1903.

6 Glenn Ligon, “Black Light: David Hammons and the Poetics of Emptiness,” *Artforum* 43, no. 1 (September 2004), 249.

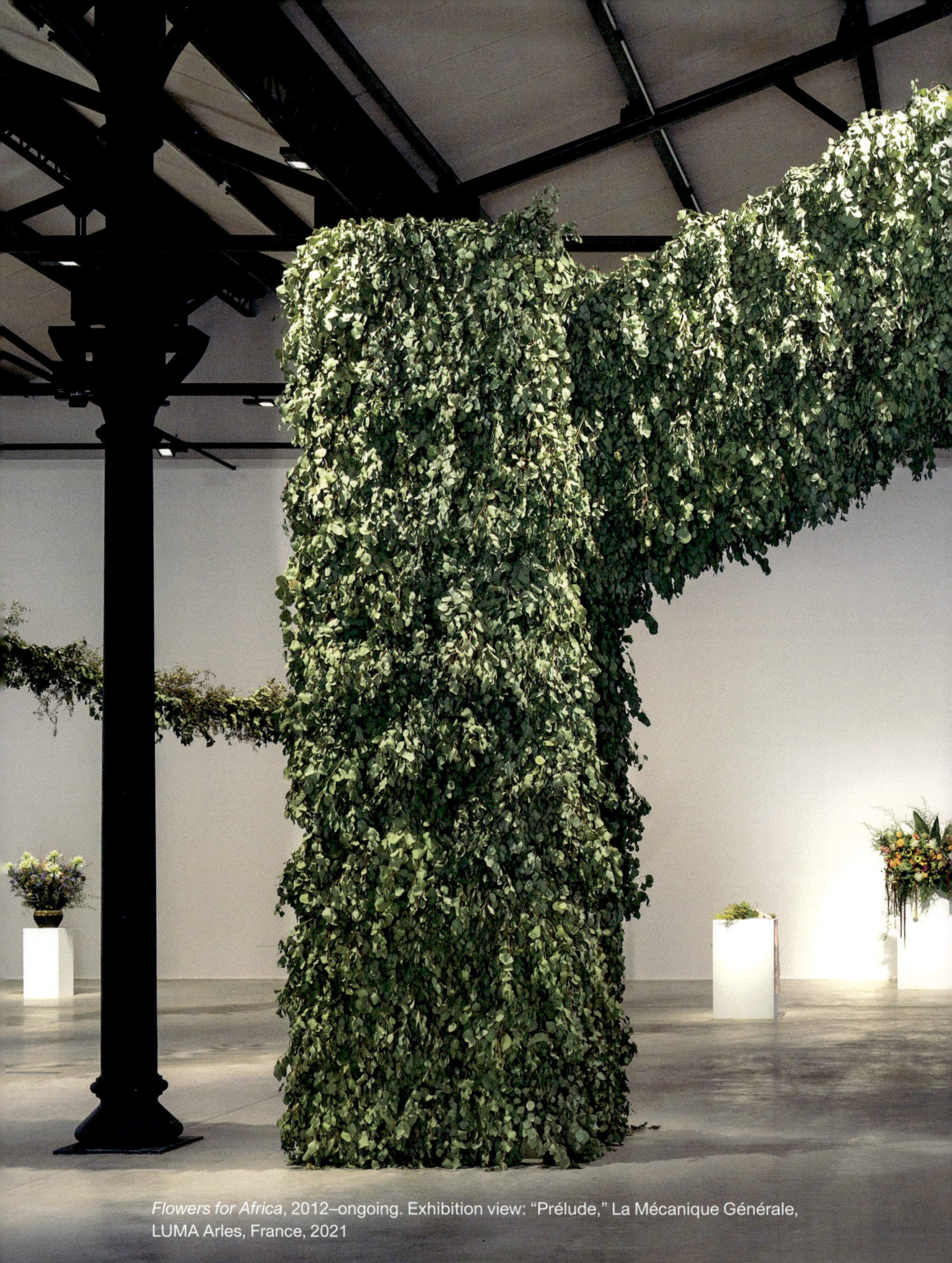

Flowers for Africa, 2012–ongoing. Exhibition view: "Prélude," La Mécanique Générale, LUMA Arles, France, 2021

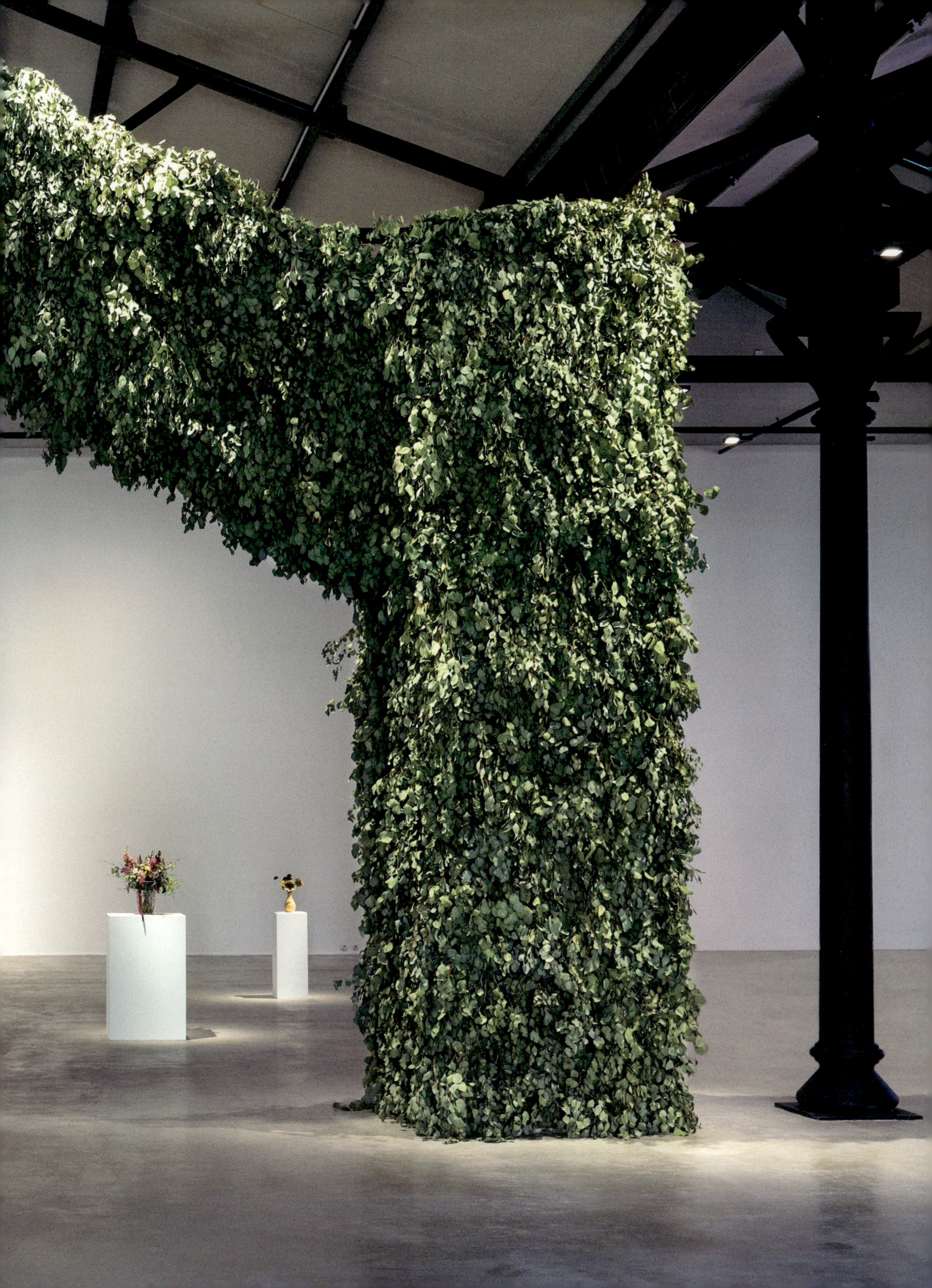

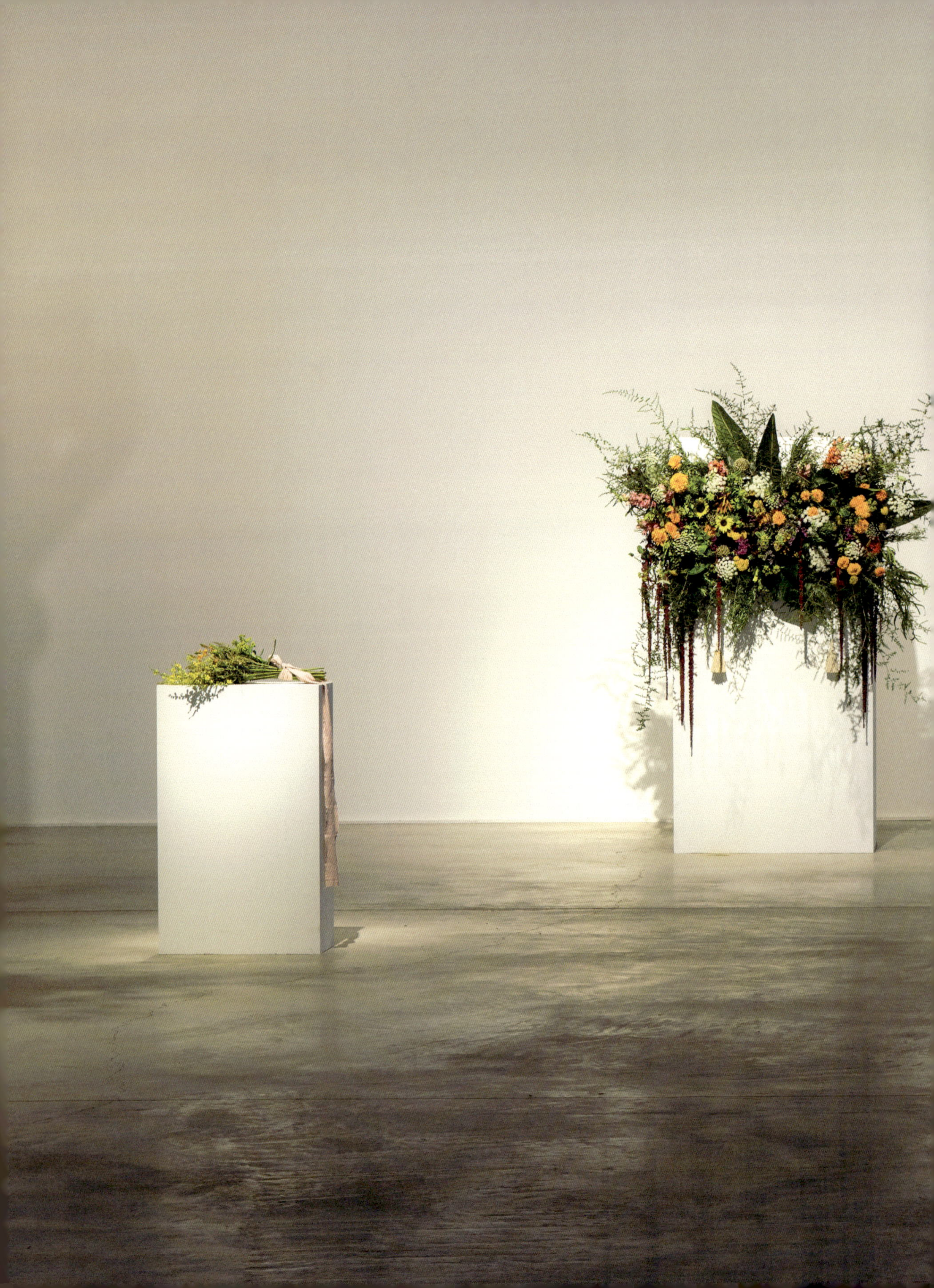

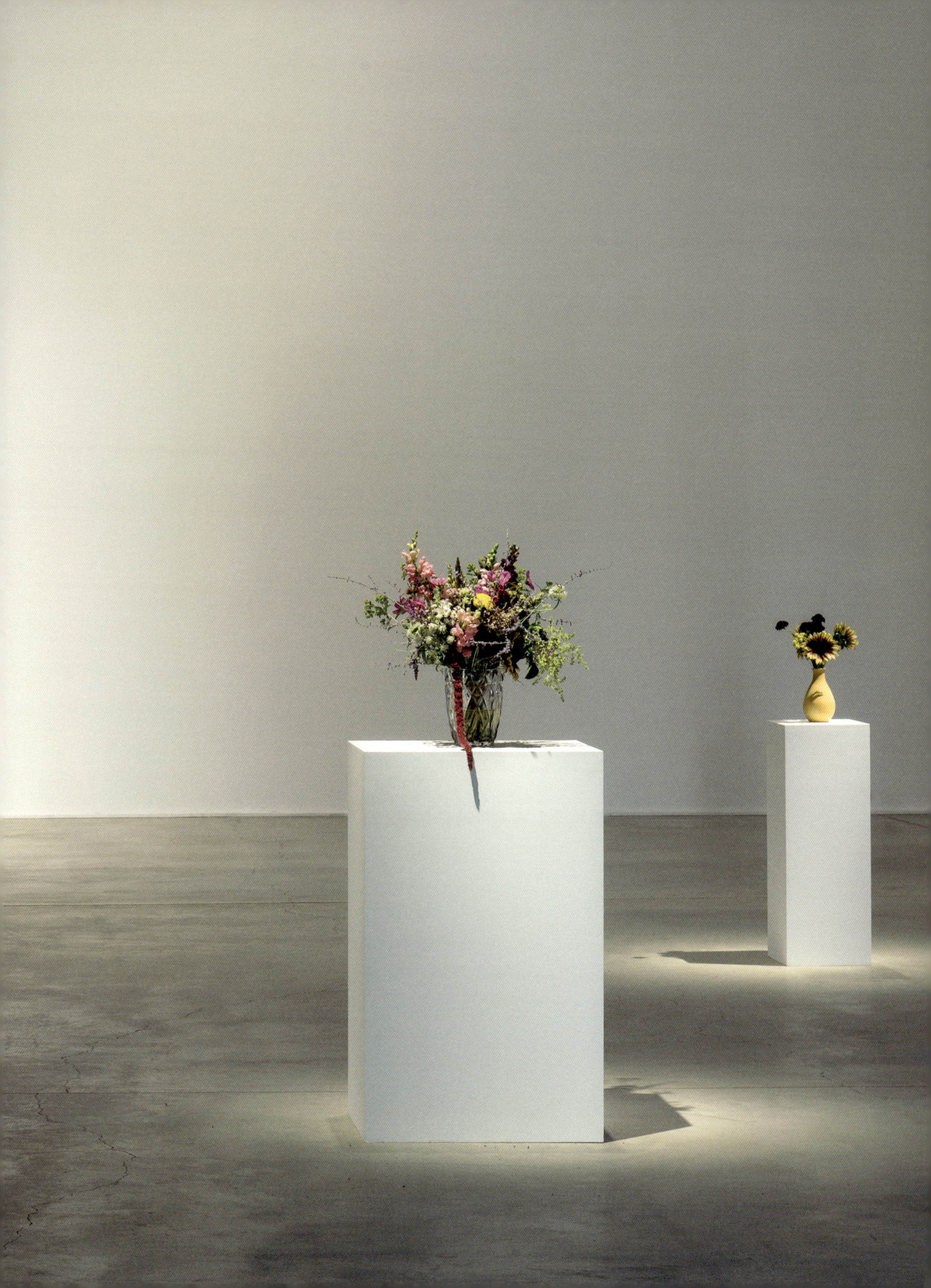

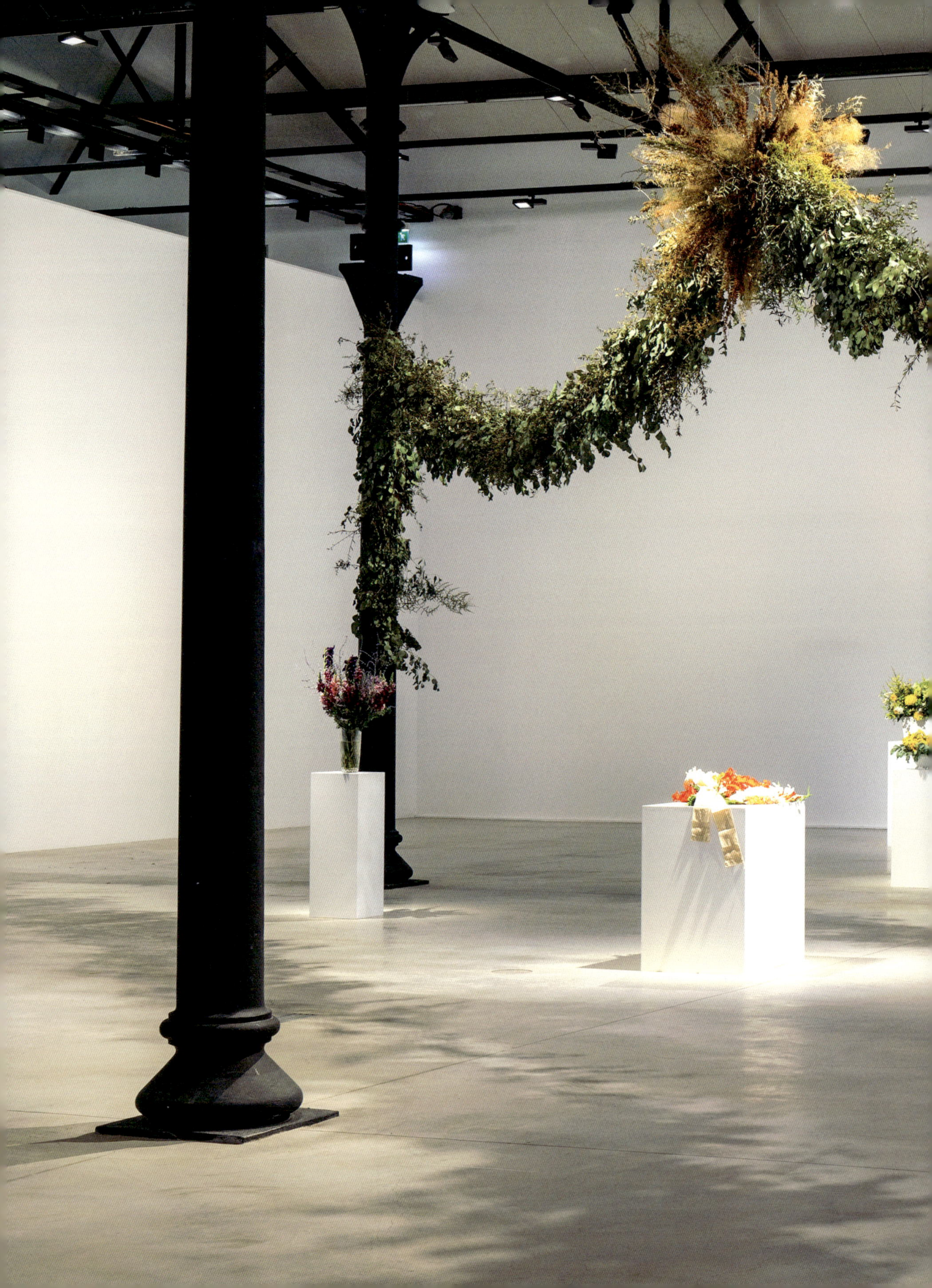

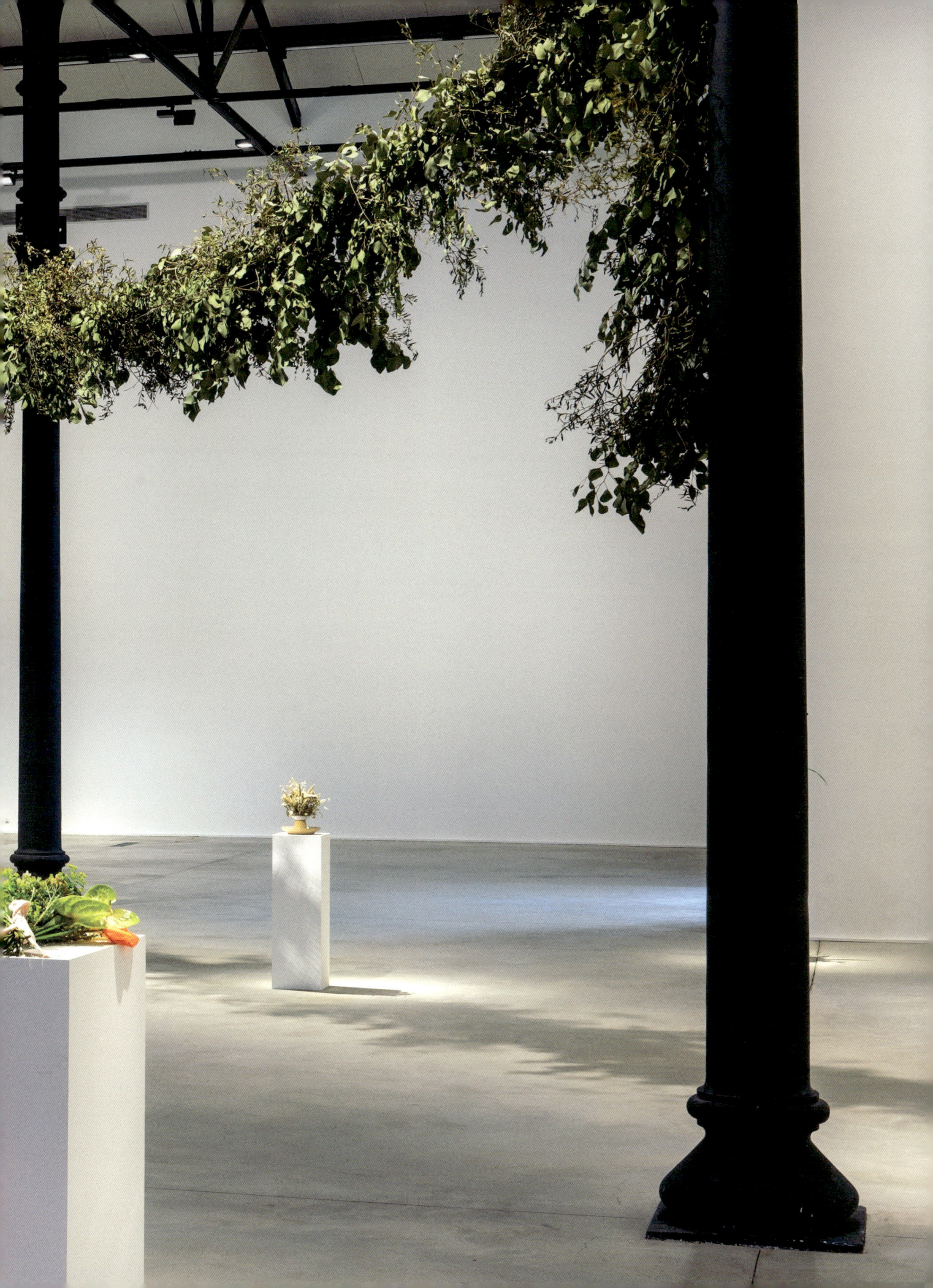

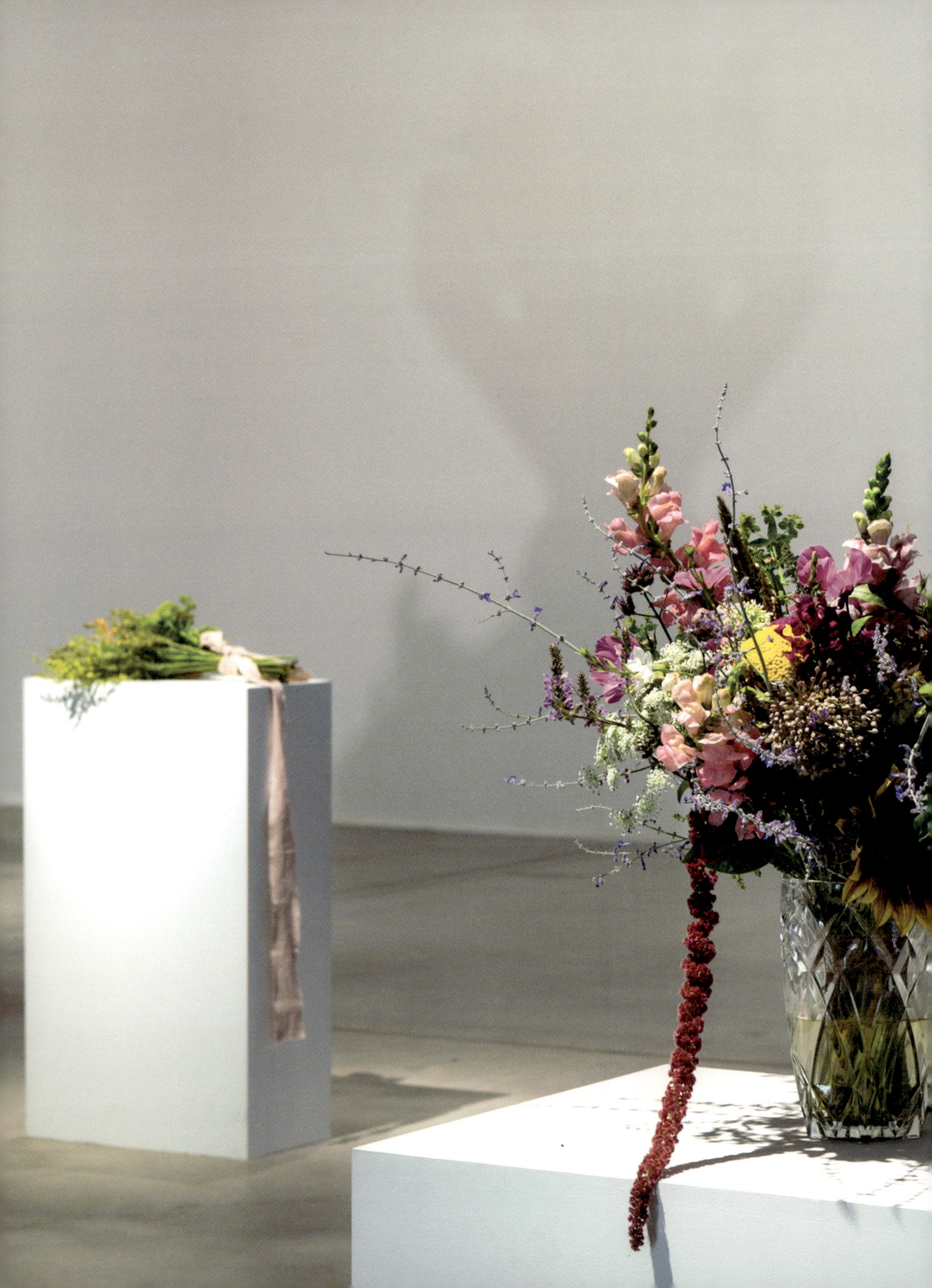

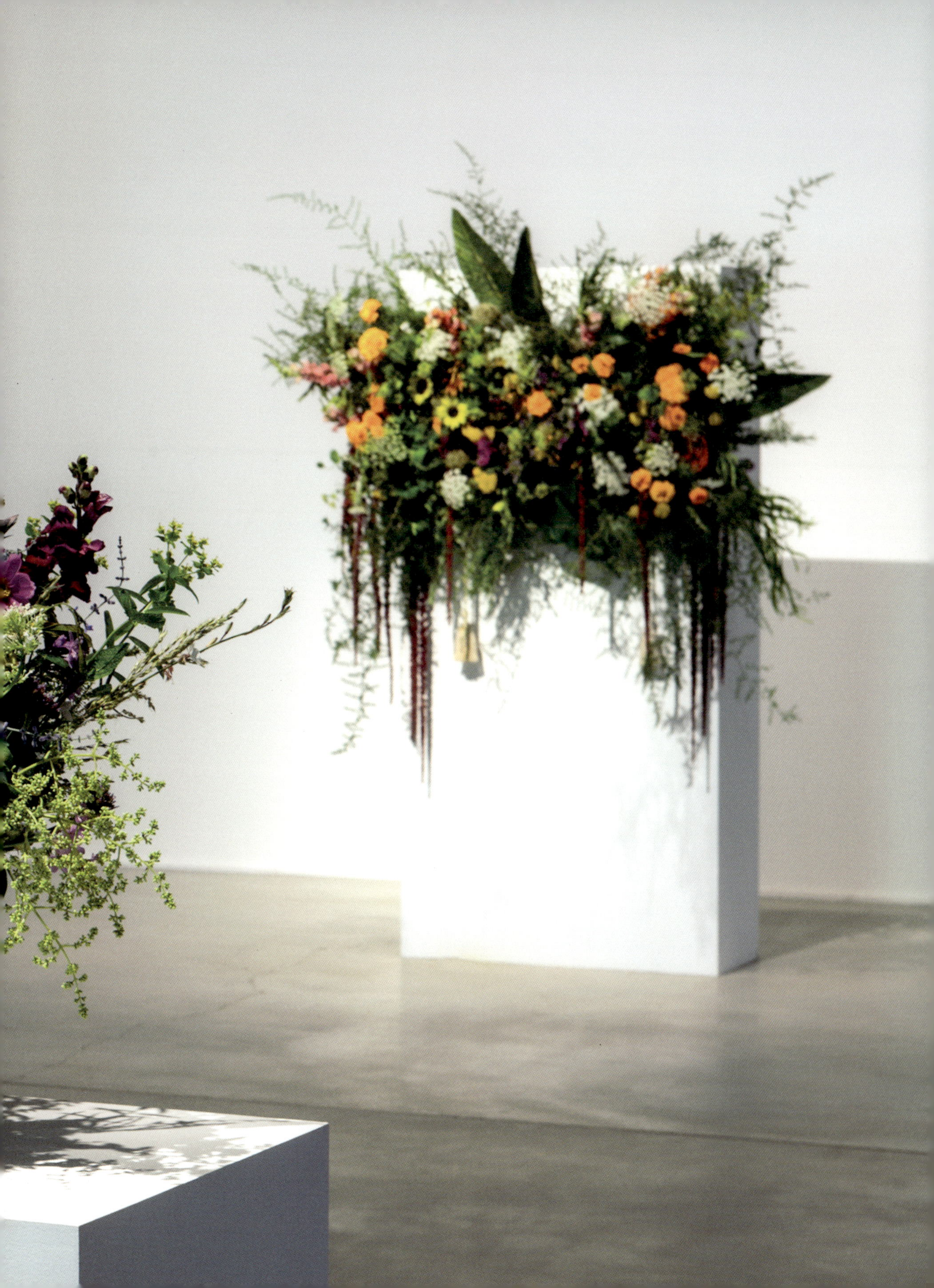

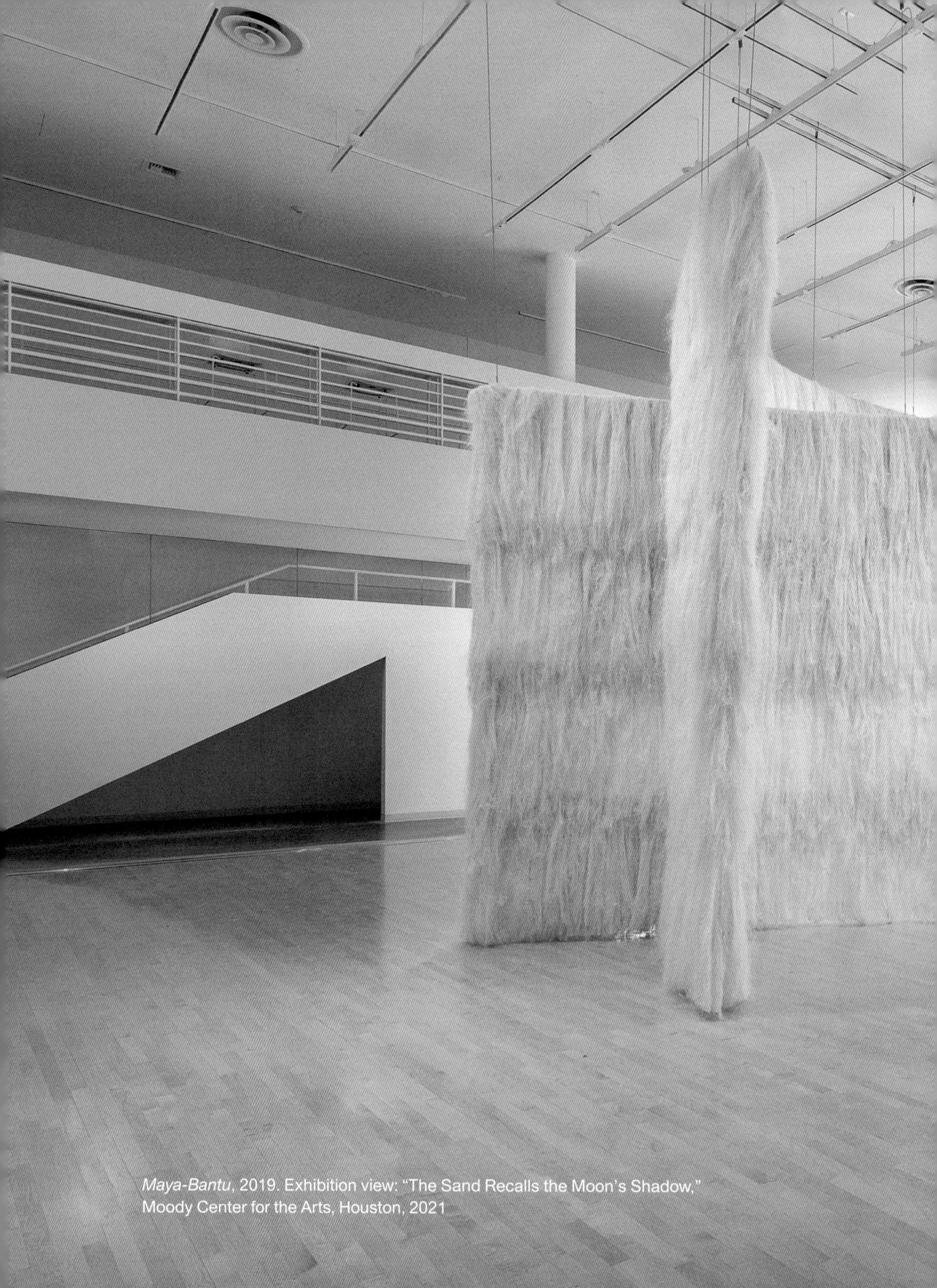

Maya-Bantu, 2019. Exhibition view: “The Sand Recalls the Moon’s Shadow,” Moody Center for the Arts, Houston, 2021

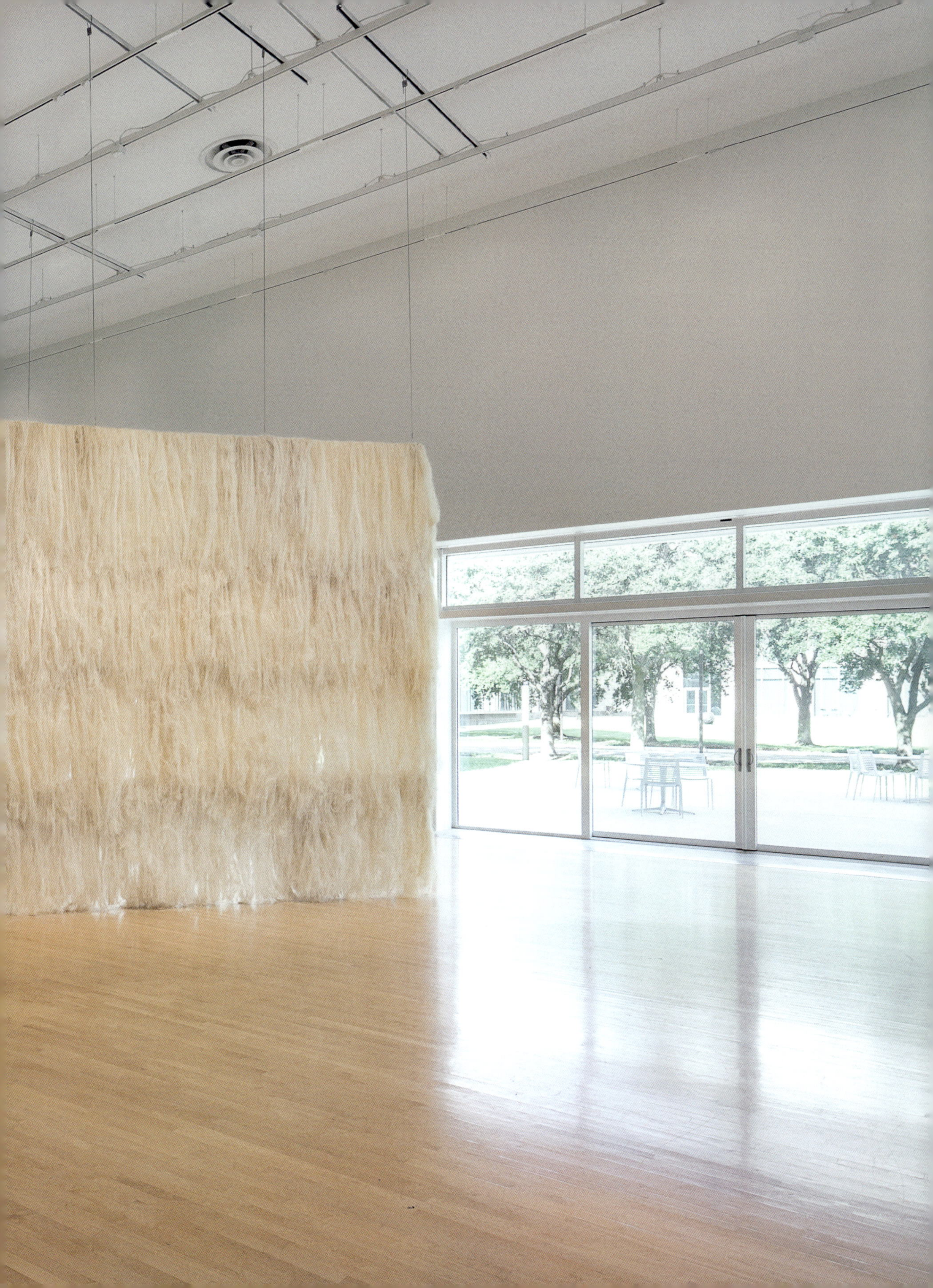

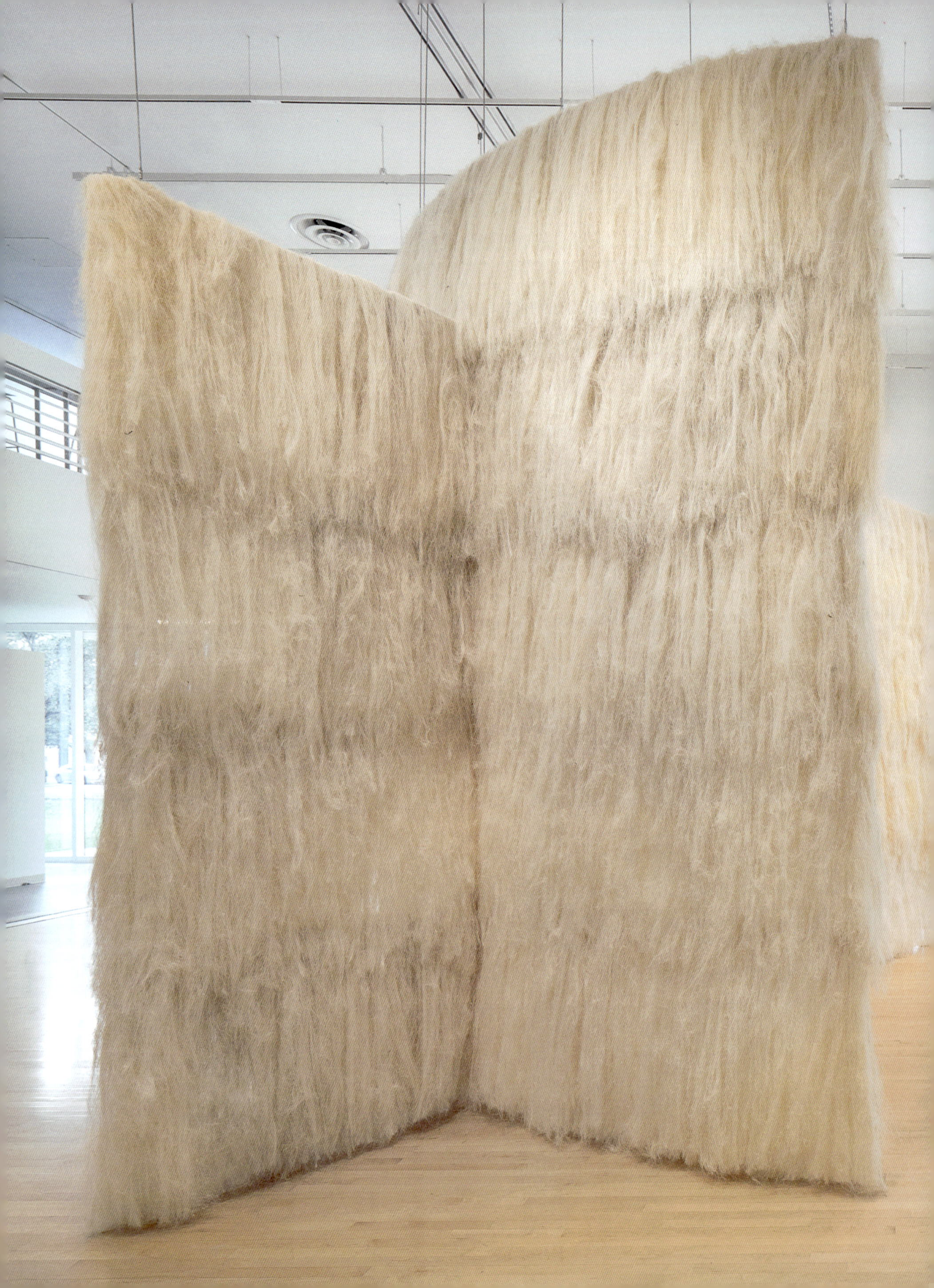

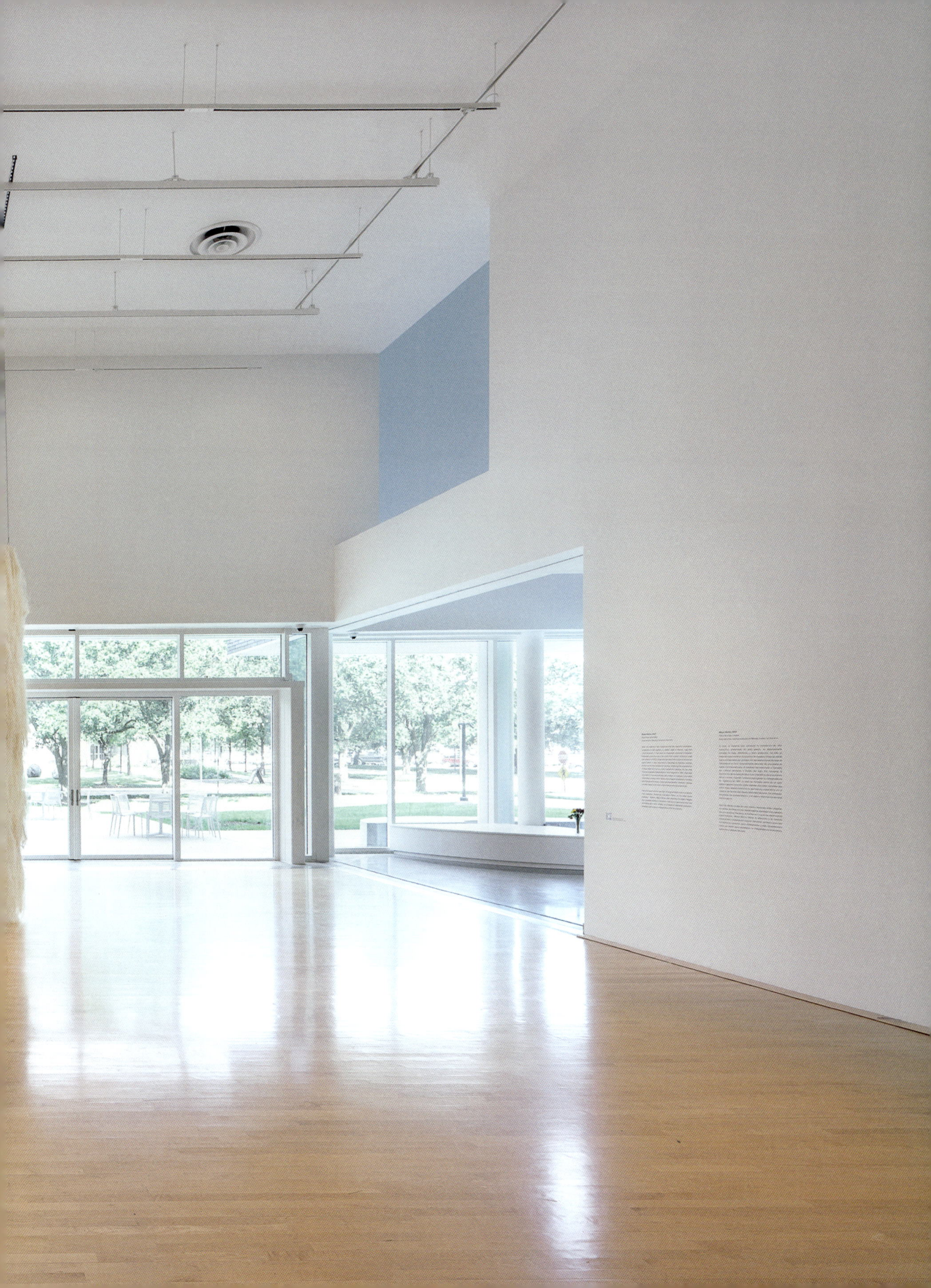

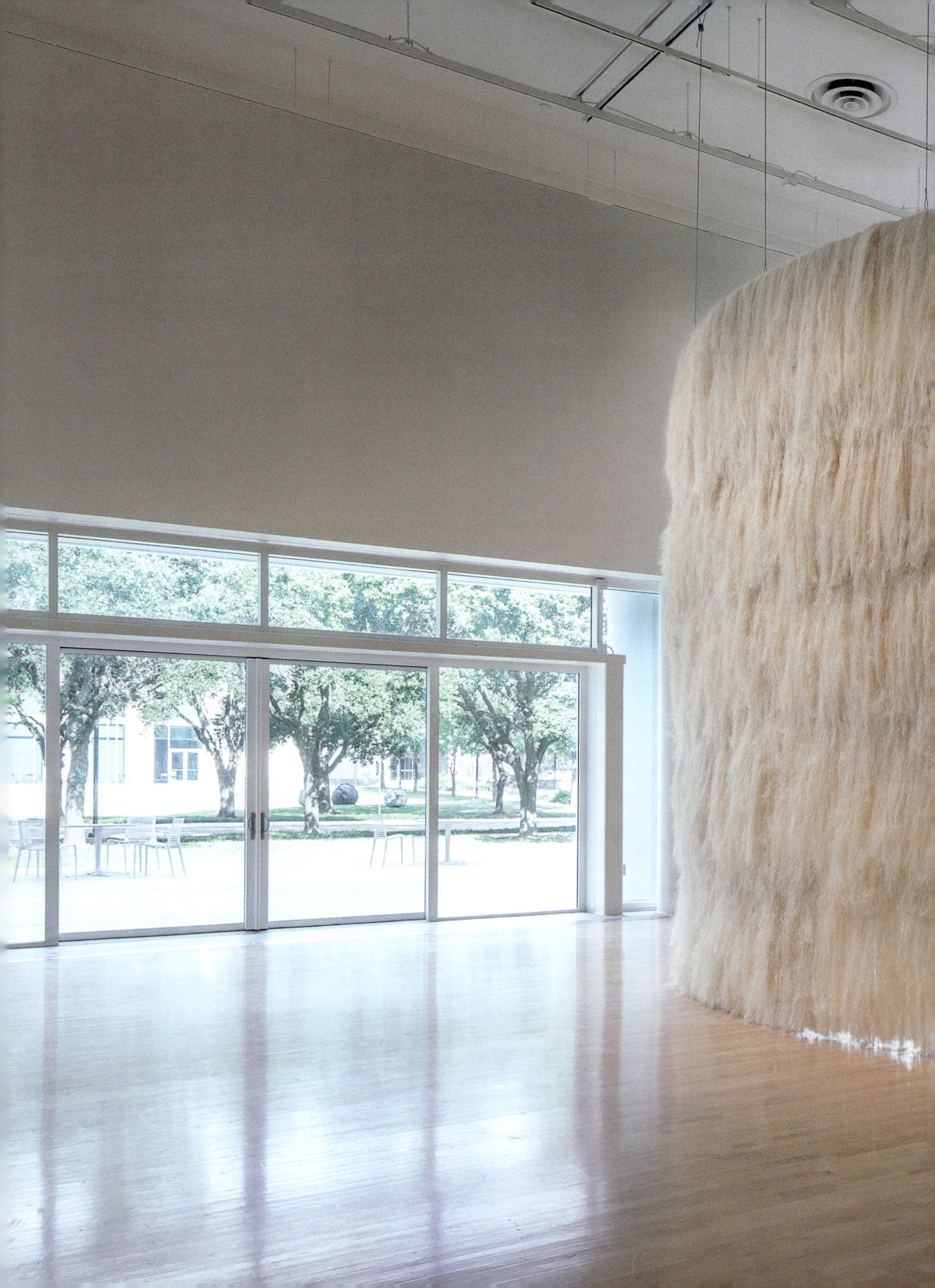

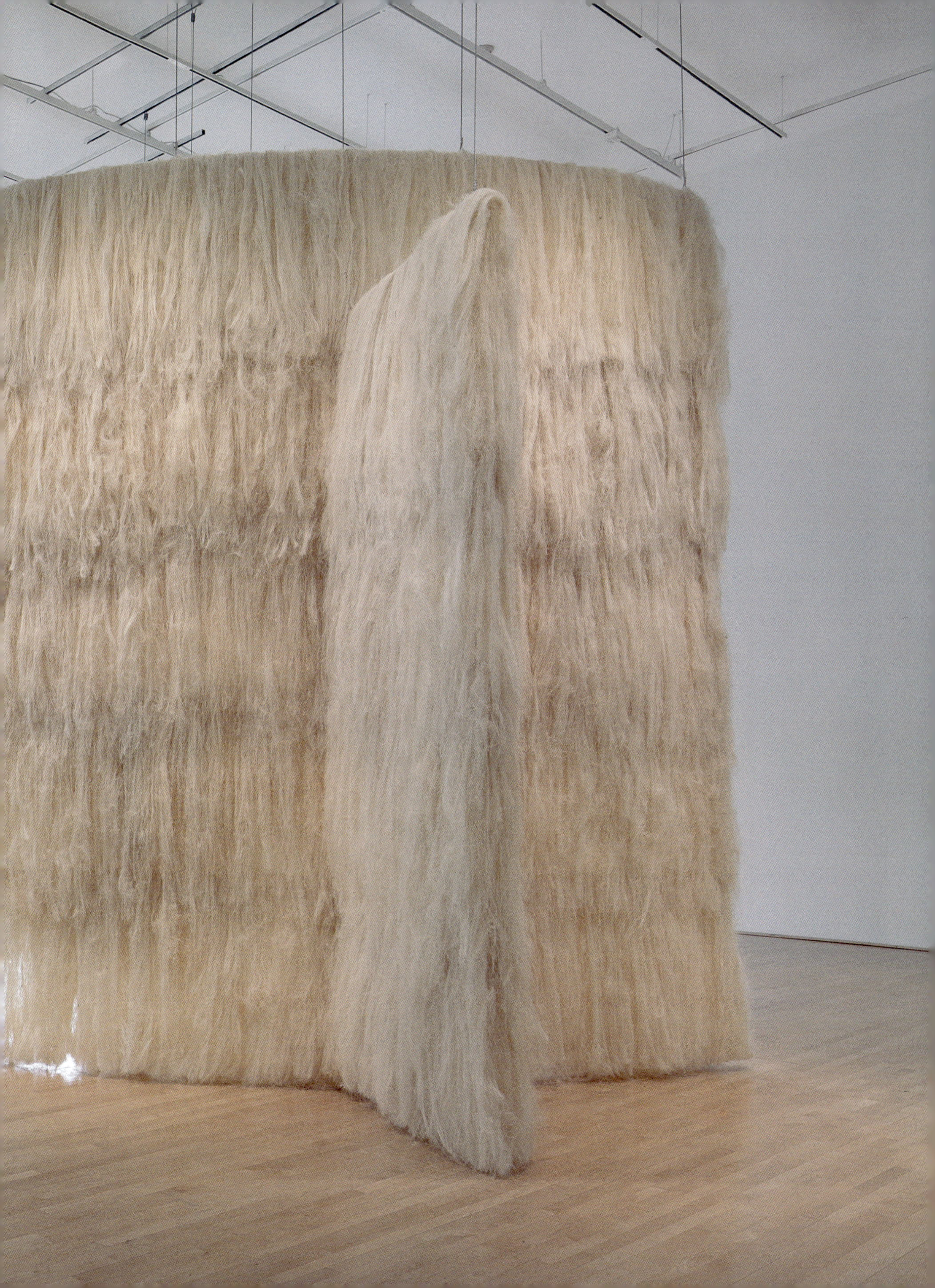

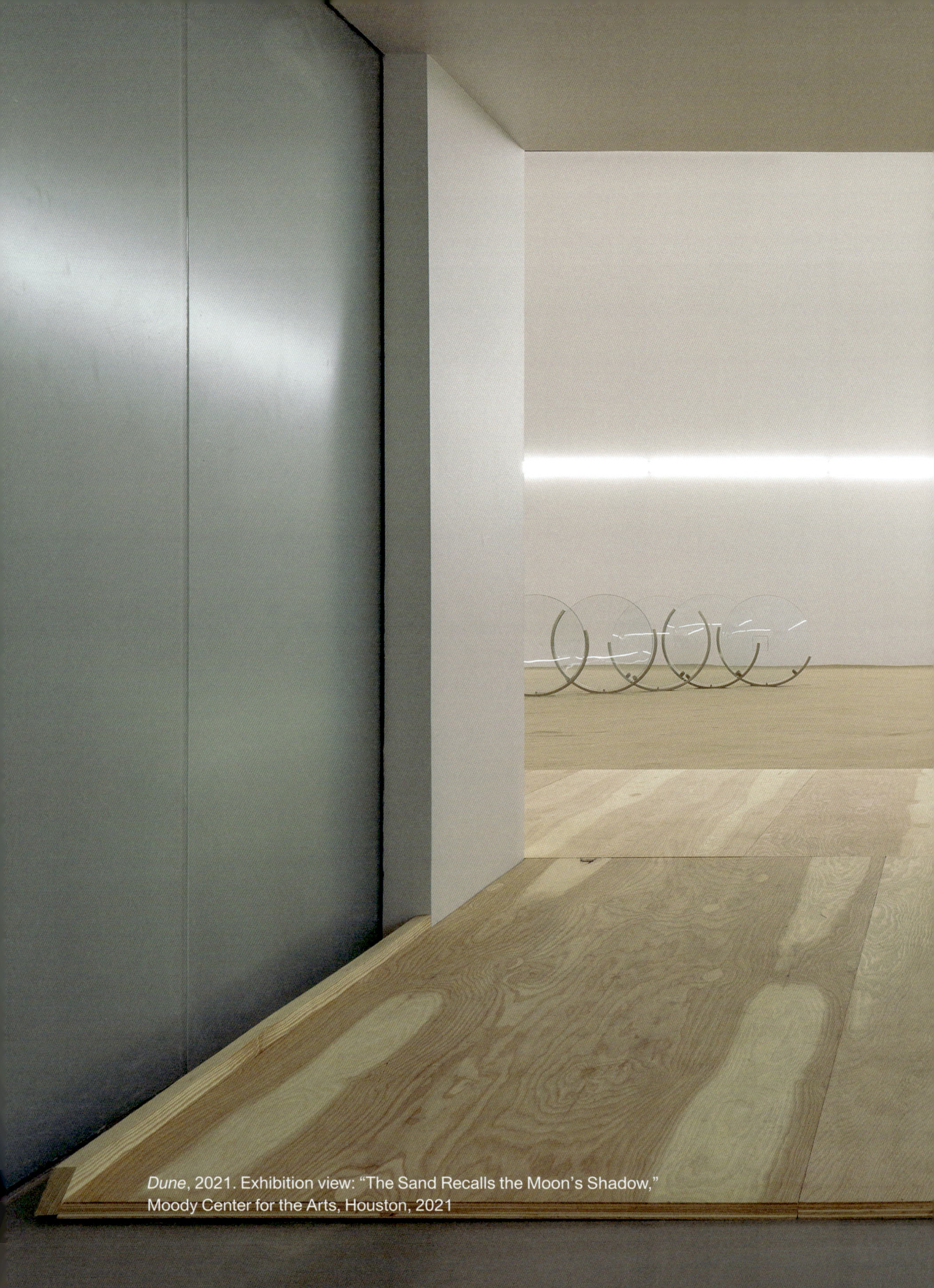

Dune, 2021. Exhibition view: "The Sand Recalls the Moon's Shadow," Moody Center for the Arts, Houston, 2021

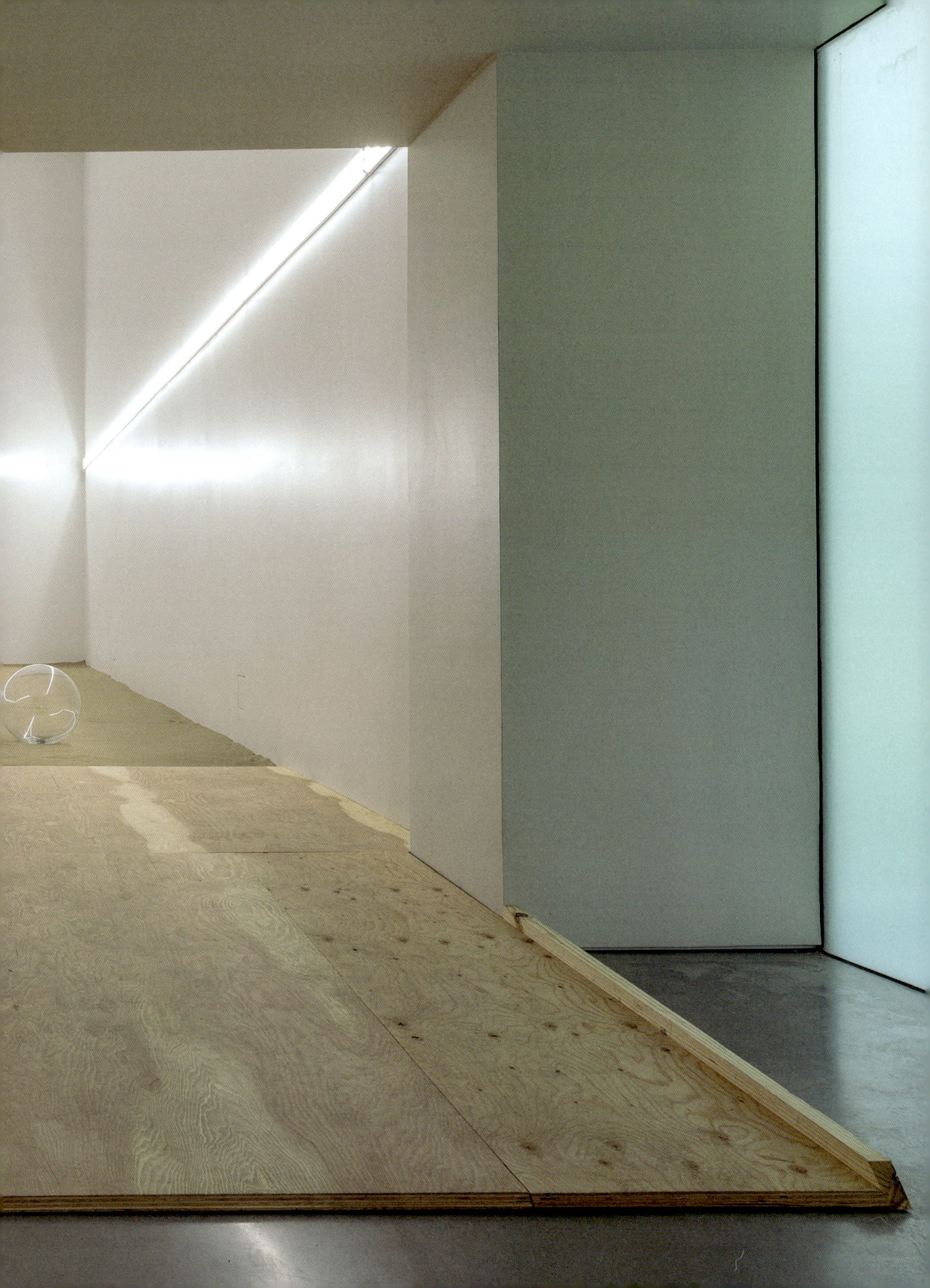

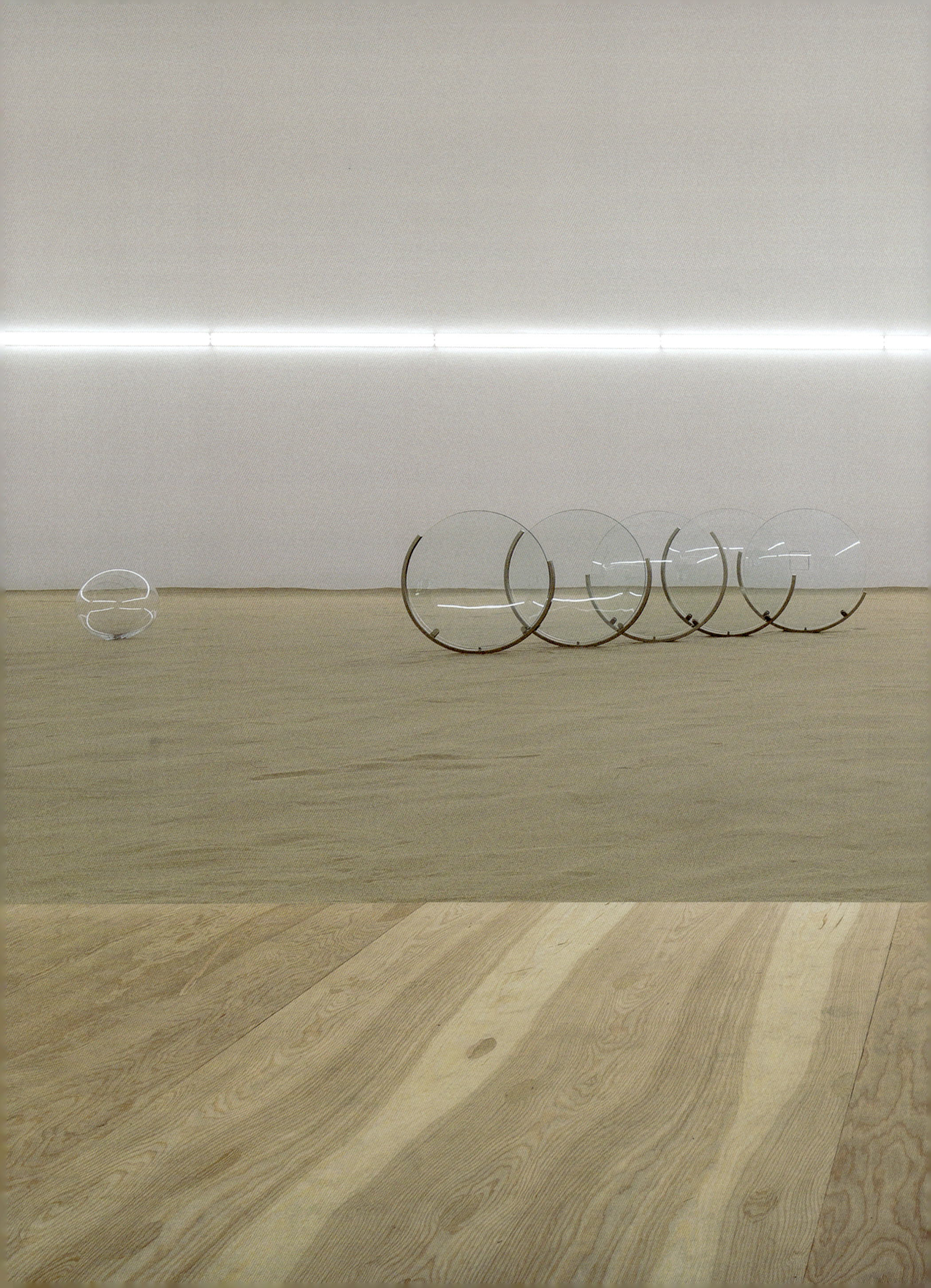

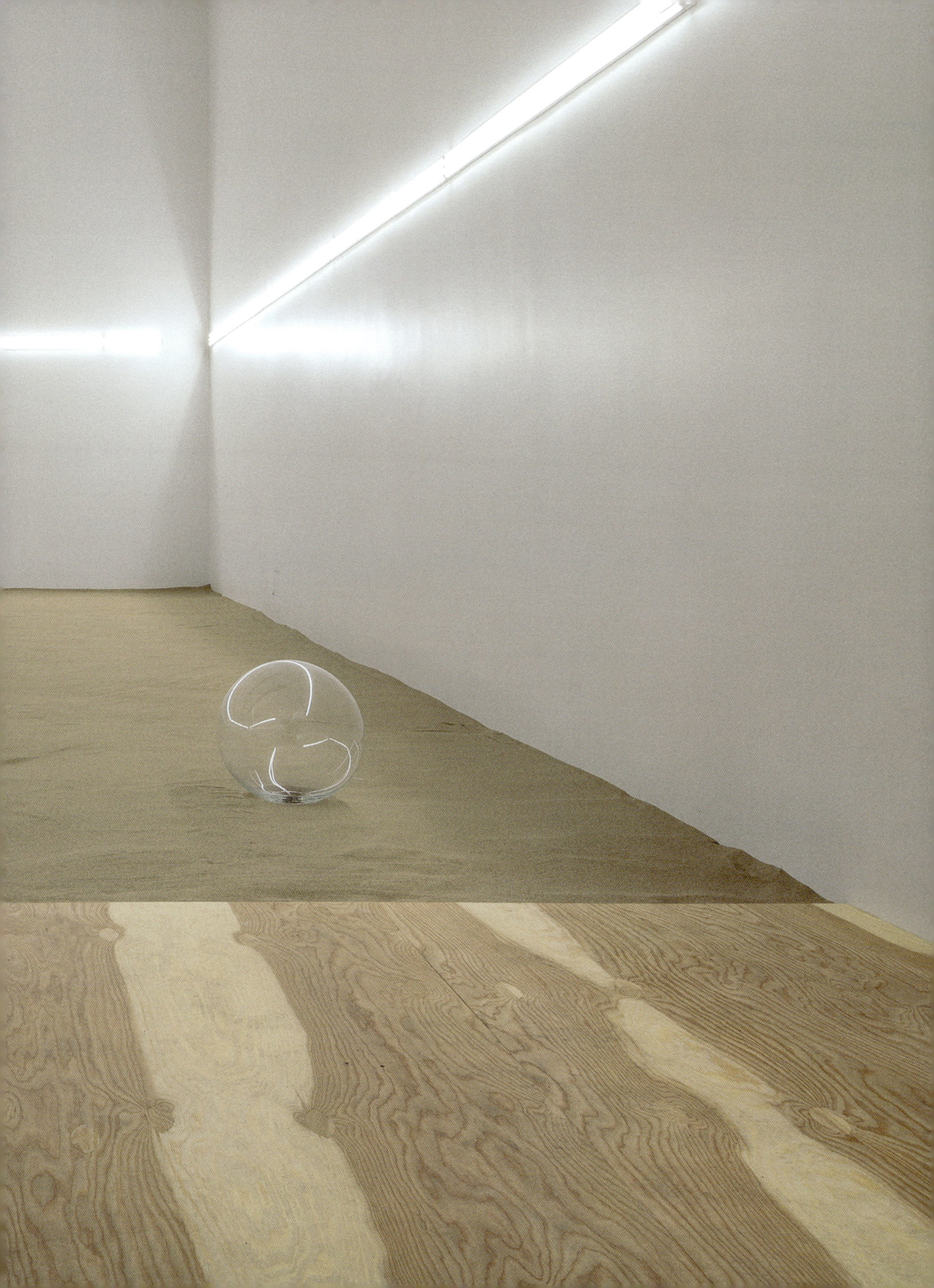

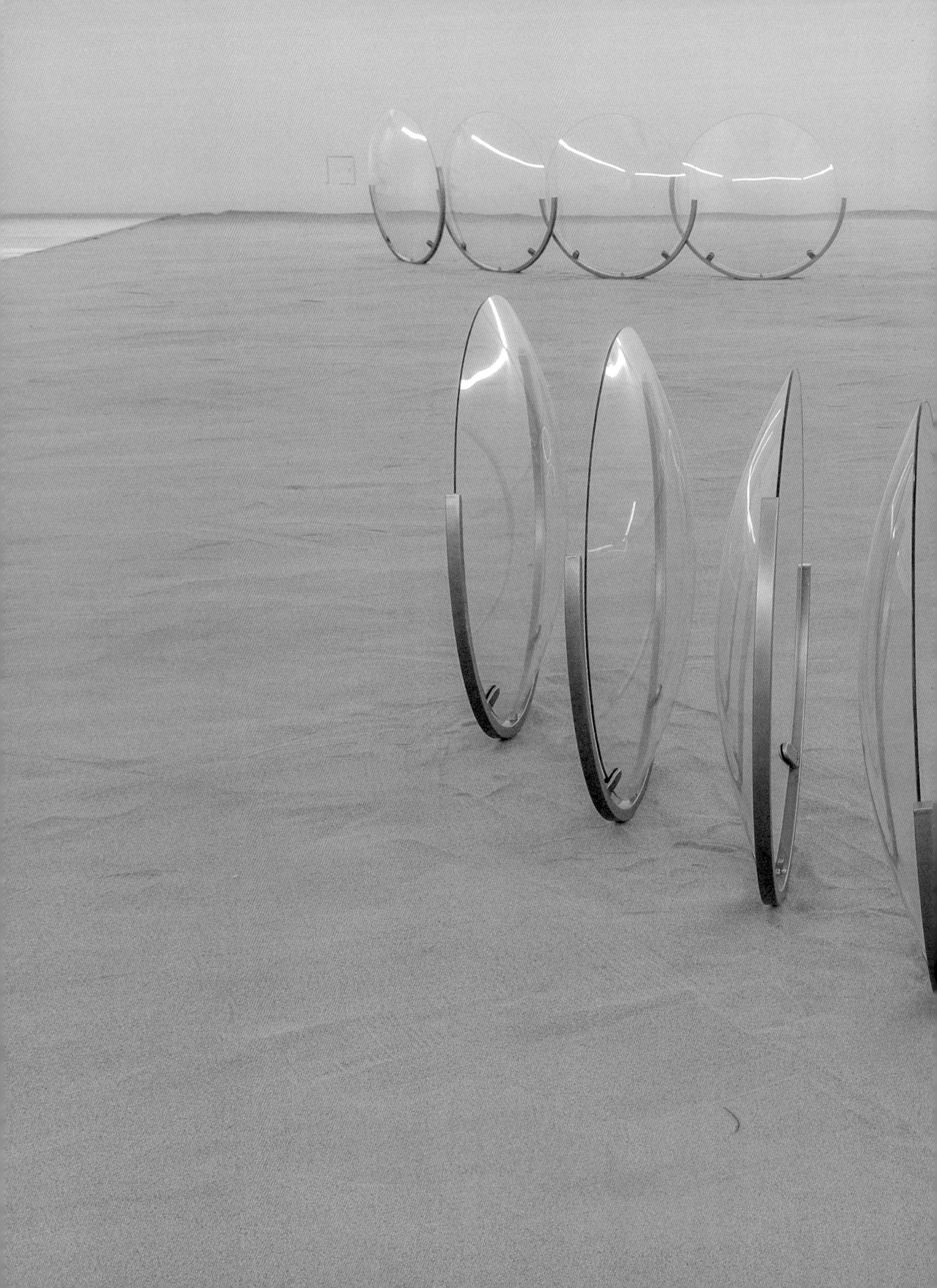

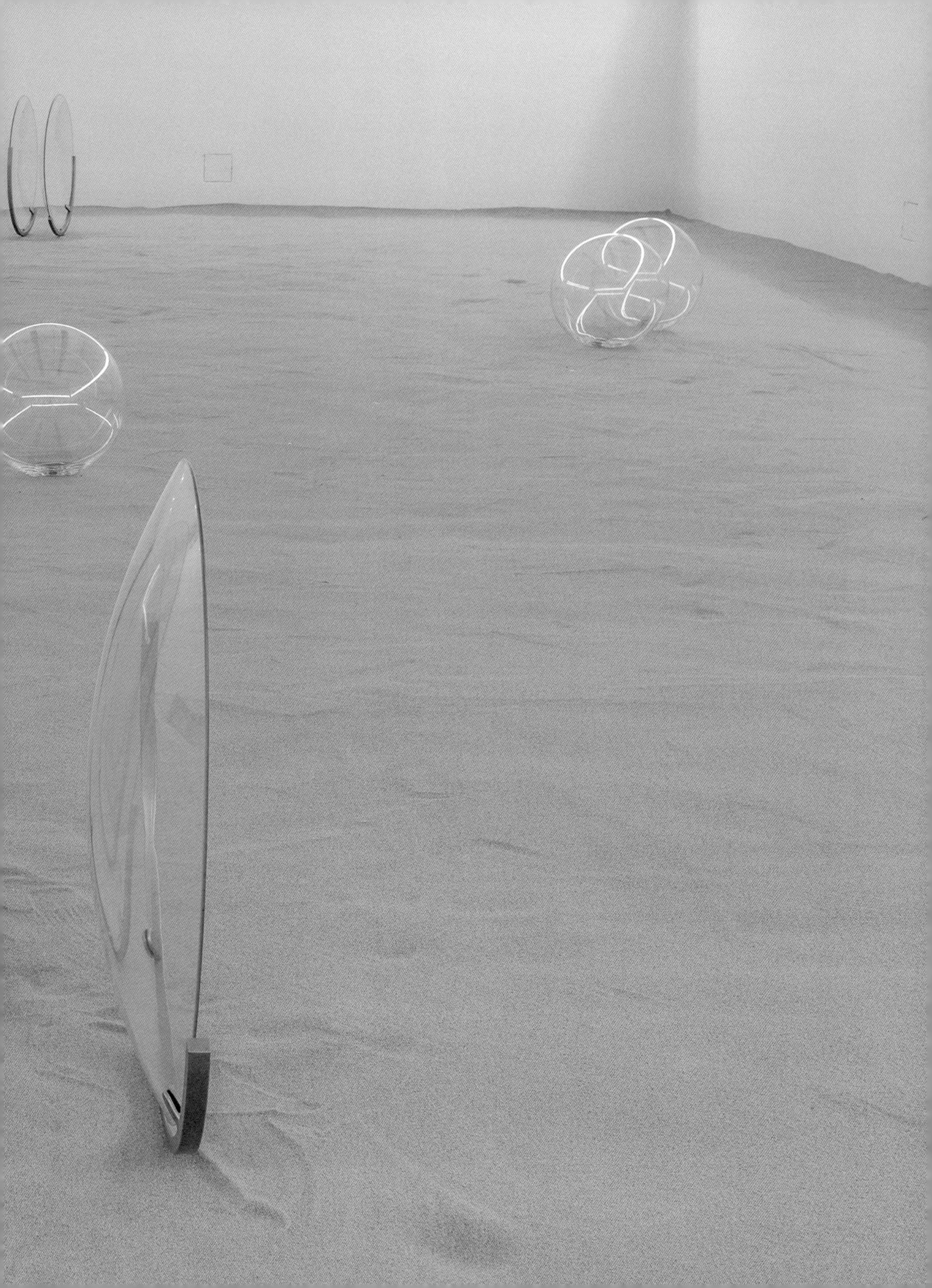

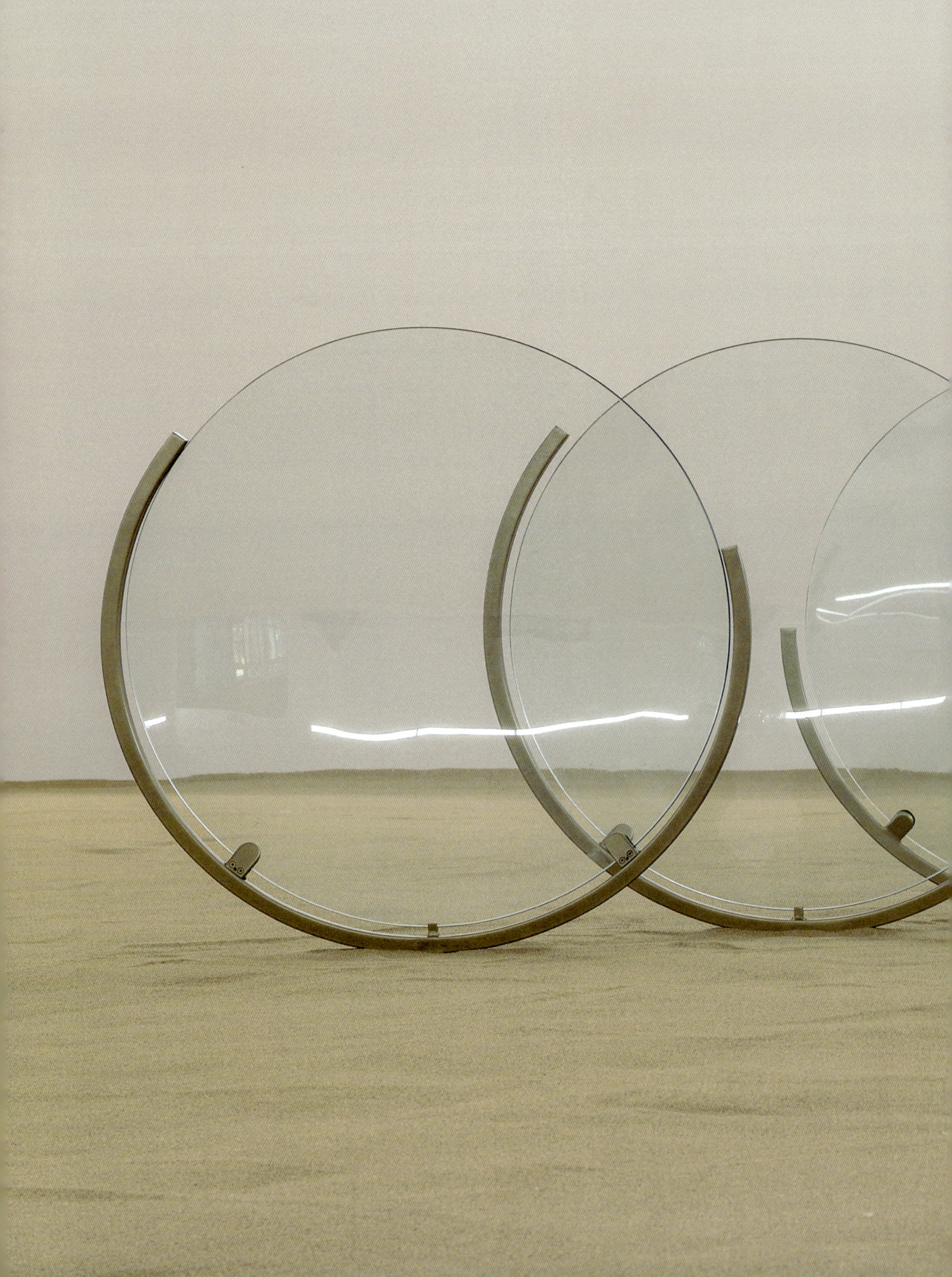

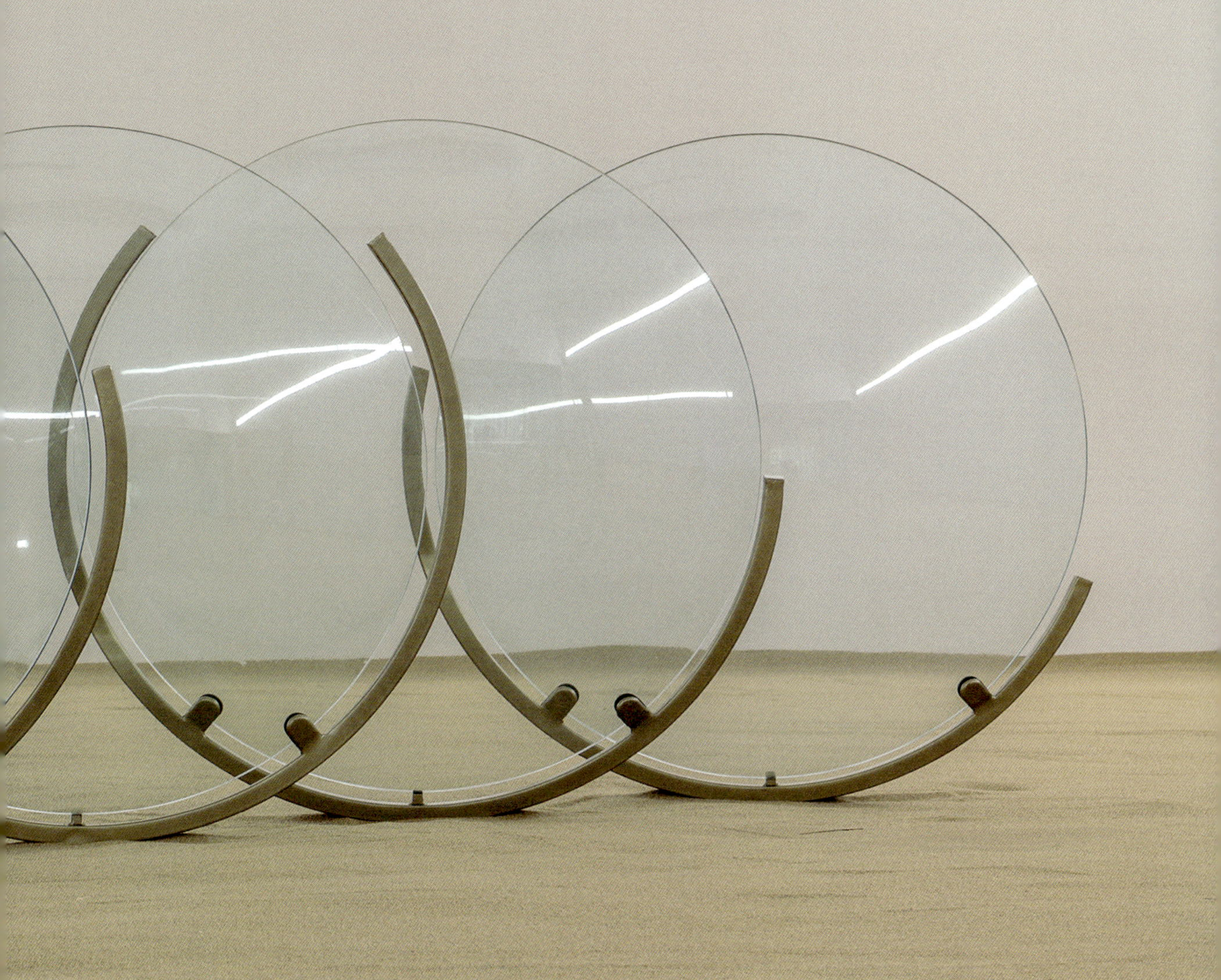

Potomitans, 2021. Exhibition view: Art Basel, Basel, Switzerland, 2021

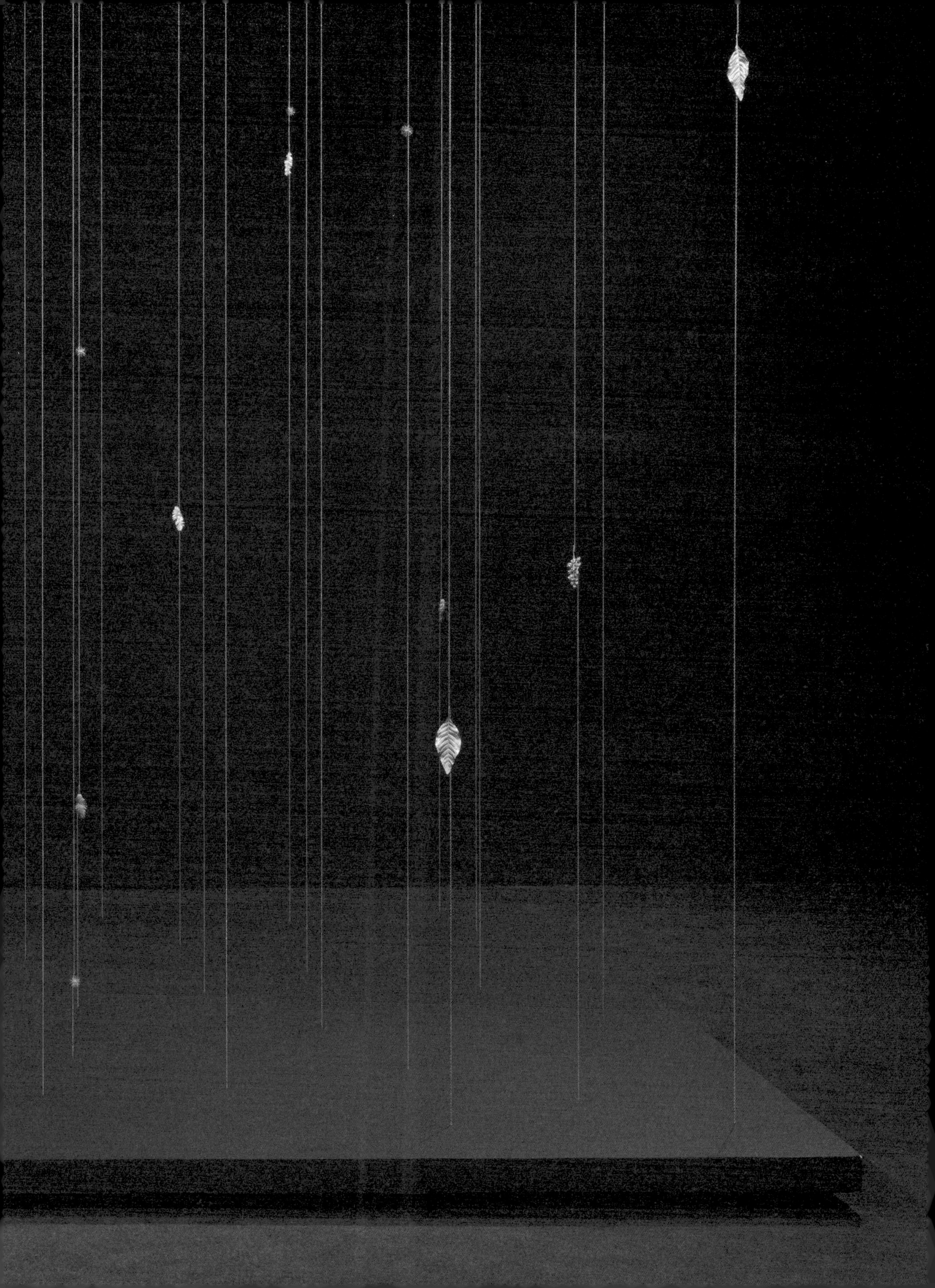

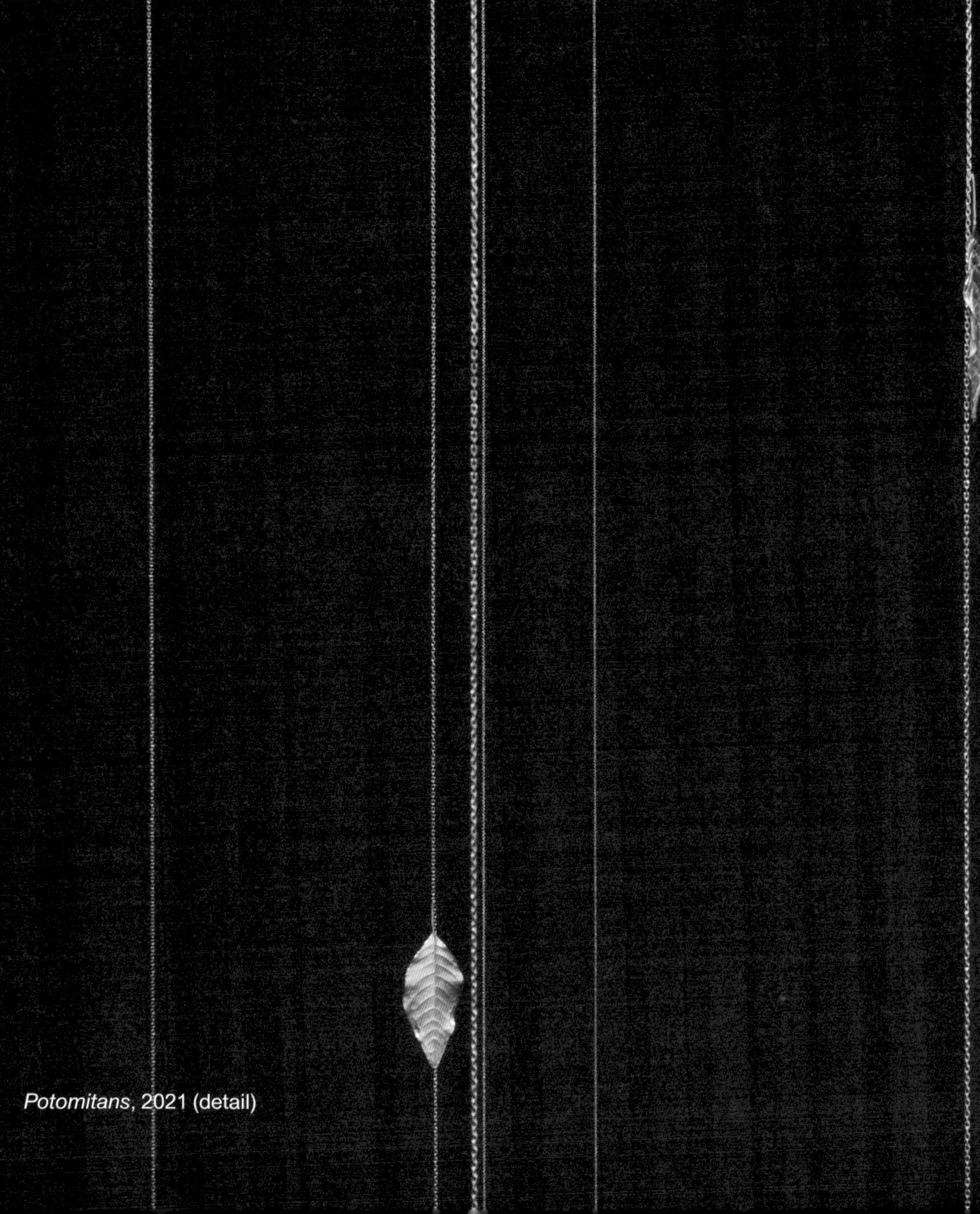

Potomitans, 2021 (detail)

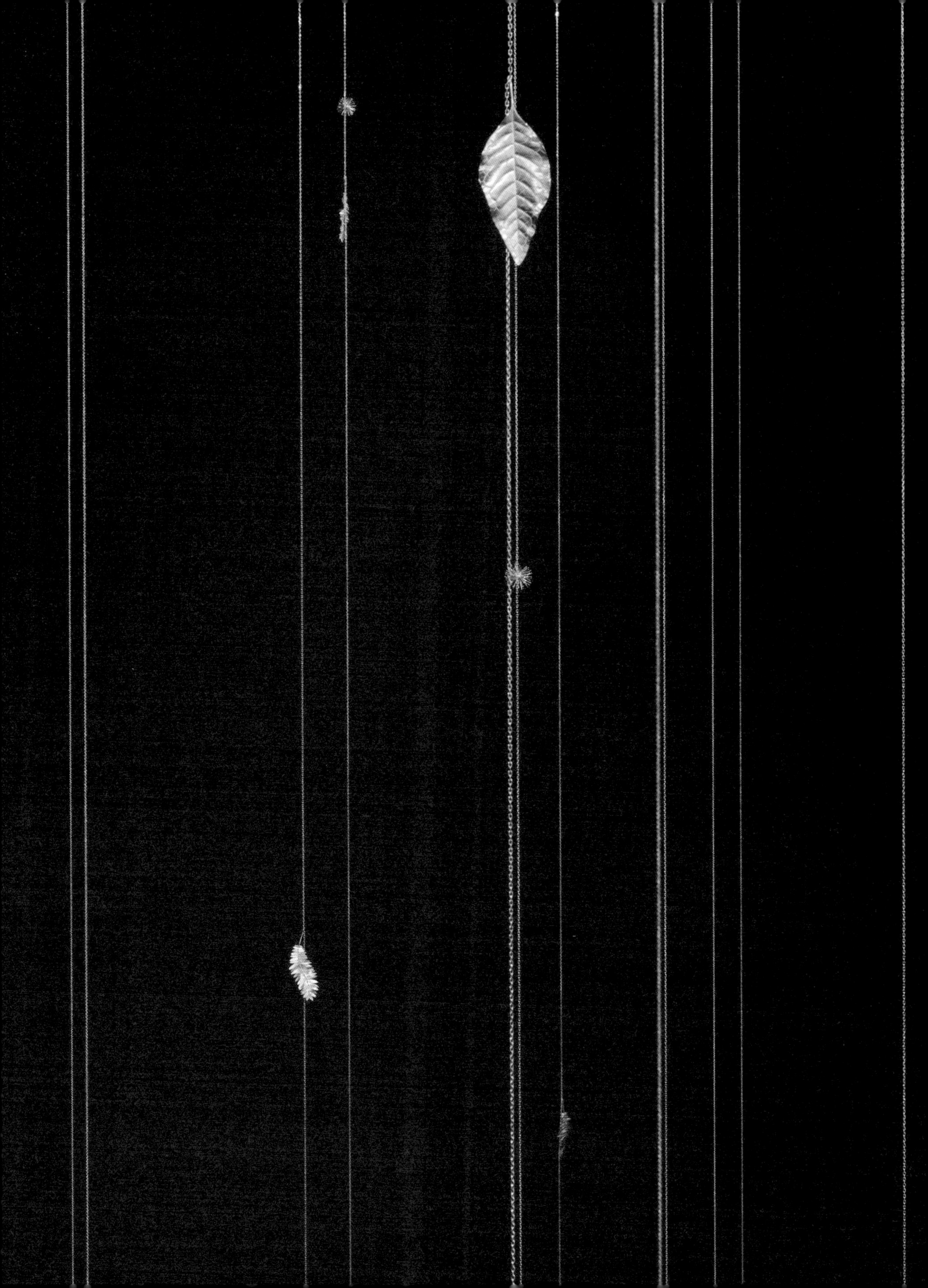

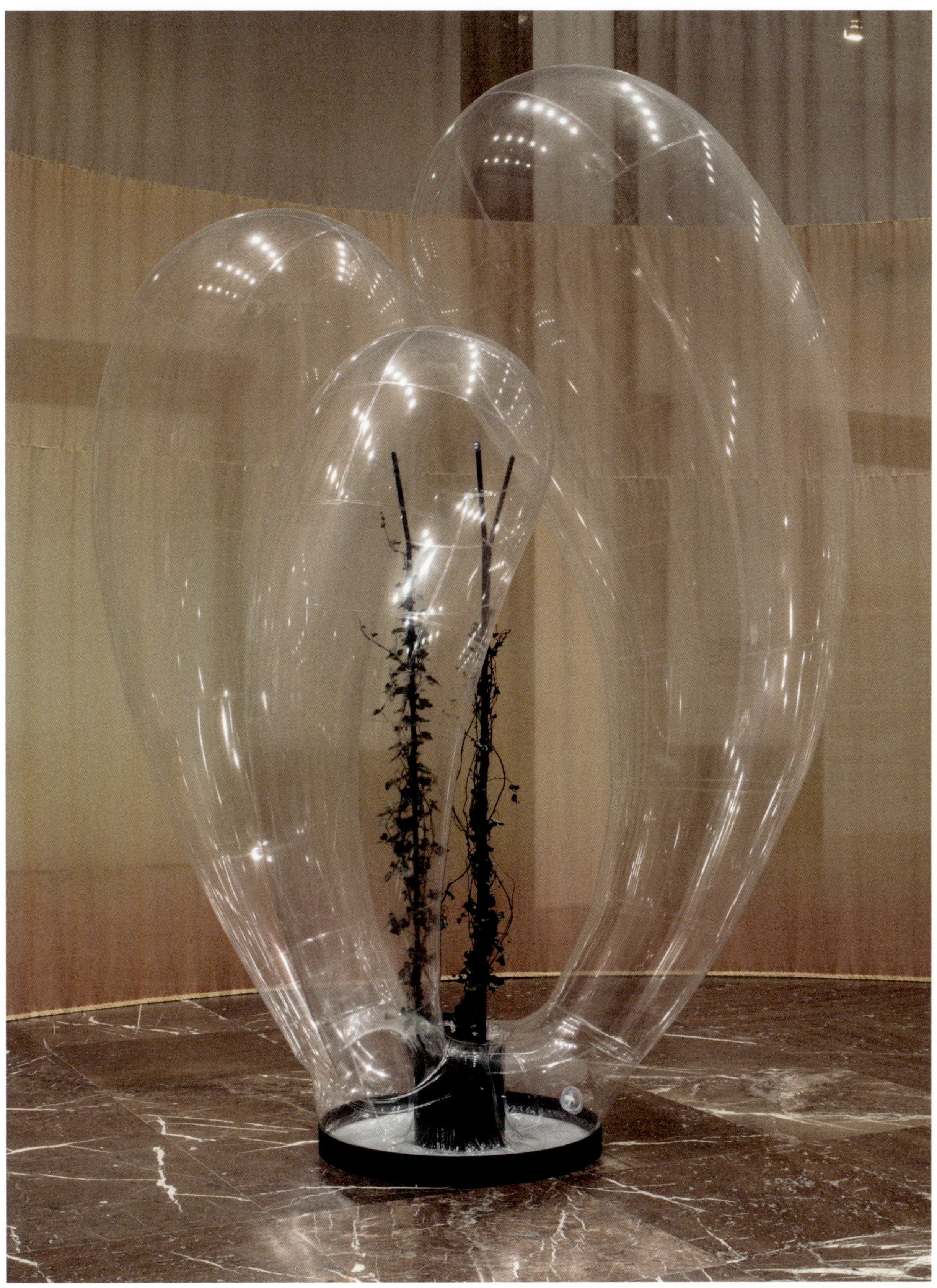

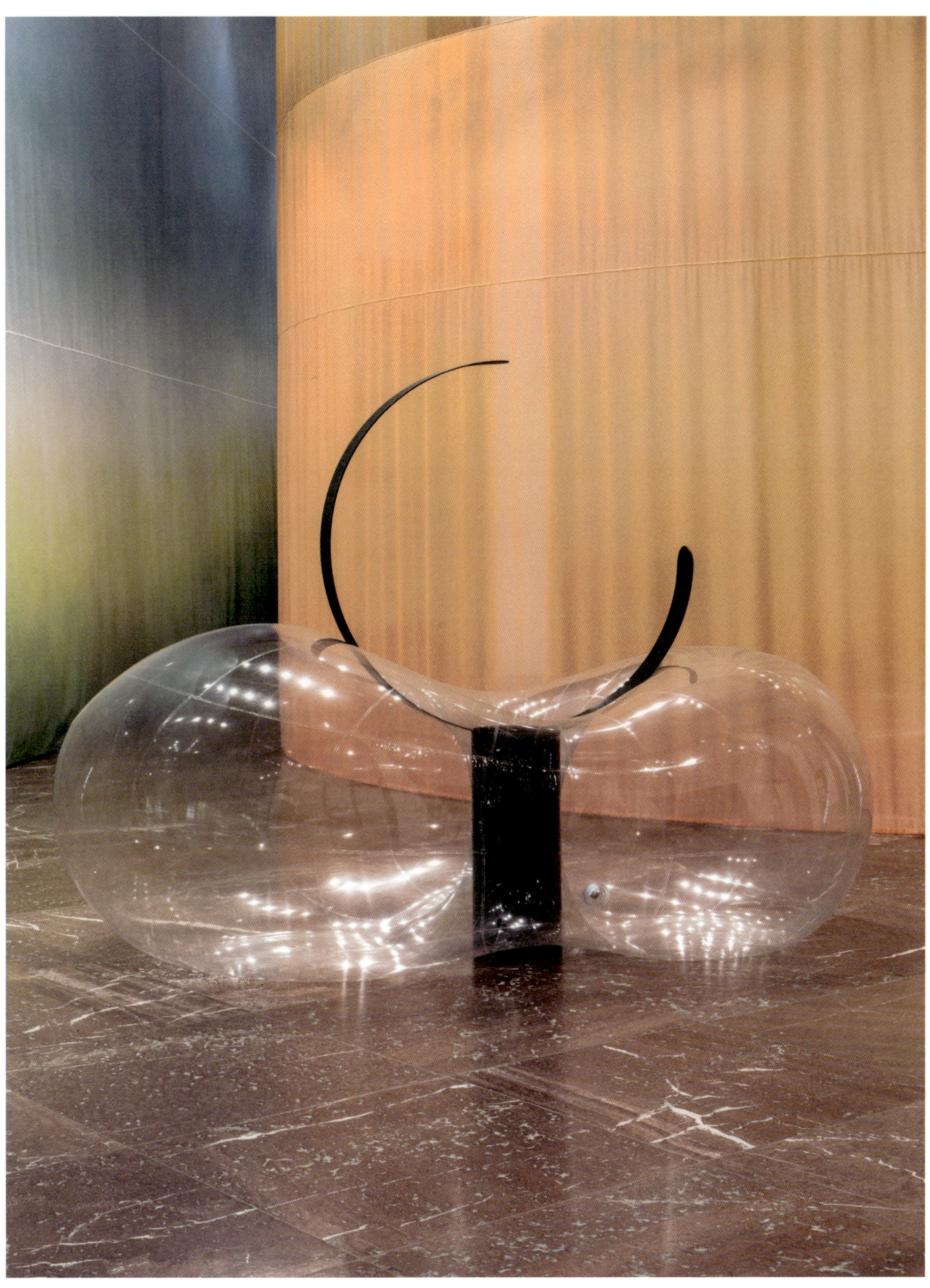

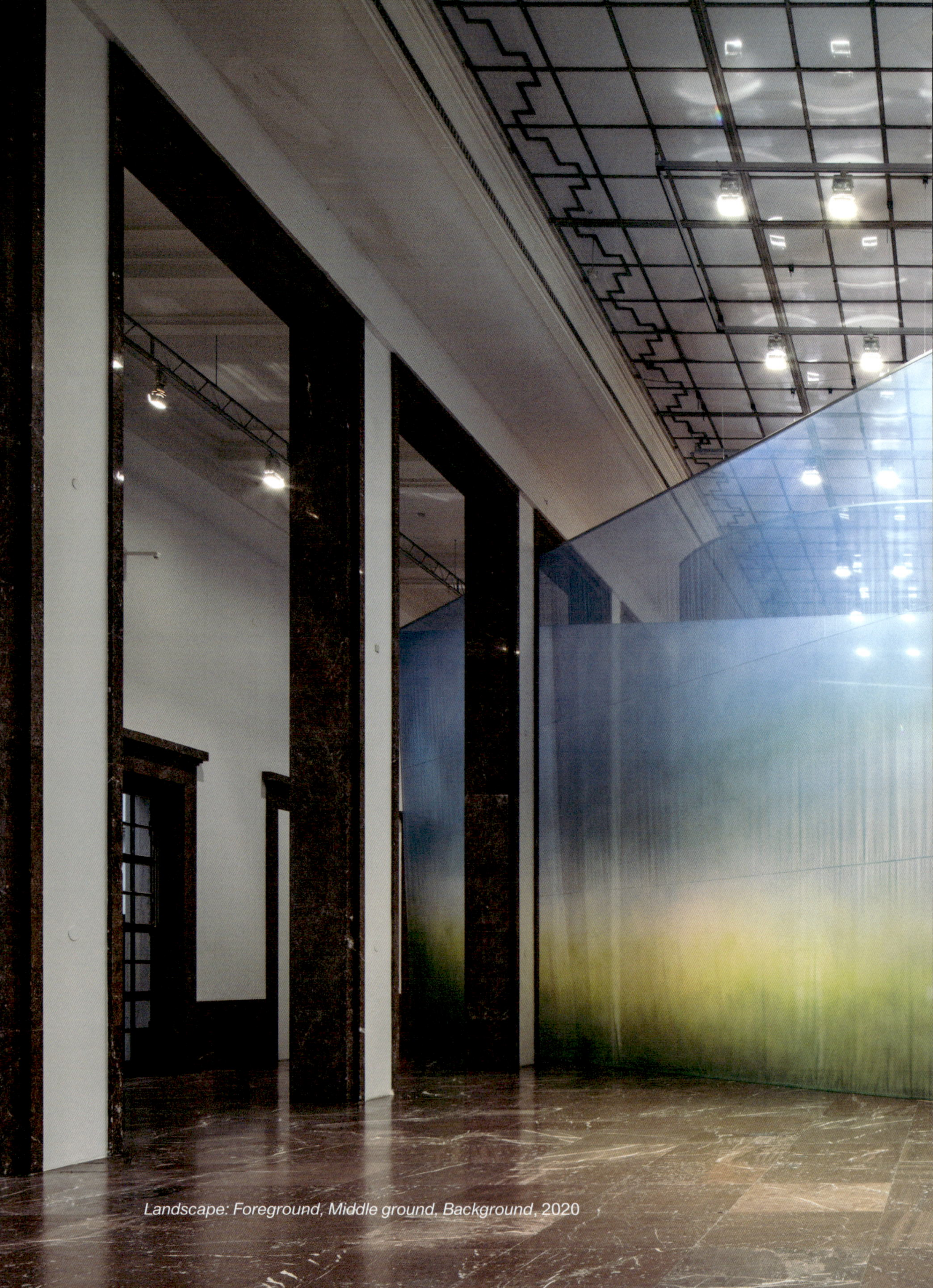

Landscape: Foreground, Middle ground, Background, 2020

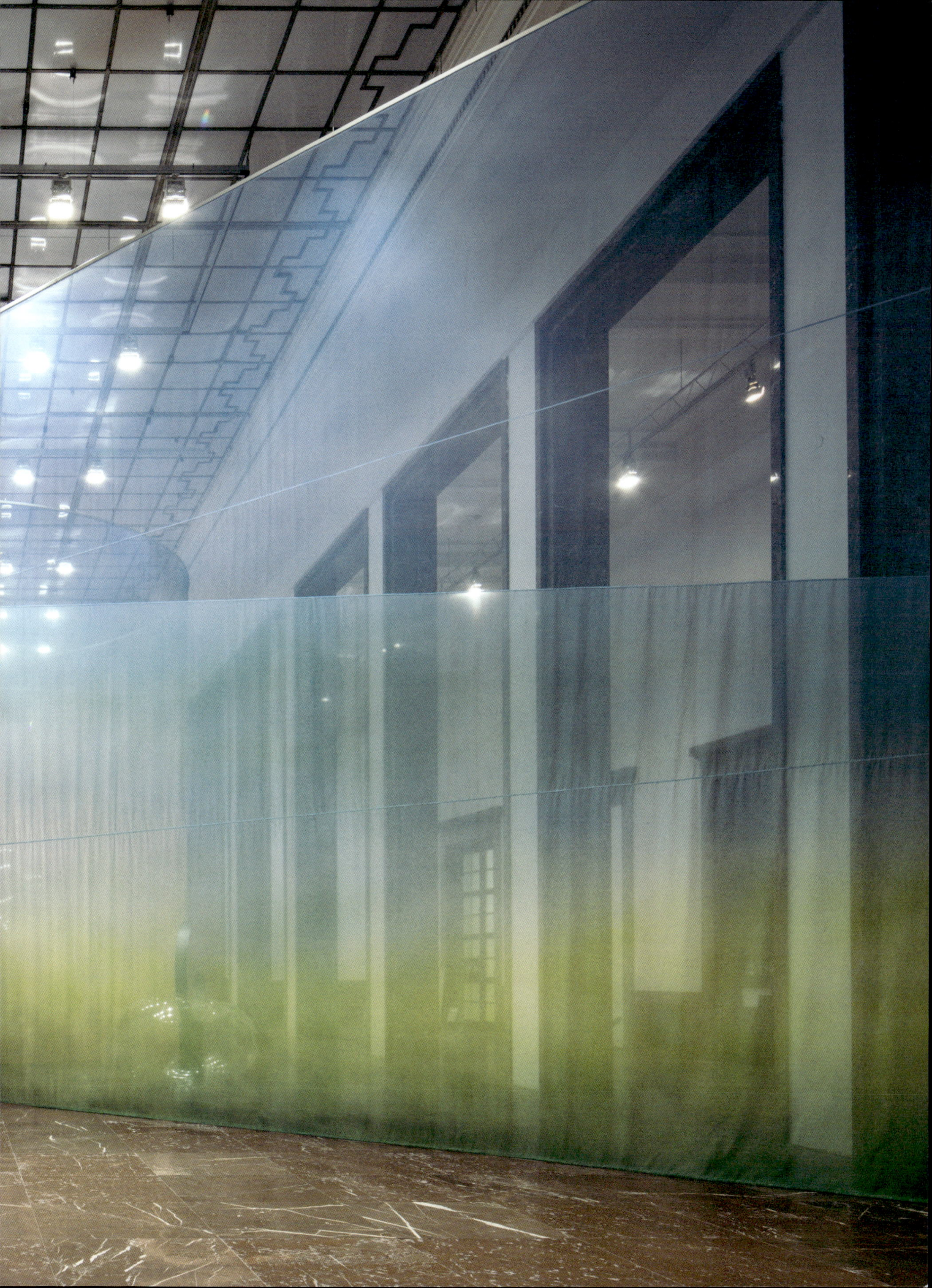

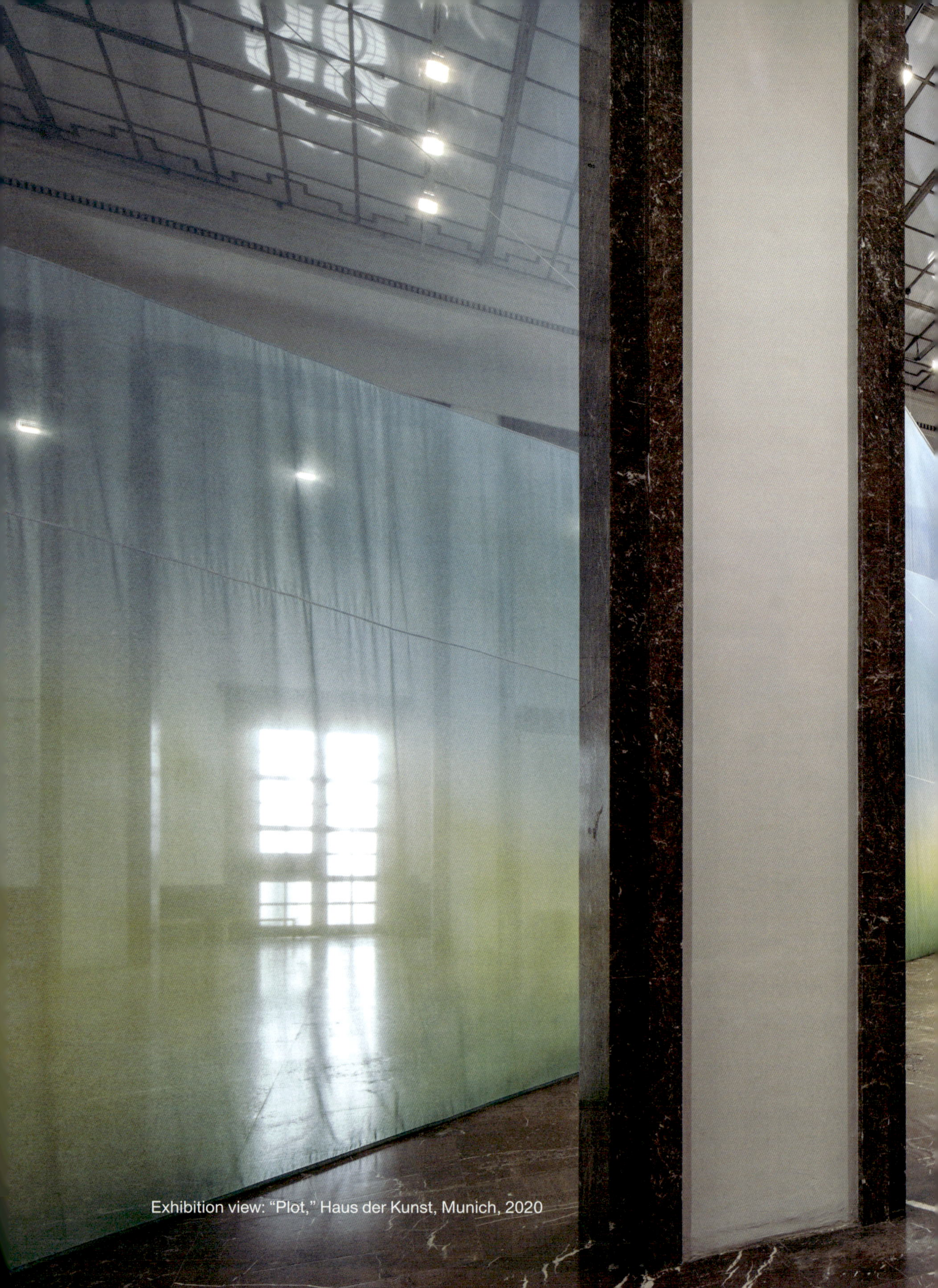

Exhibition view: "Plot," Haus der Kunst, Munich, 2020

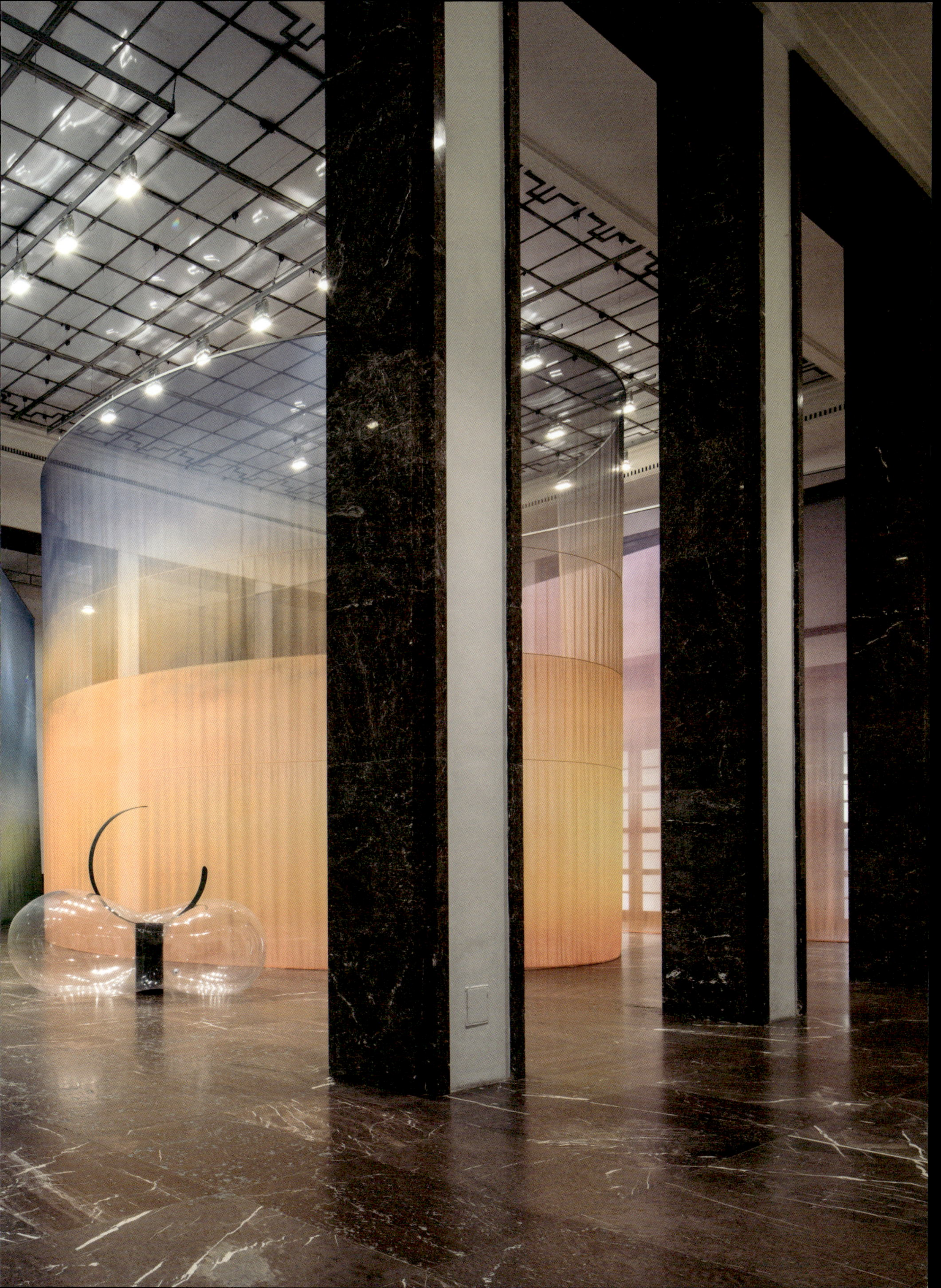

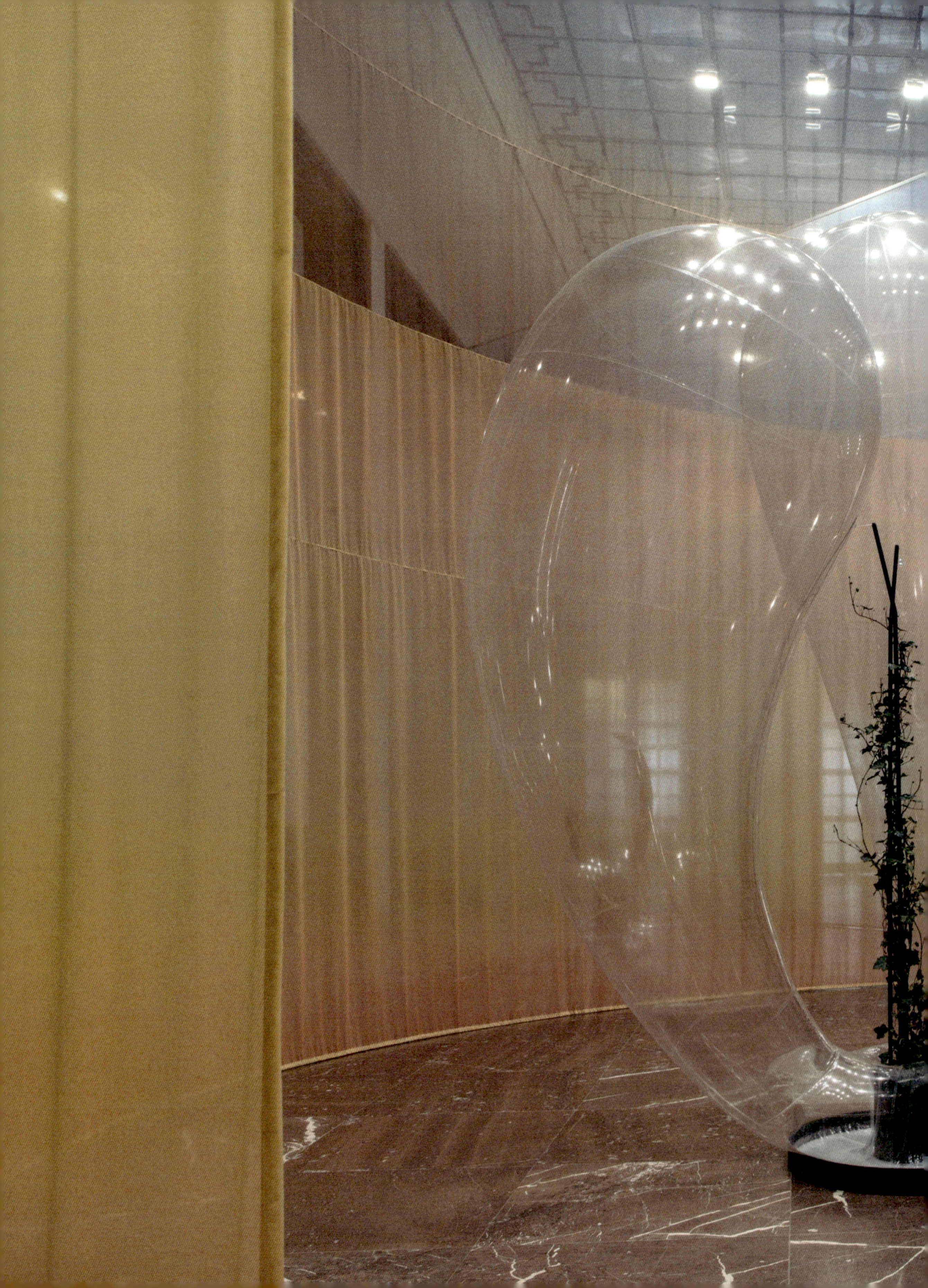

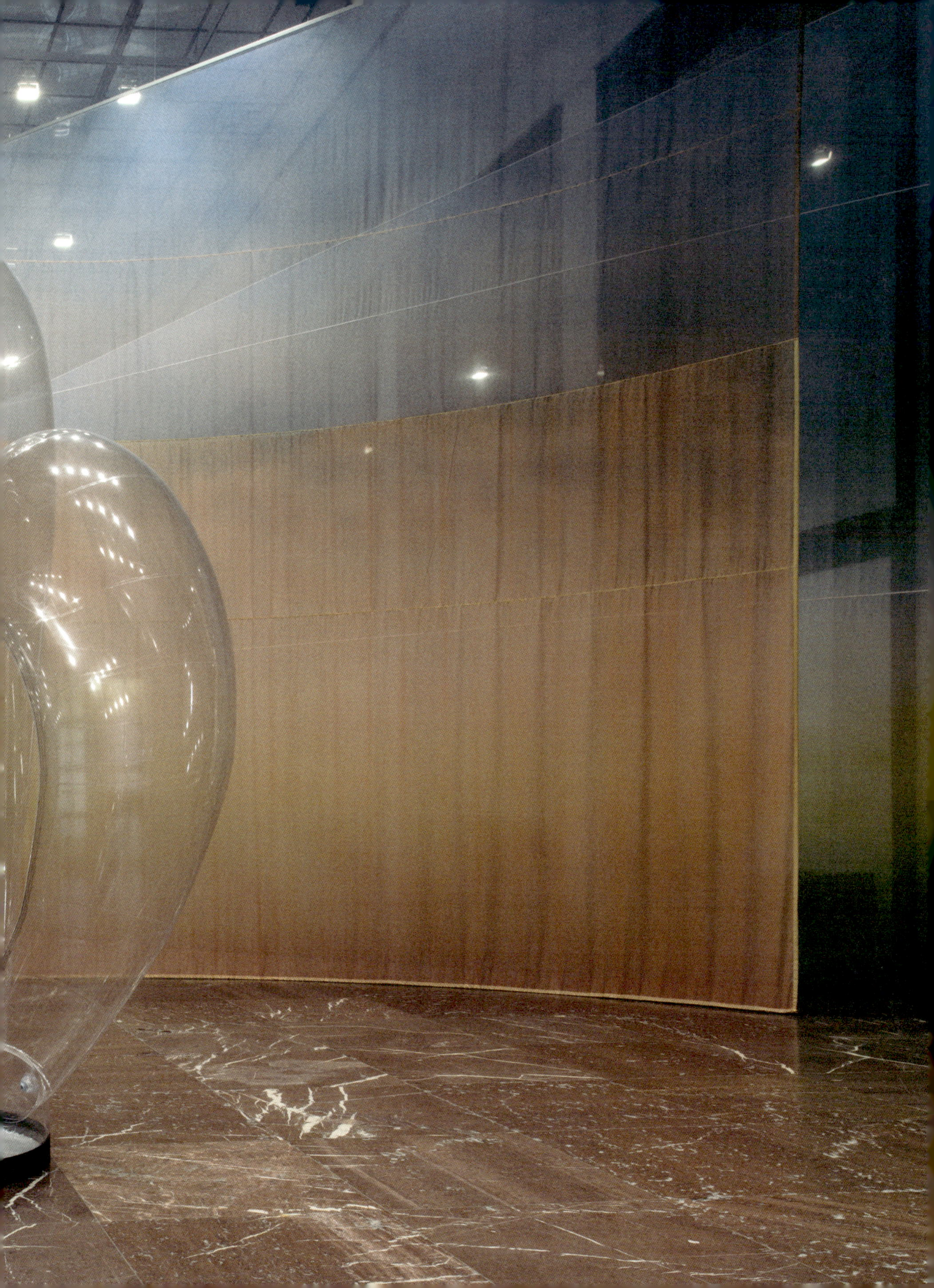

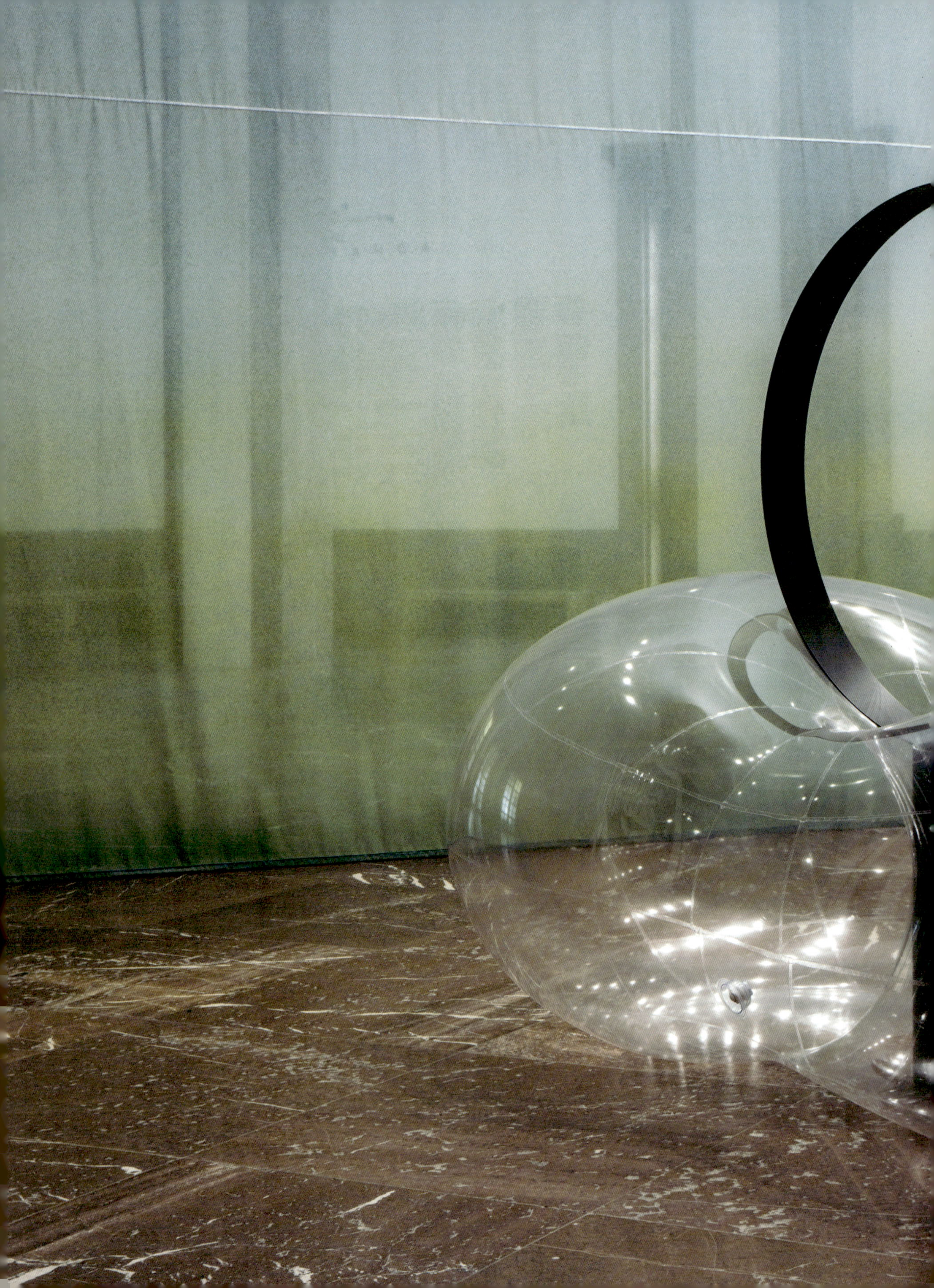

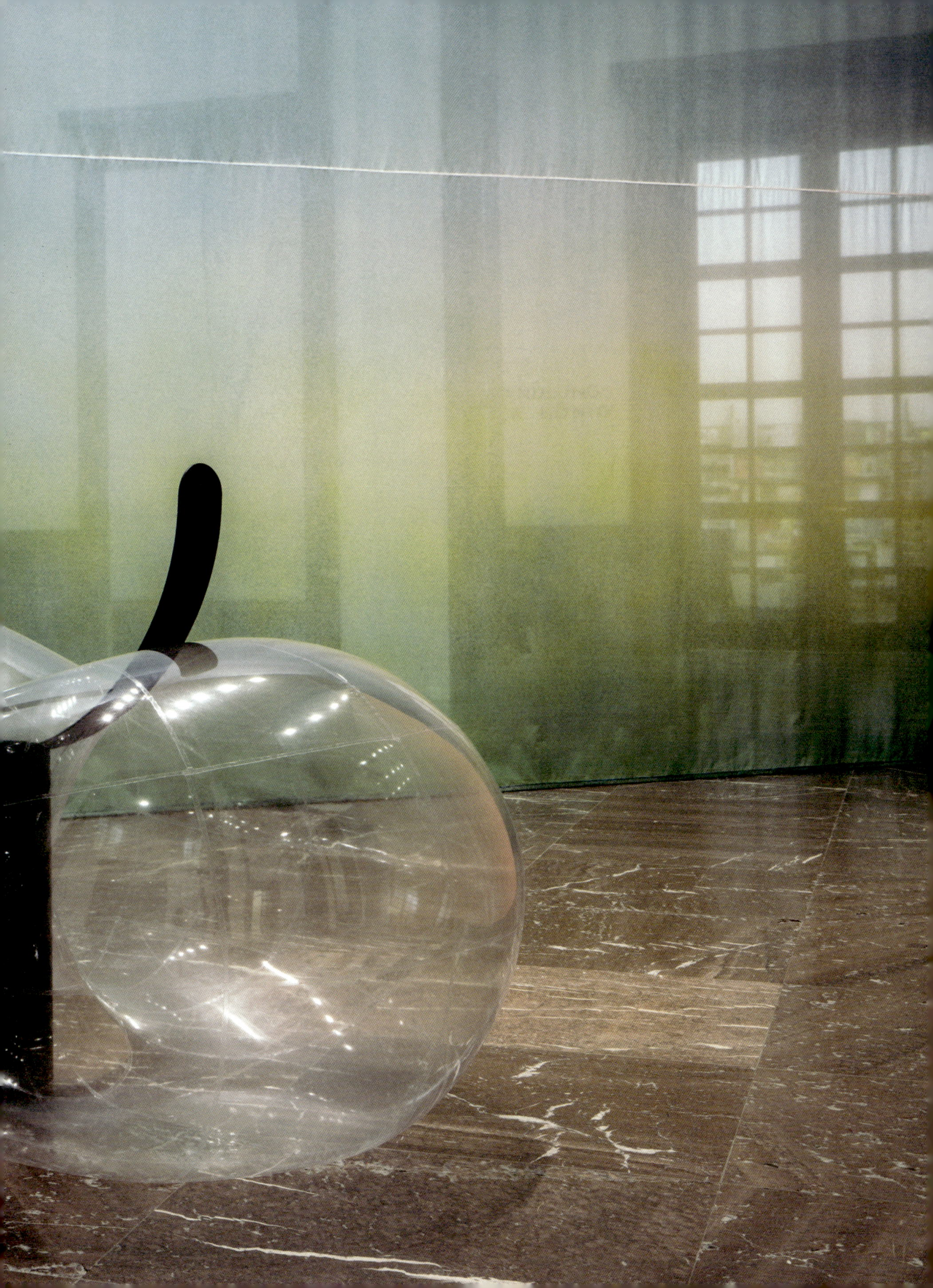

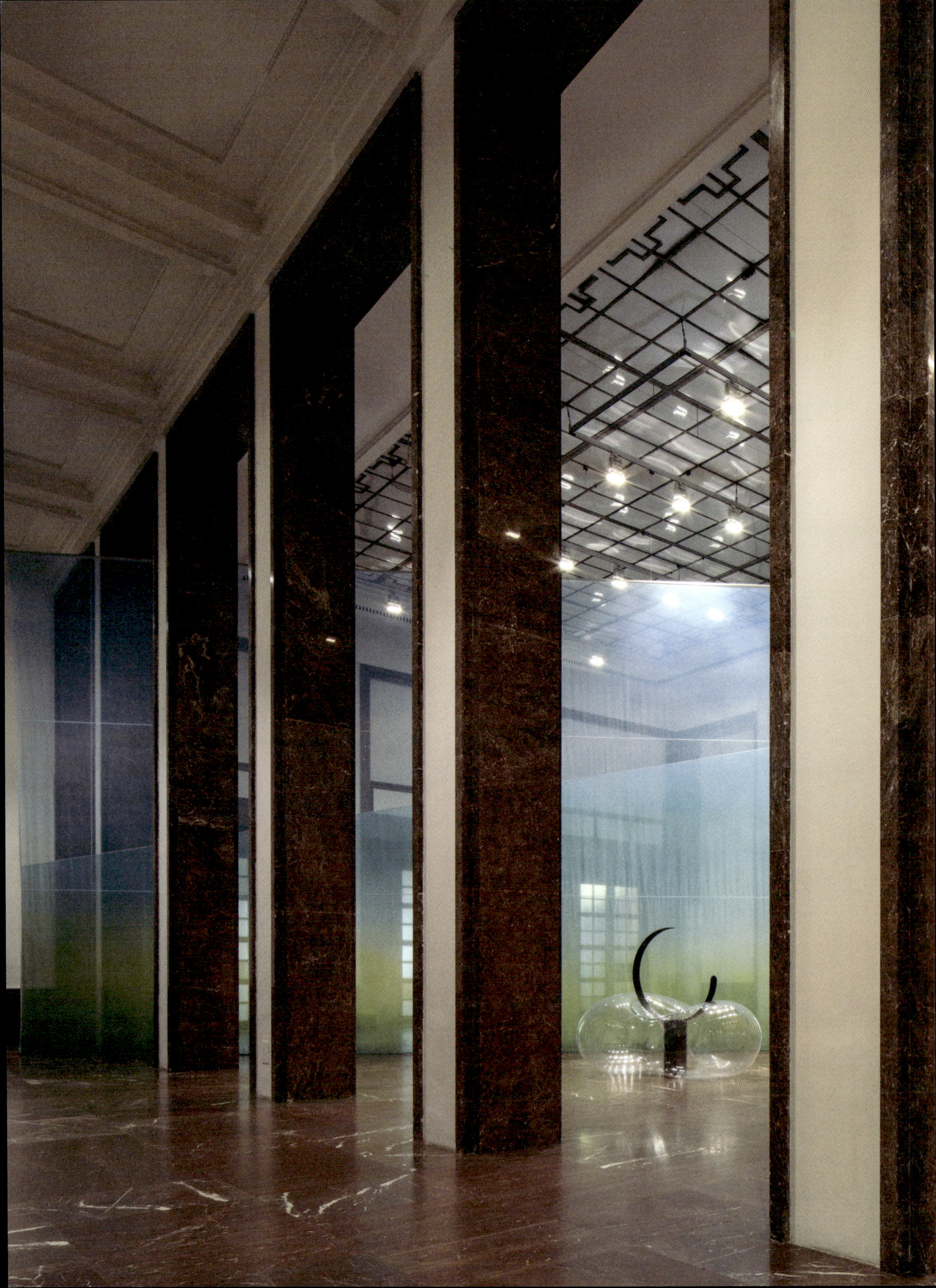

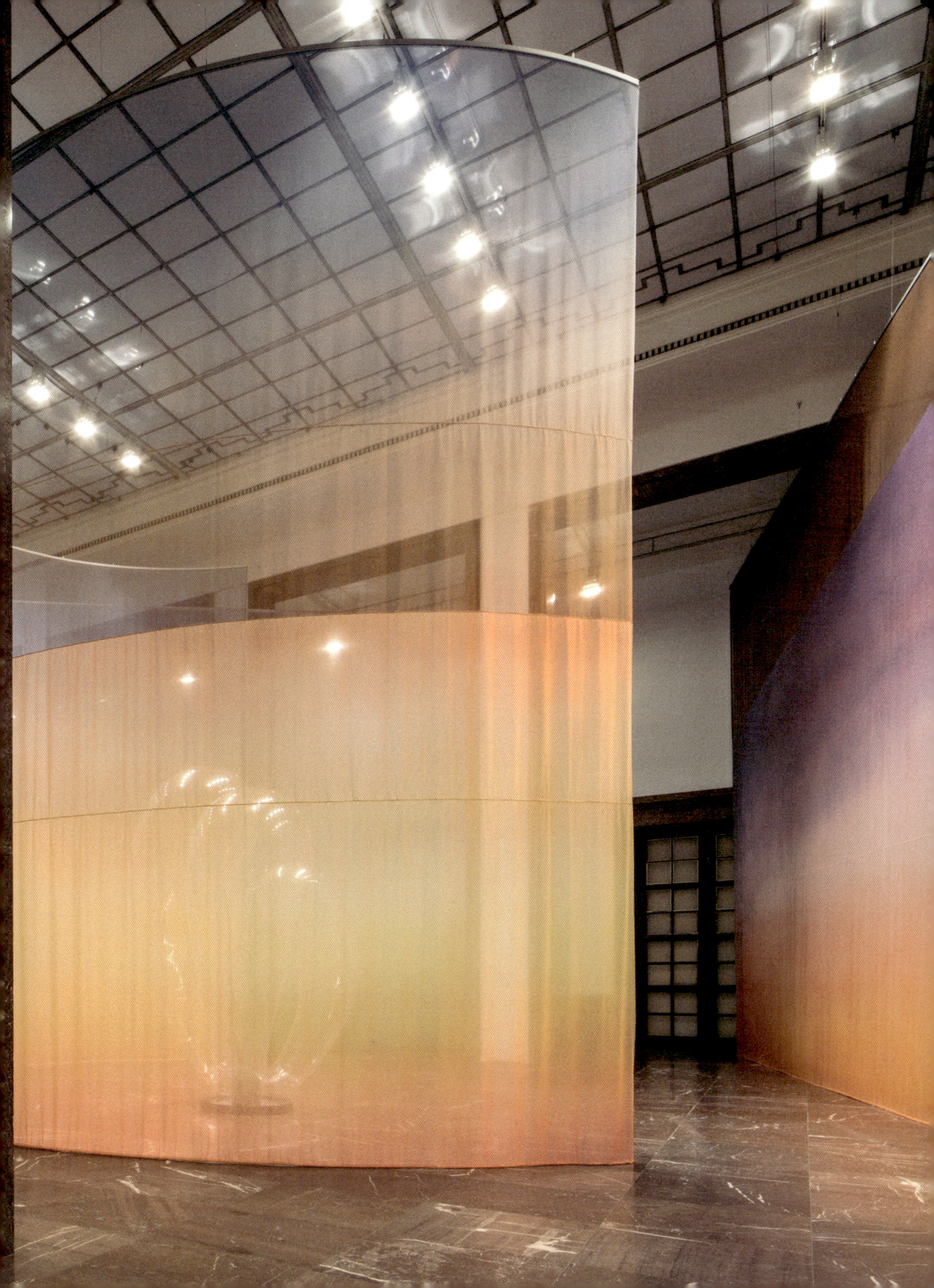

The Marias, 2020. Exhibition view: “An apology, a pill, a ritual, a resistance,” Remai Modern, Saskatoon, 2021

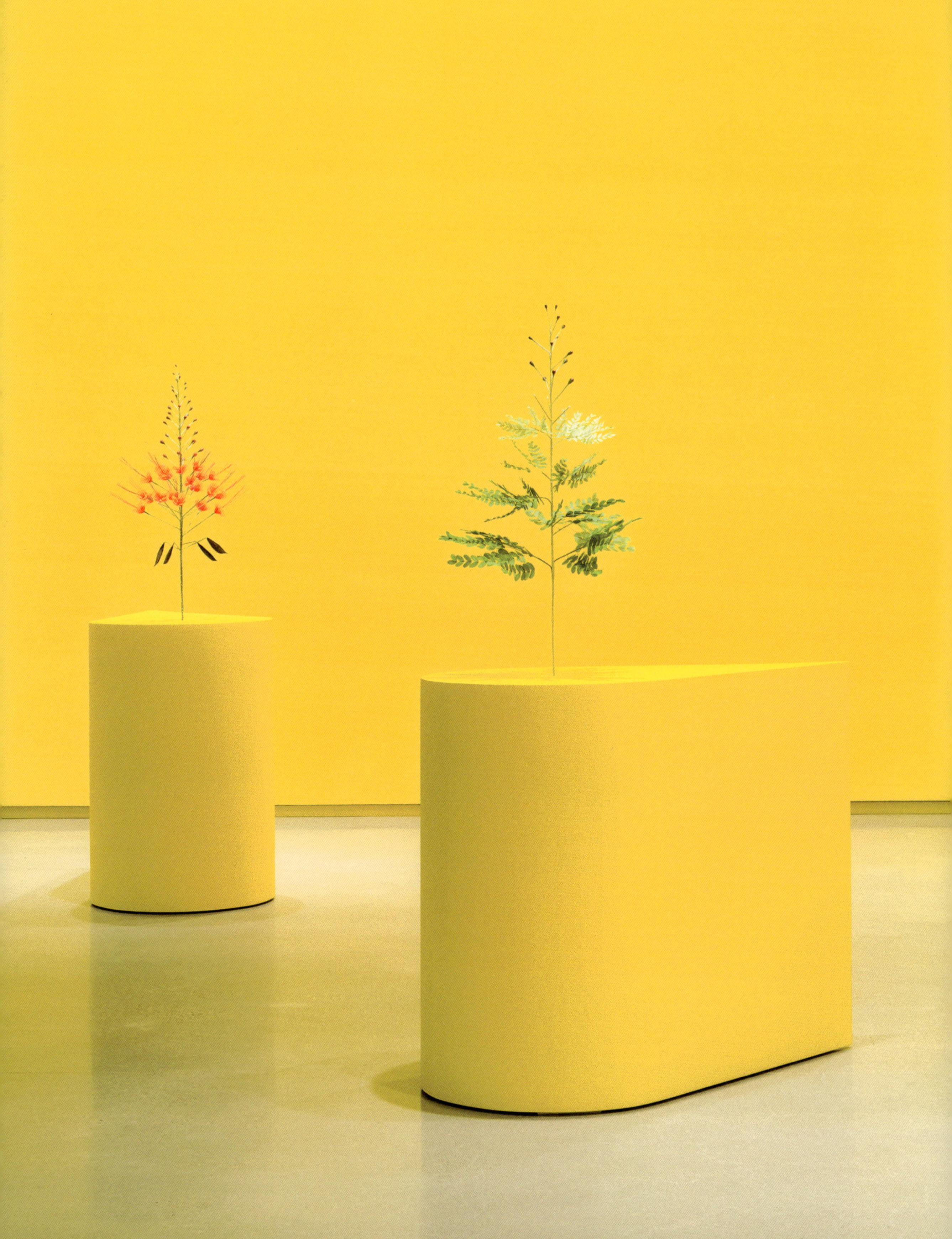

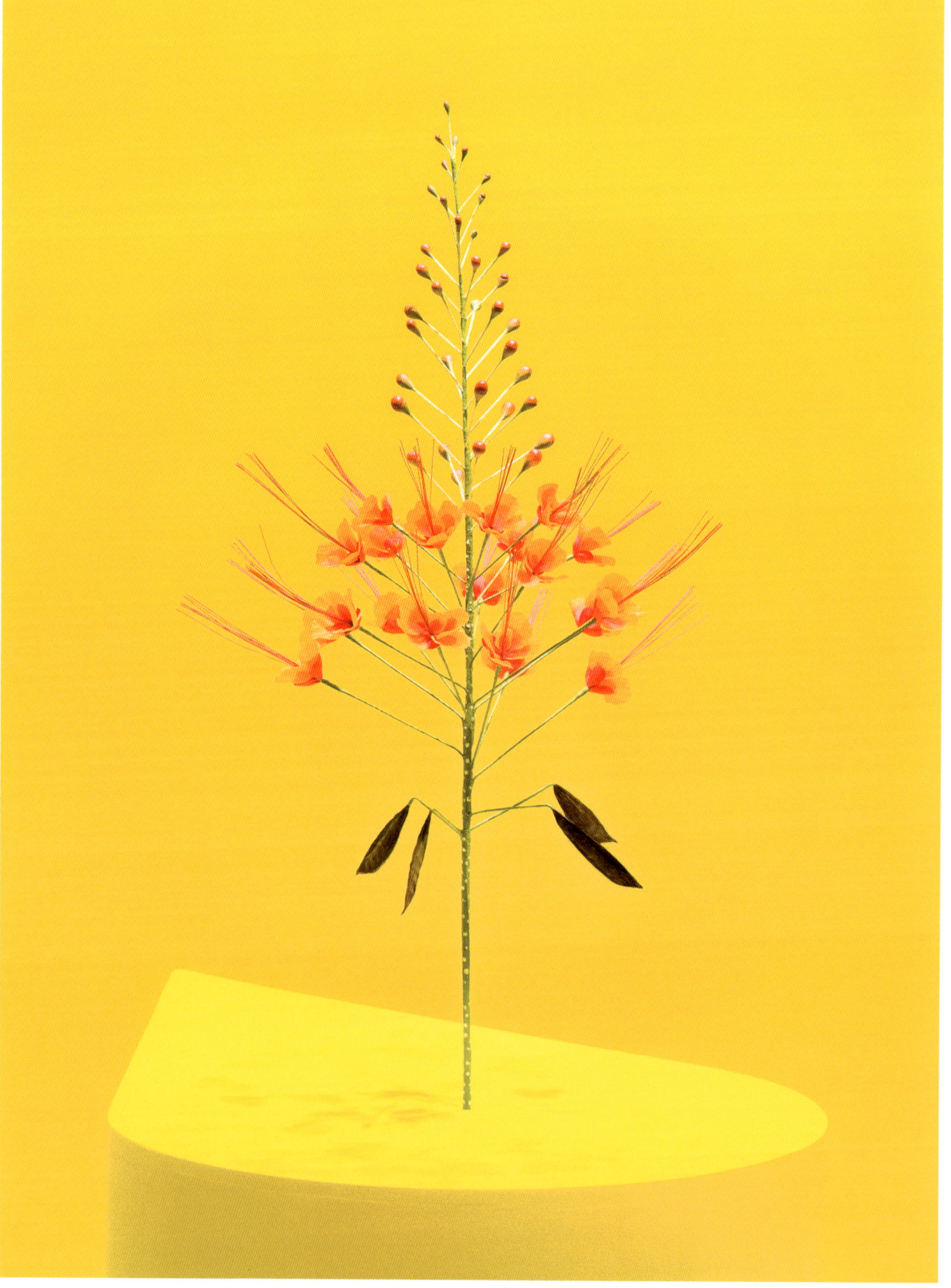

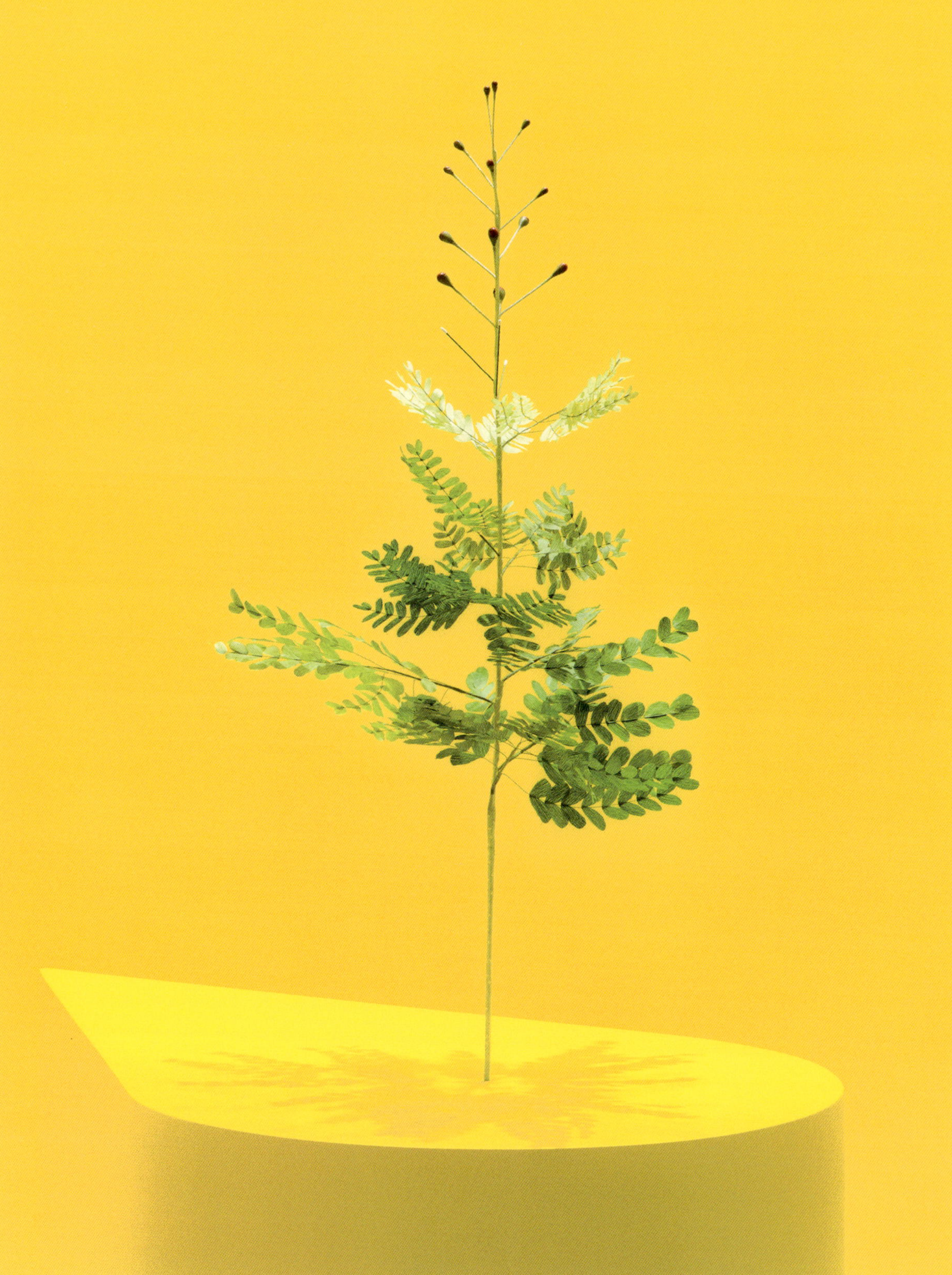

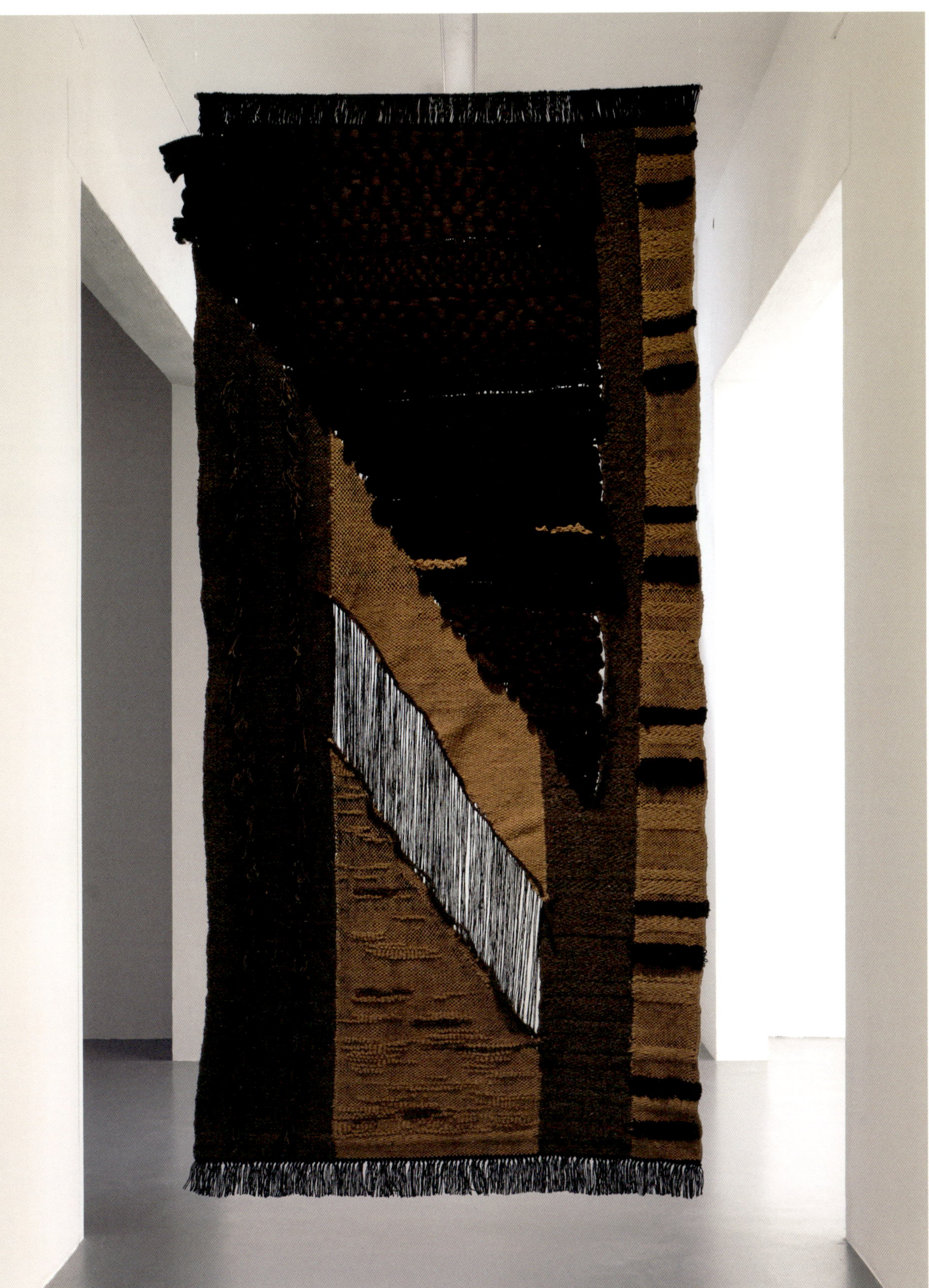

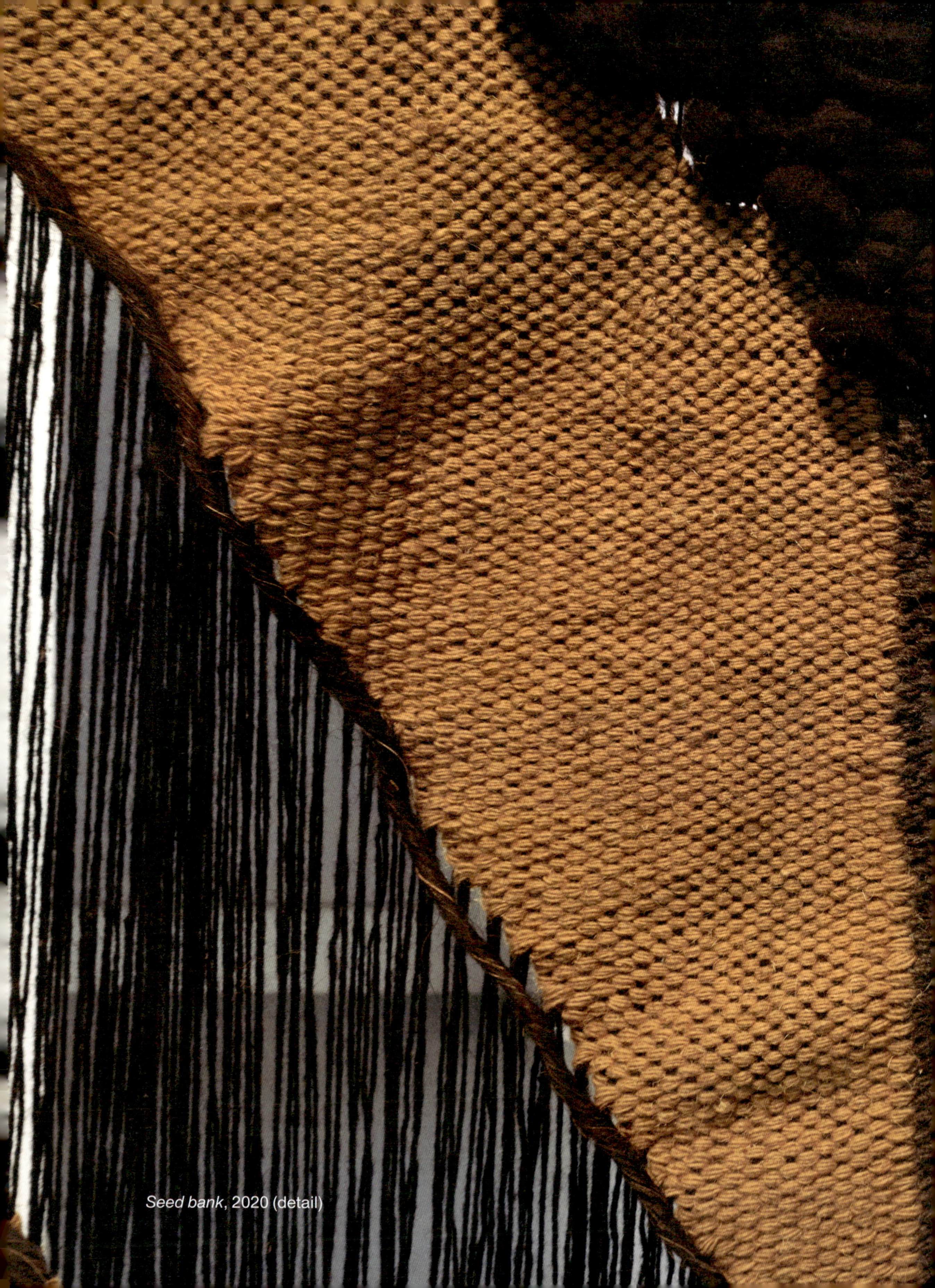

Seed bank, 2020 (detail)

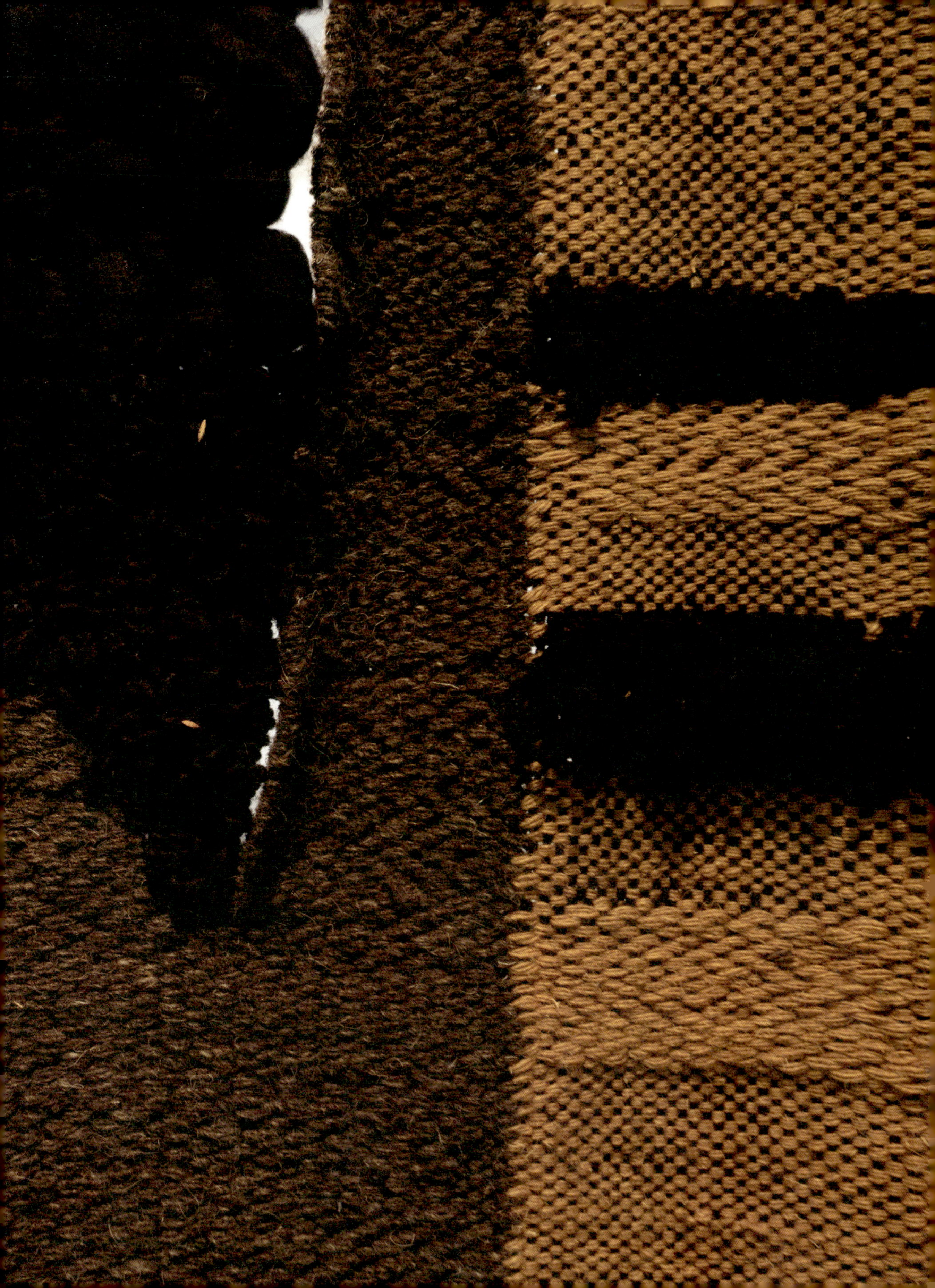

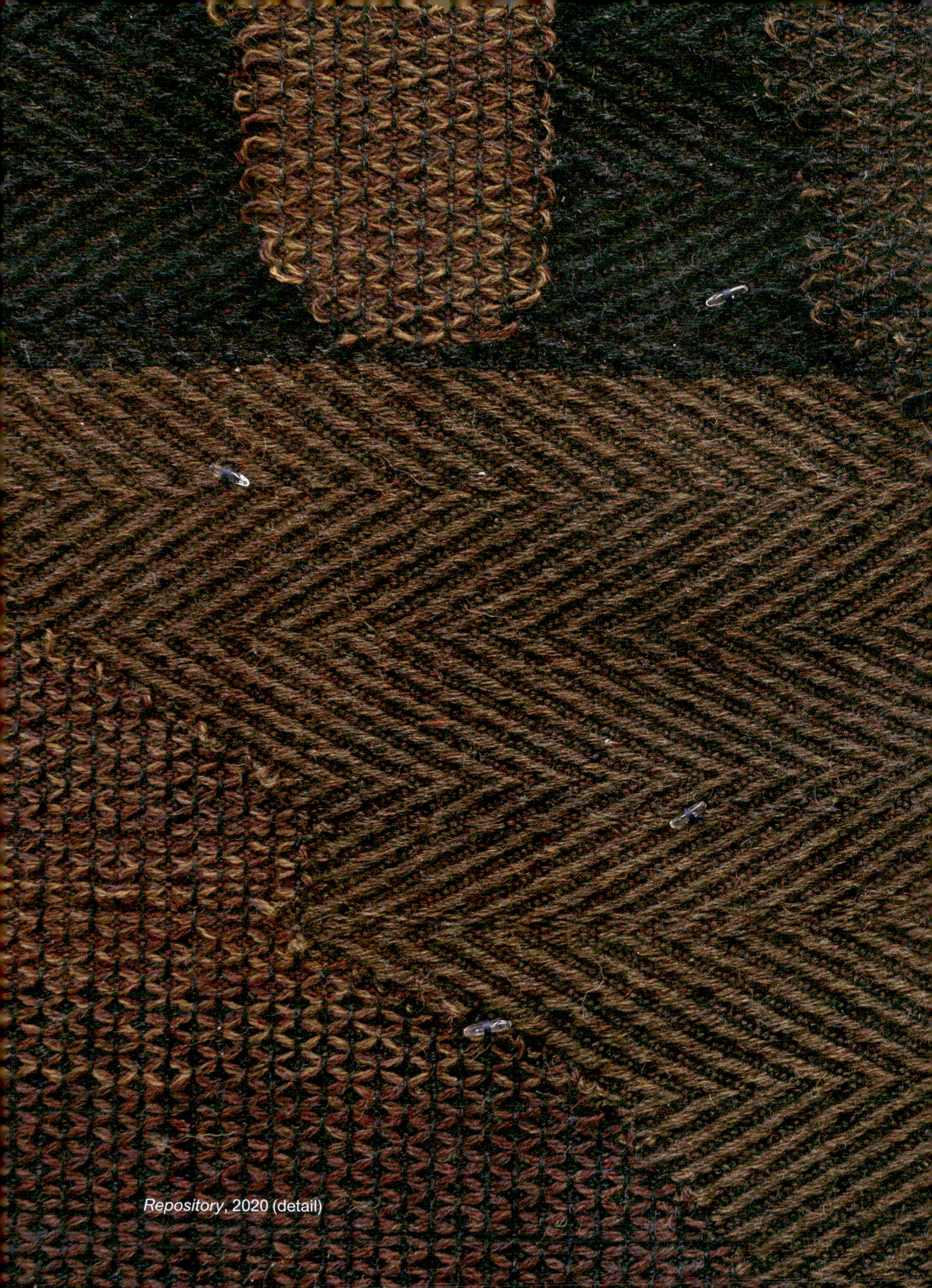

Repository, 2020 (detail)

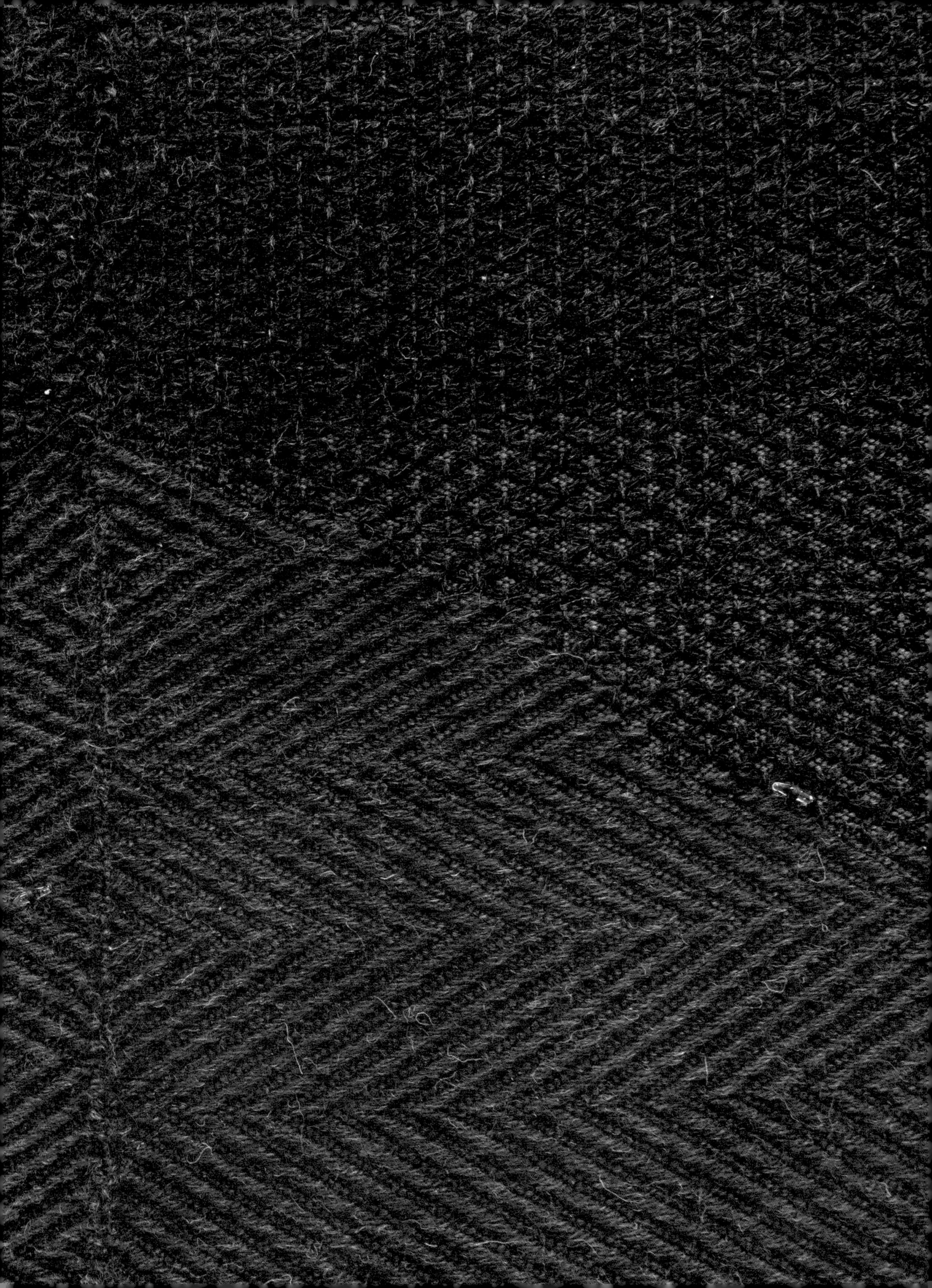

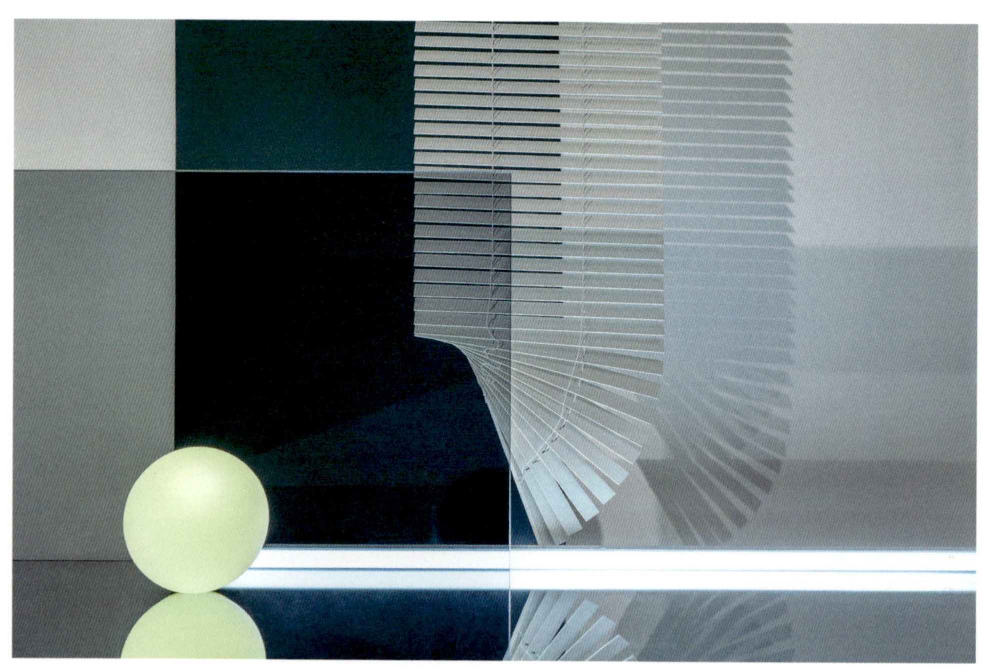

Counter-Illumination #1, 2020

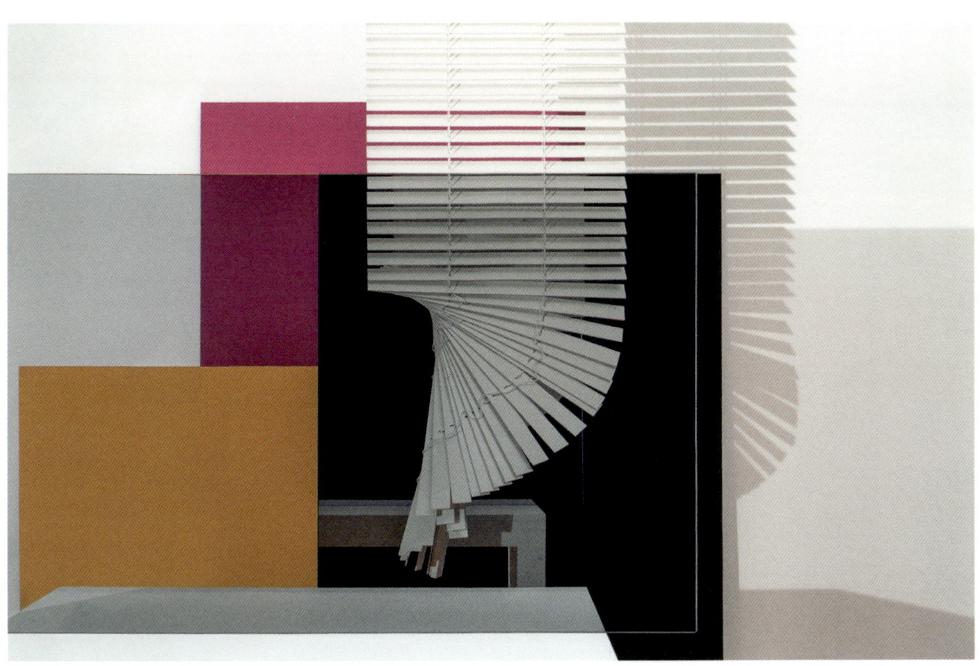

Counter-Illumination #2, 2020

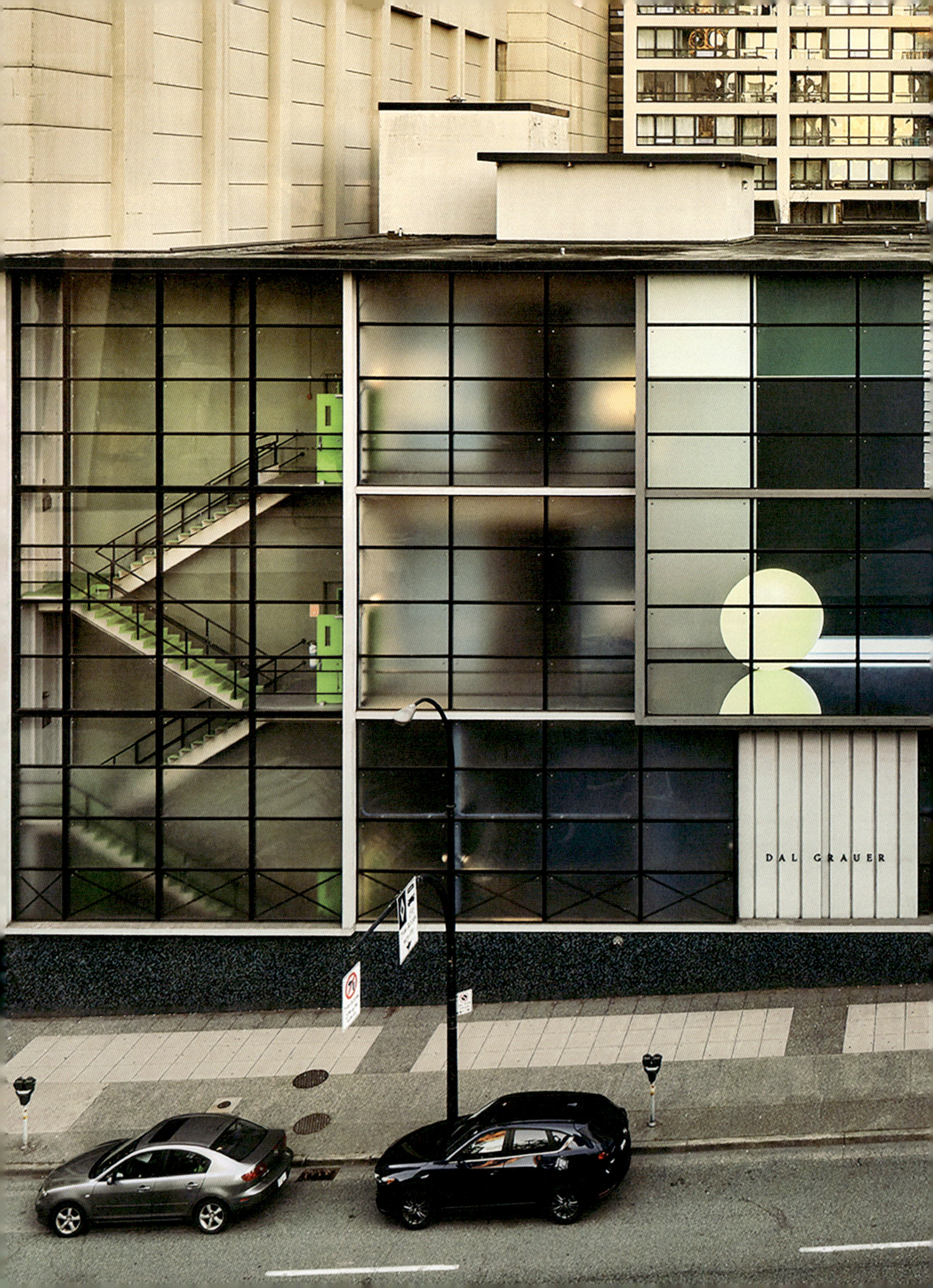
DAL GRAUER

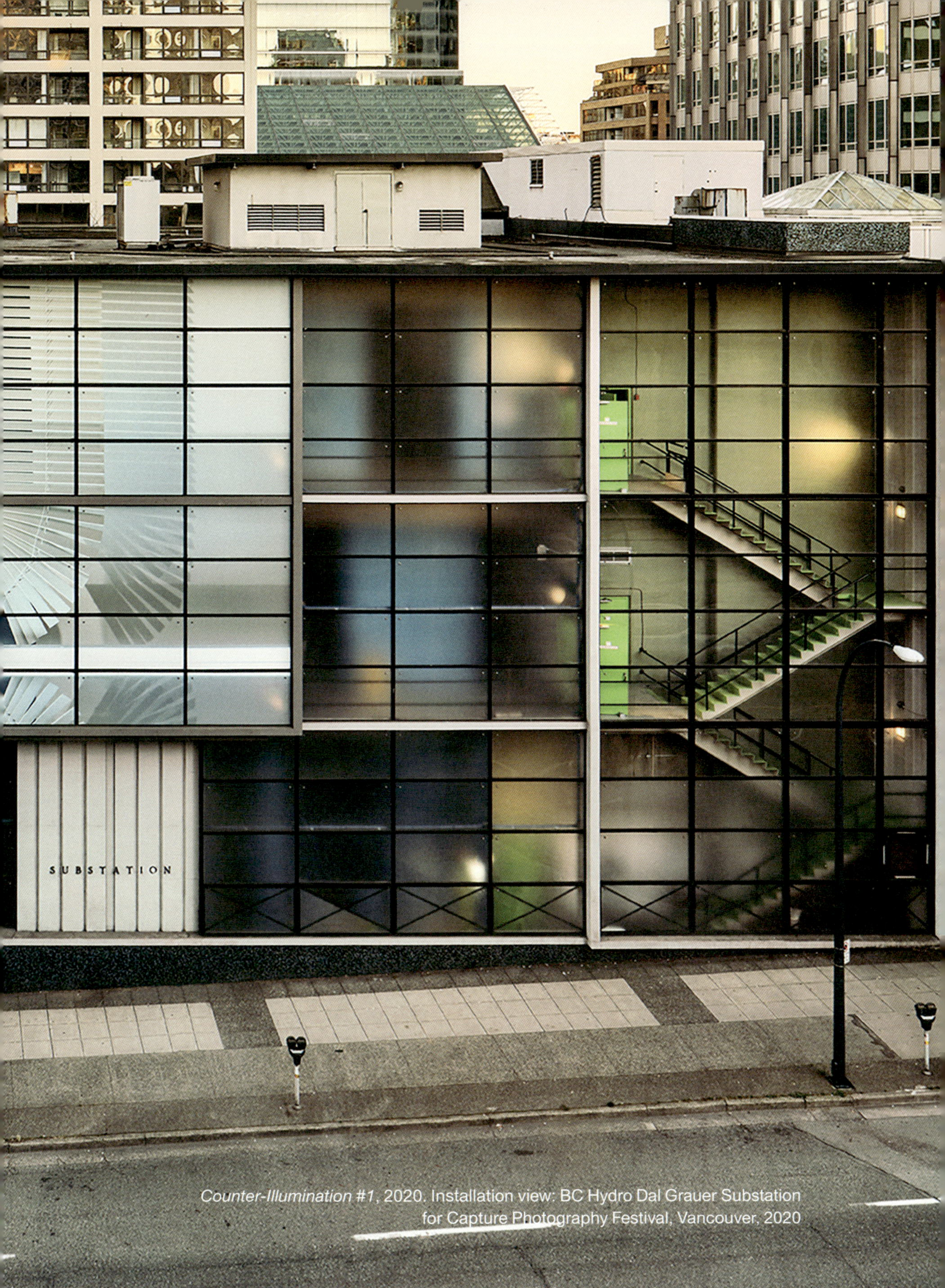

Counter-Illumination #1, 2020. Installation view: BC Hydro Dal Grauer Substation for Capture Photography Festival, Vancouver, 2020

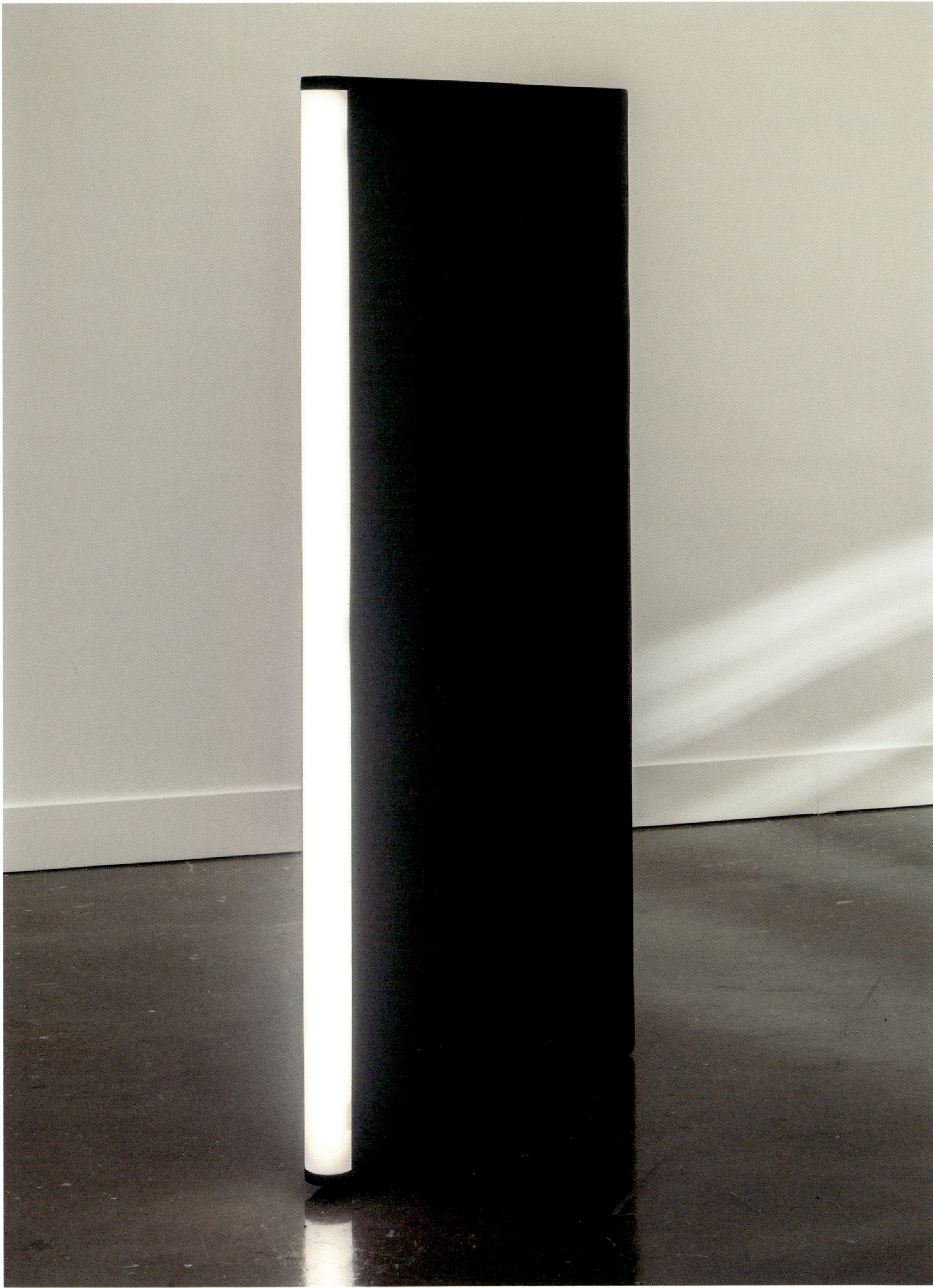

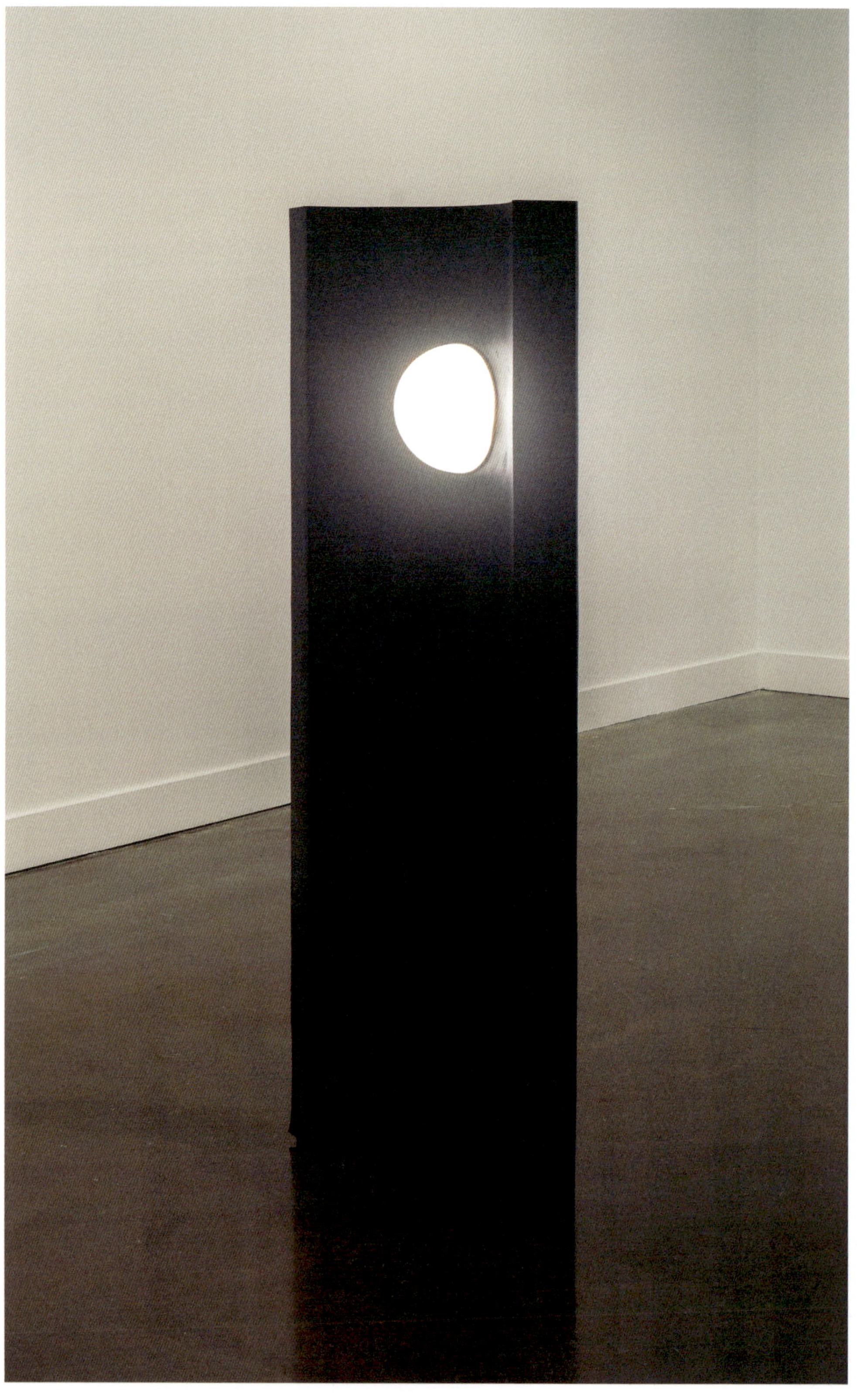

Glow #2, 2019

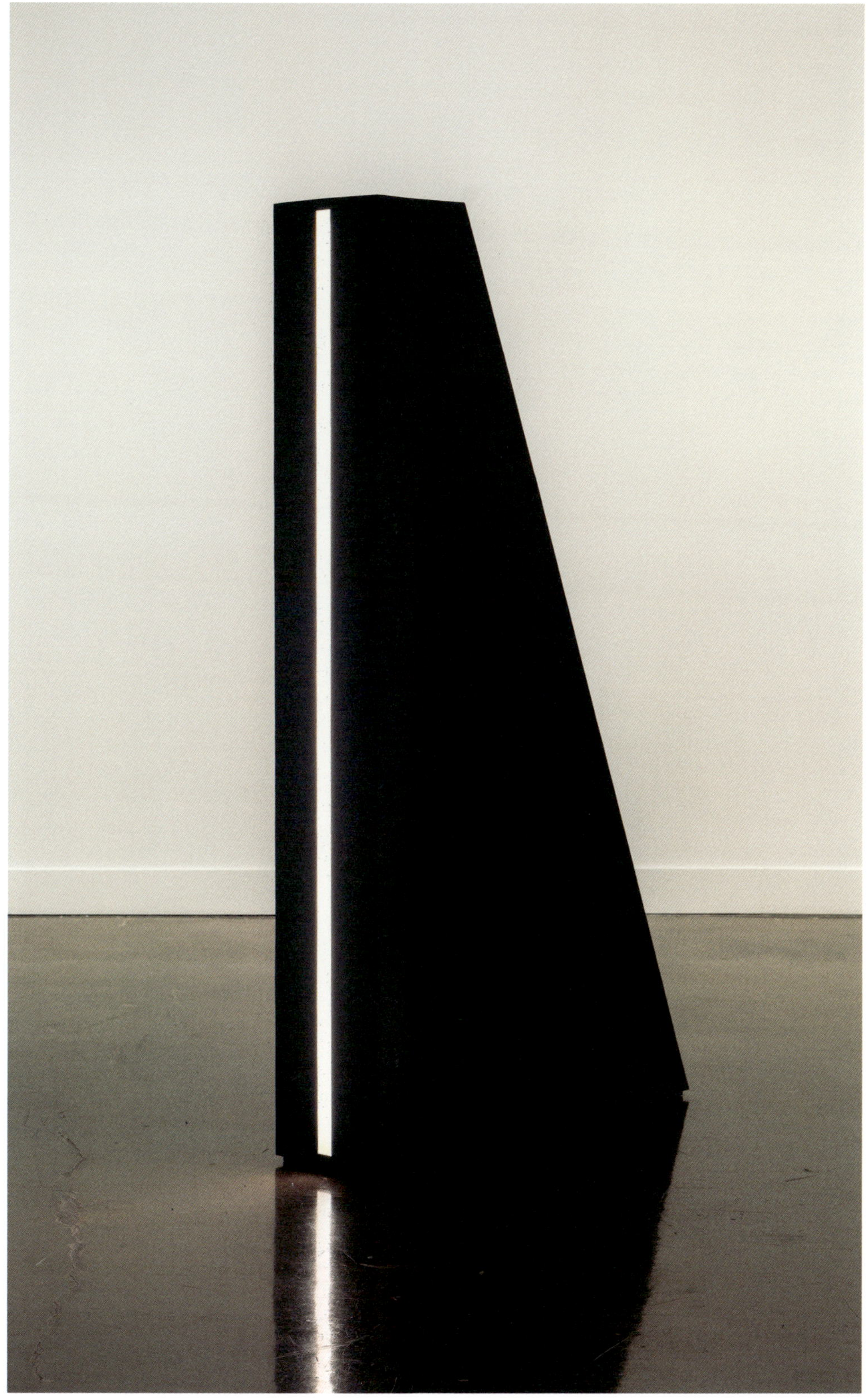

Glow #3, 2019

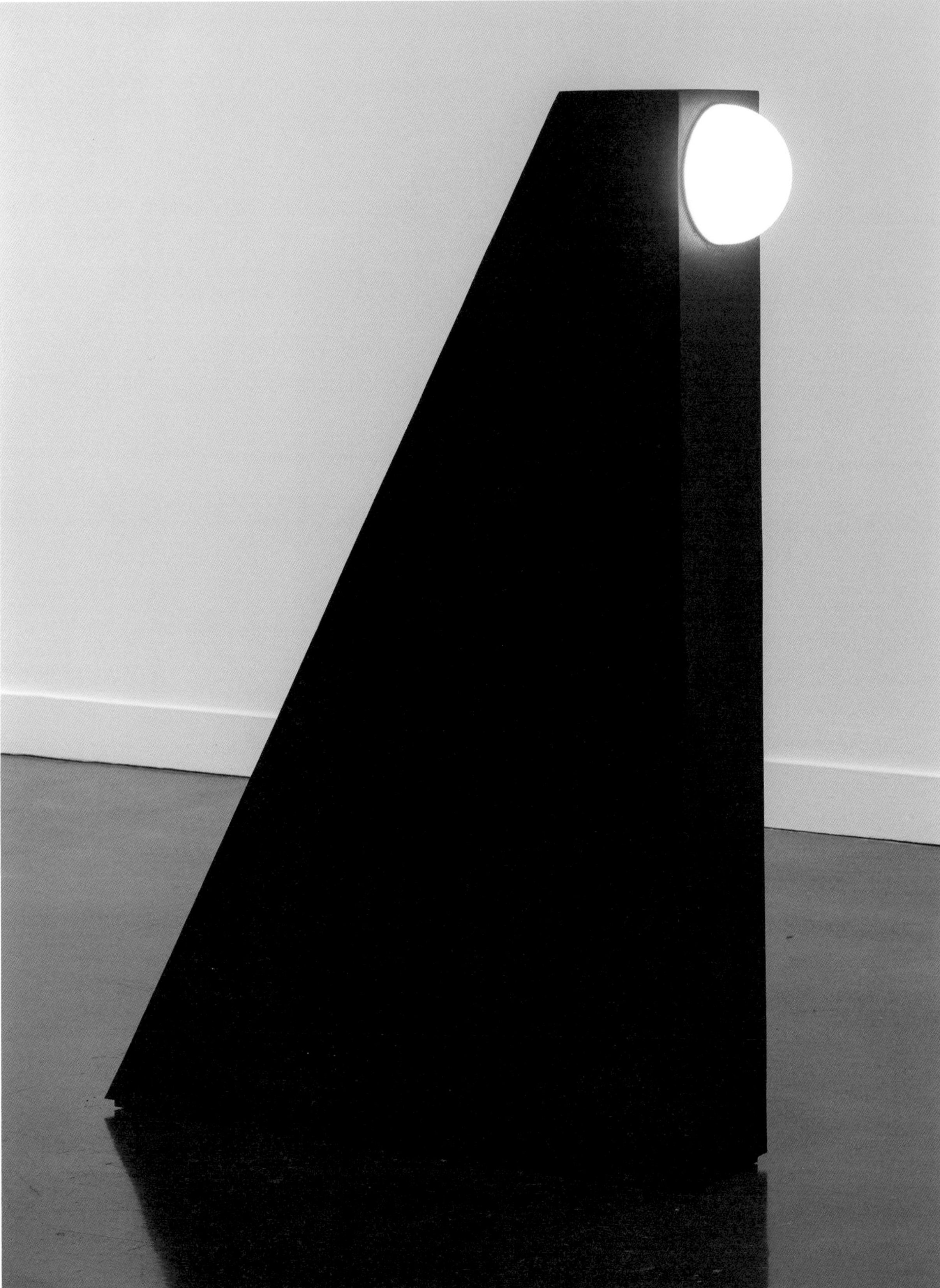

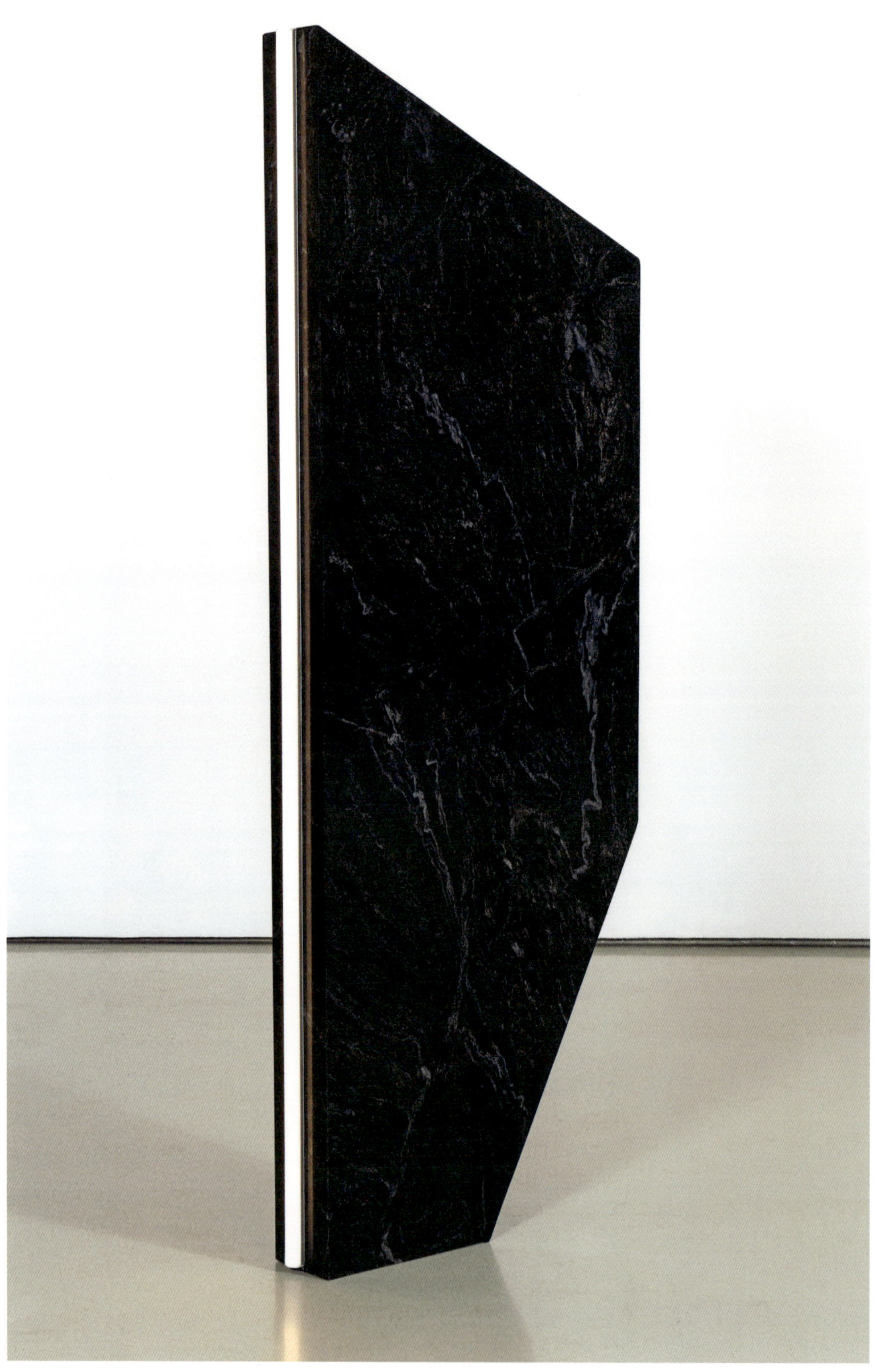

Glow #8, 2019

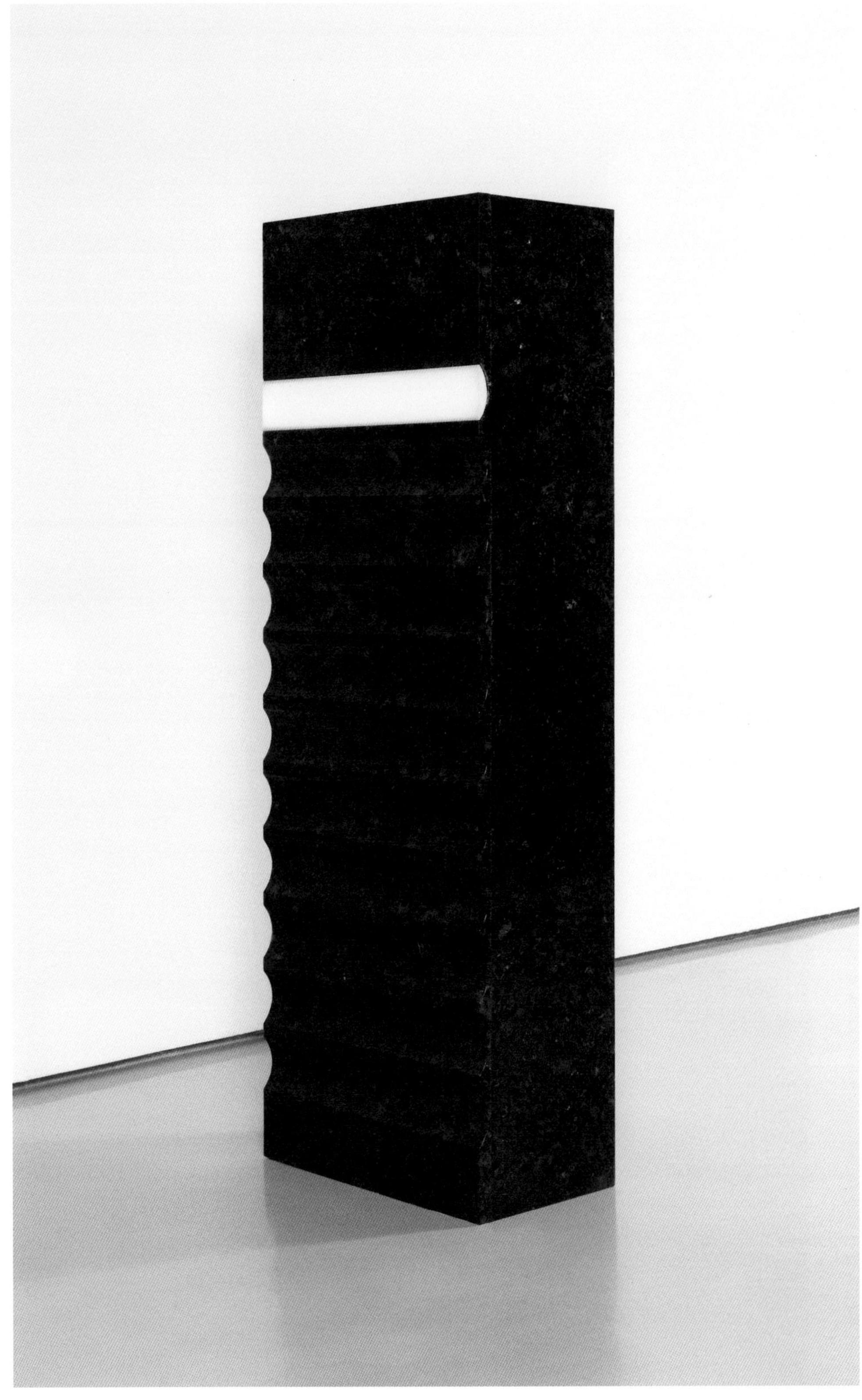

Glow #9, 2019

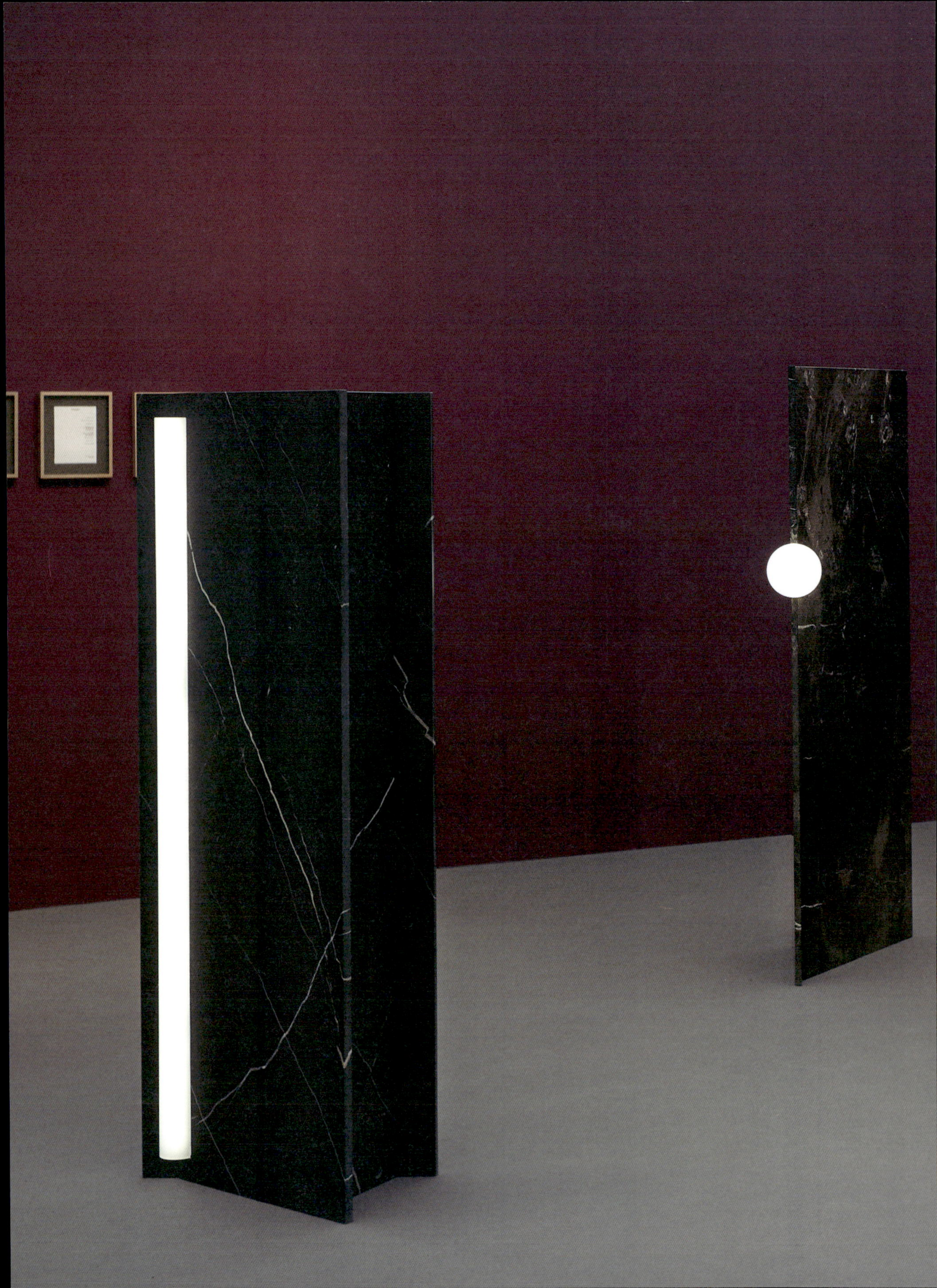

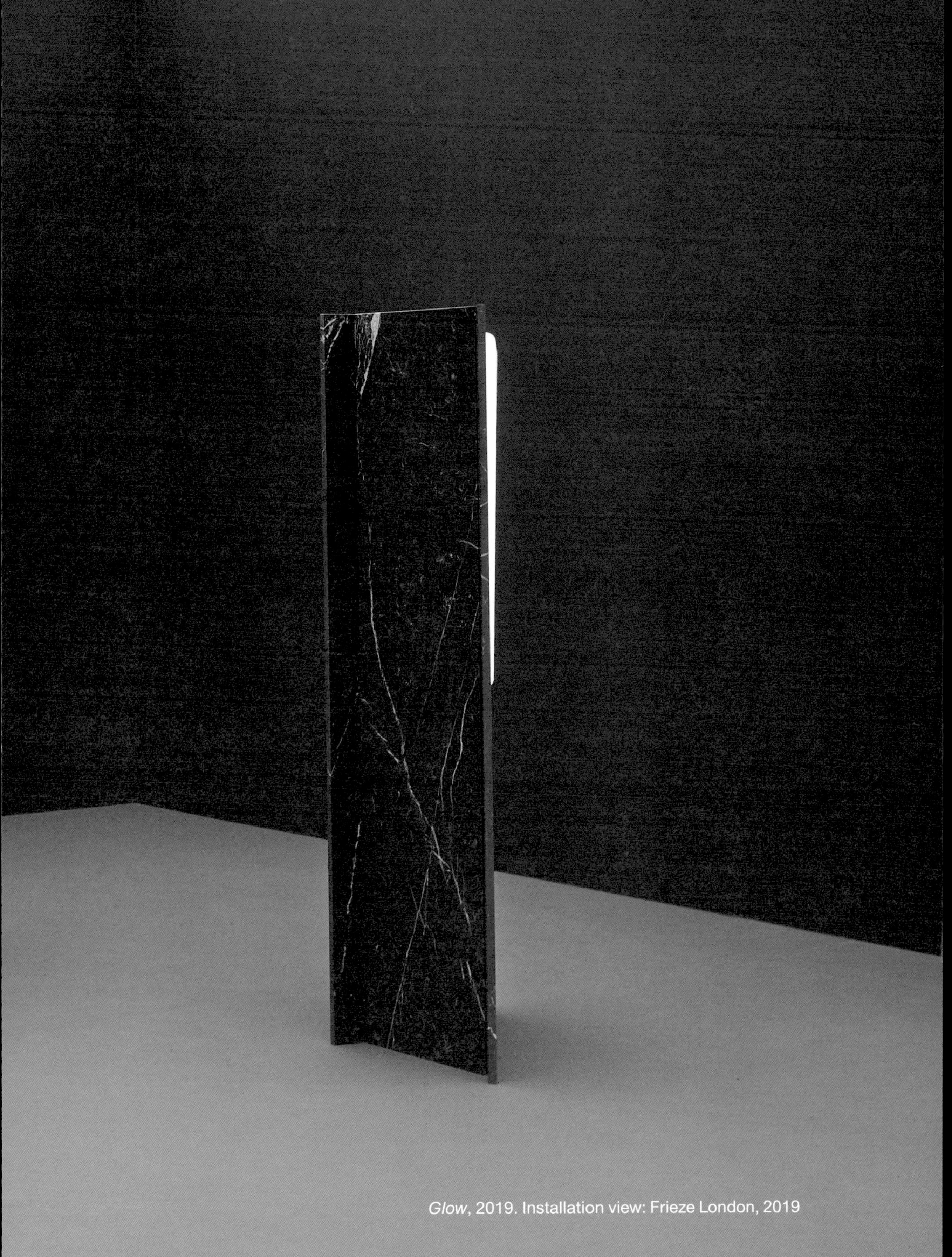

Glow, 2019. Installation view: Frieze London, 2019

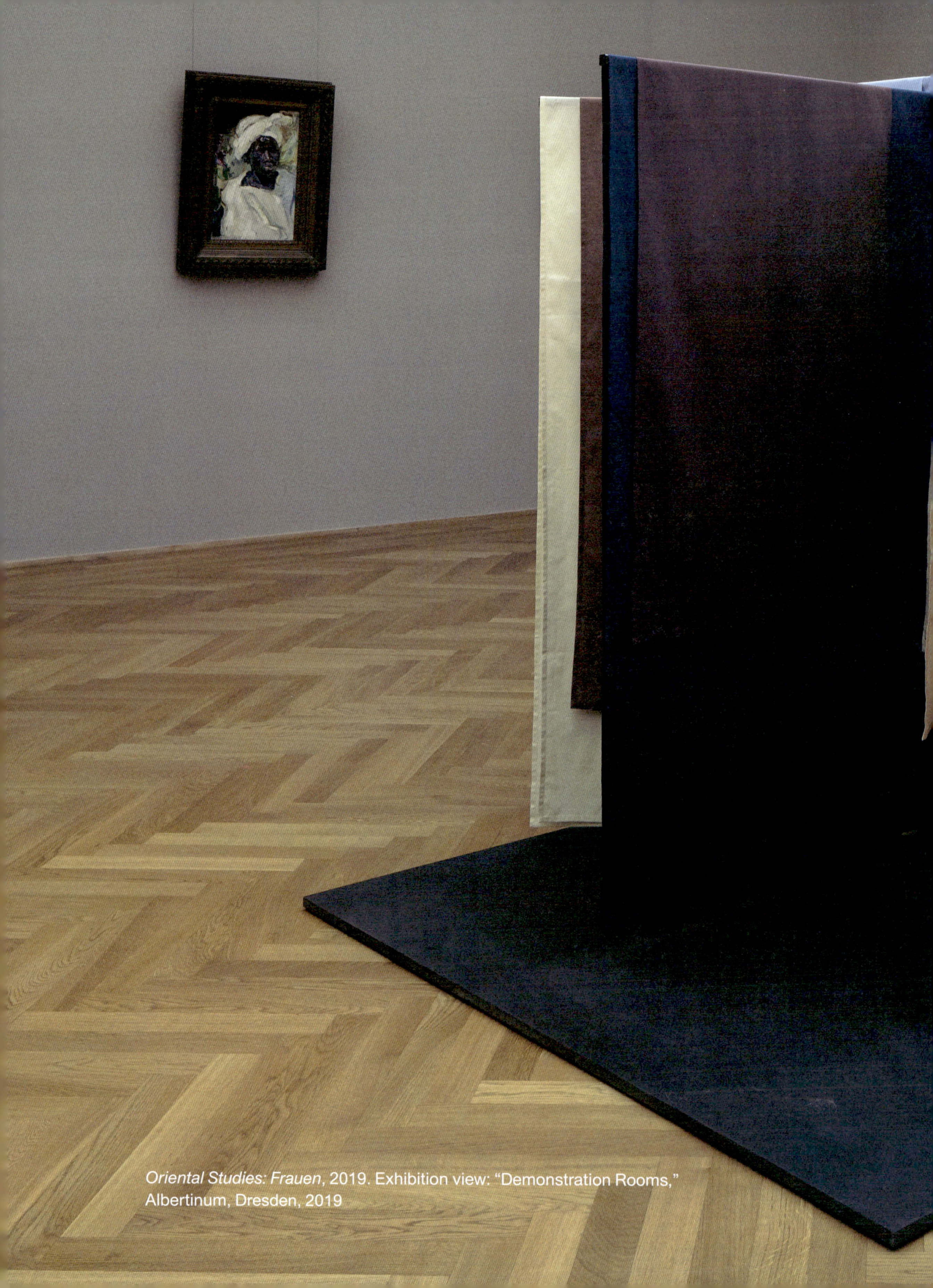

Oriental Studies: Frauen, 2019. Exhibition view: "Demonstration Rooms," Albertinum, Dresden, 2019

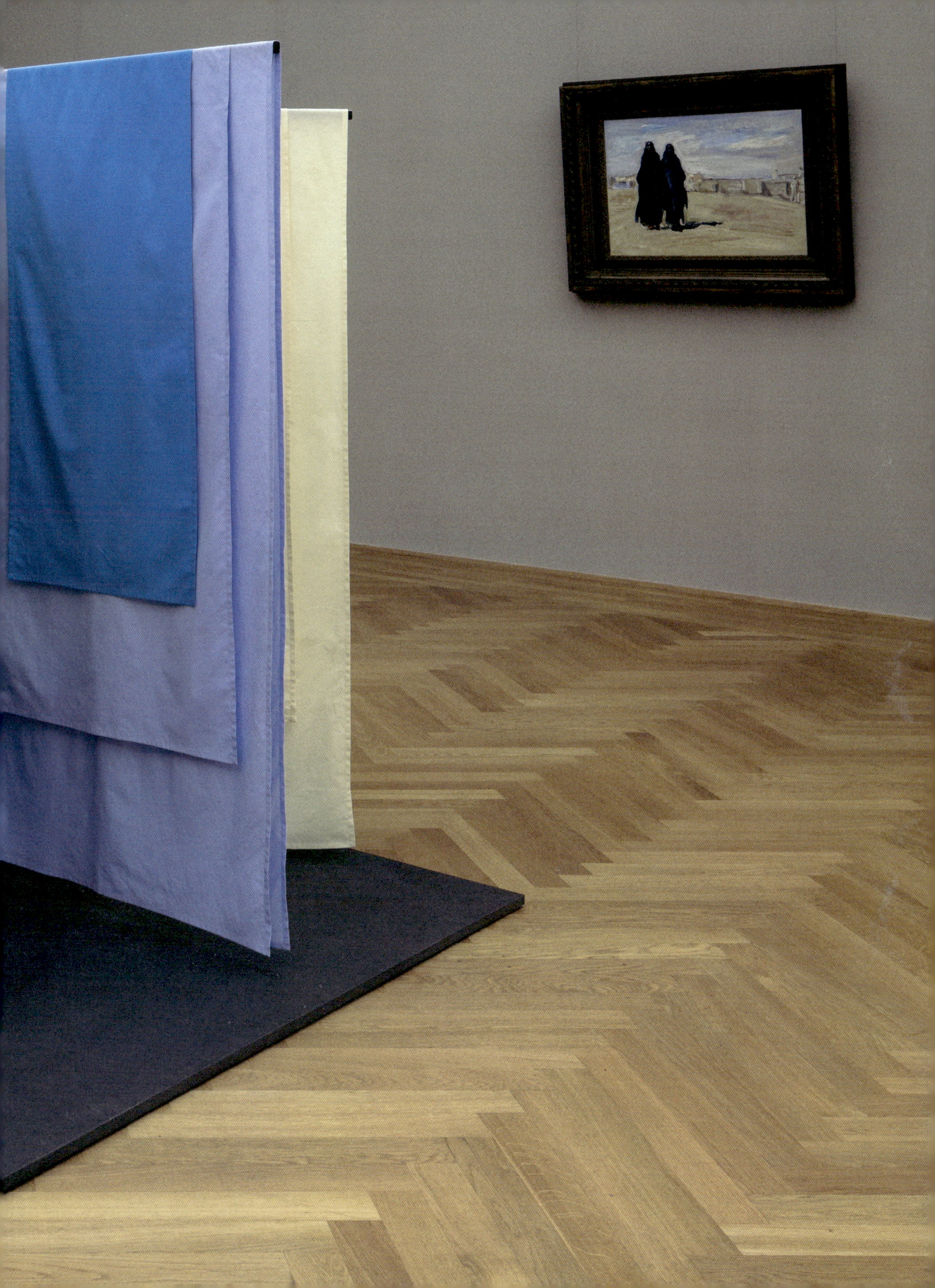

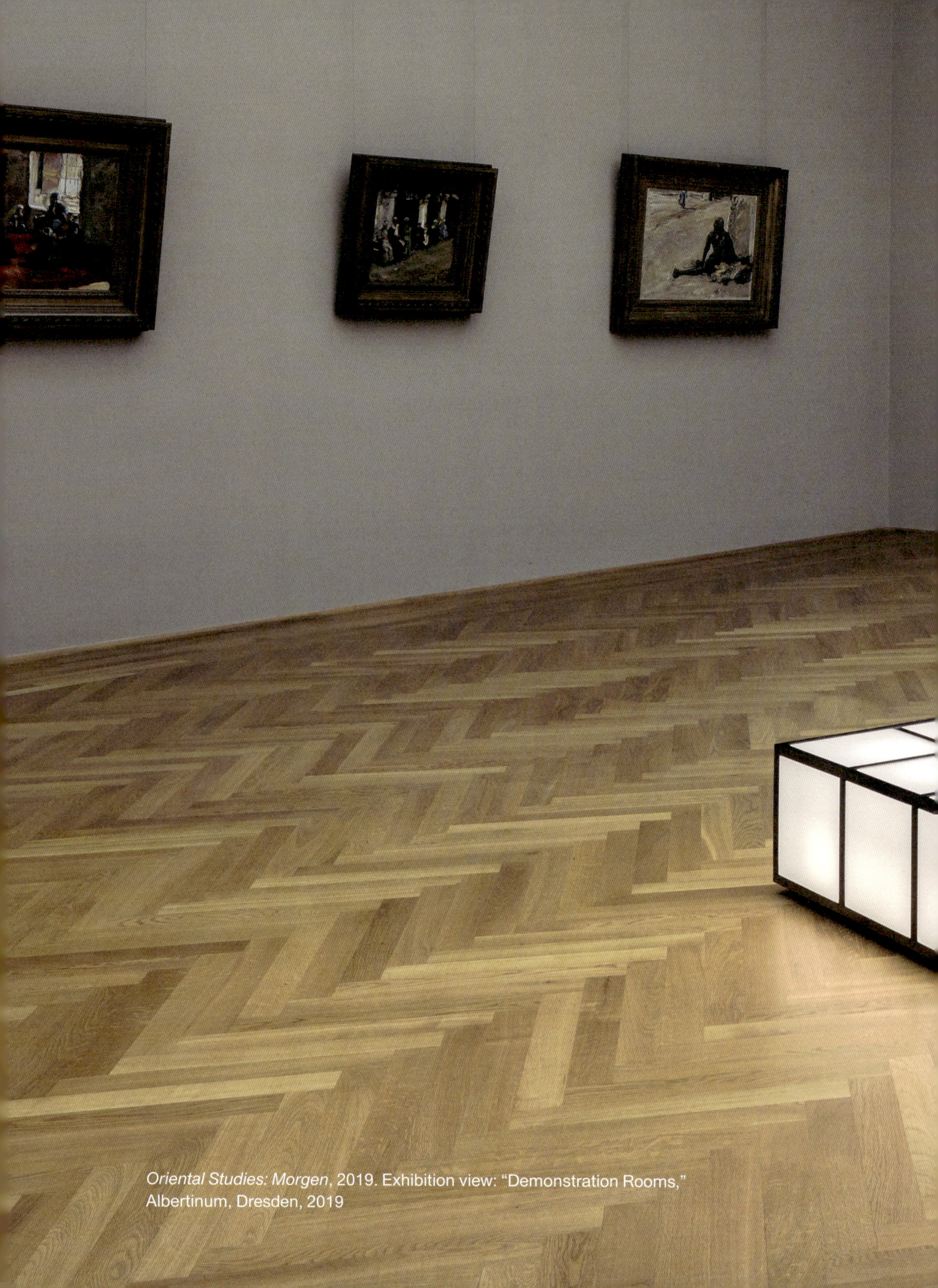

Oriental Studies: Morgen, 2019. Exhibition view: "Demonstration Rooms," Albertinum, Dresden, 2019

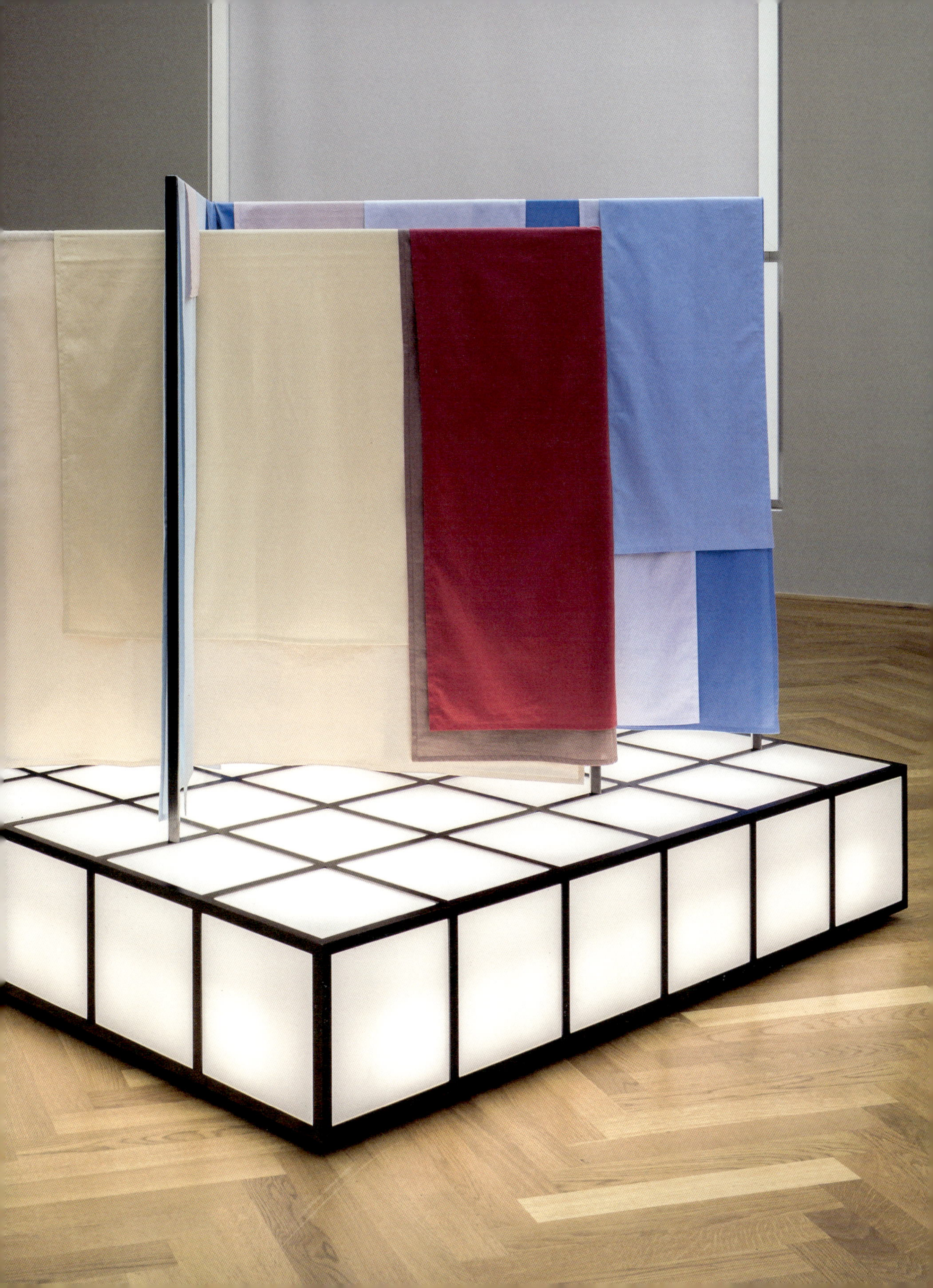

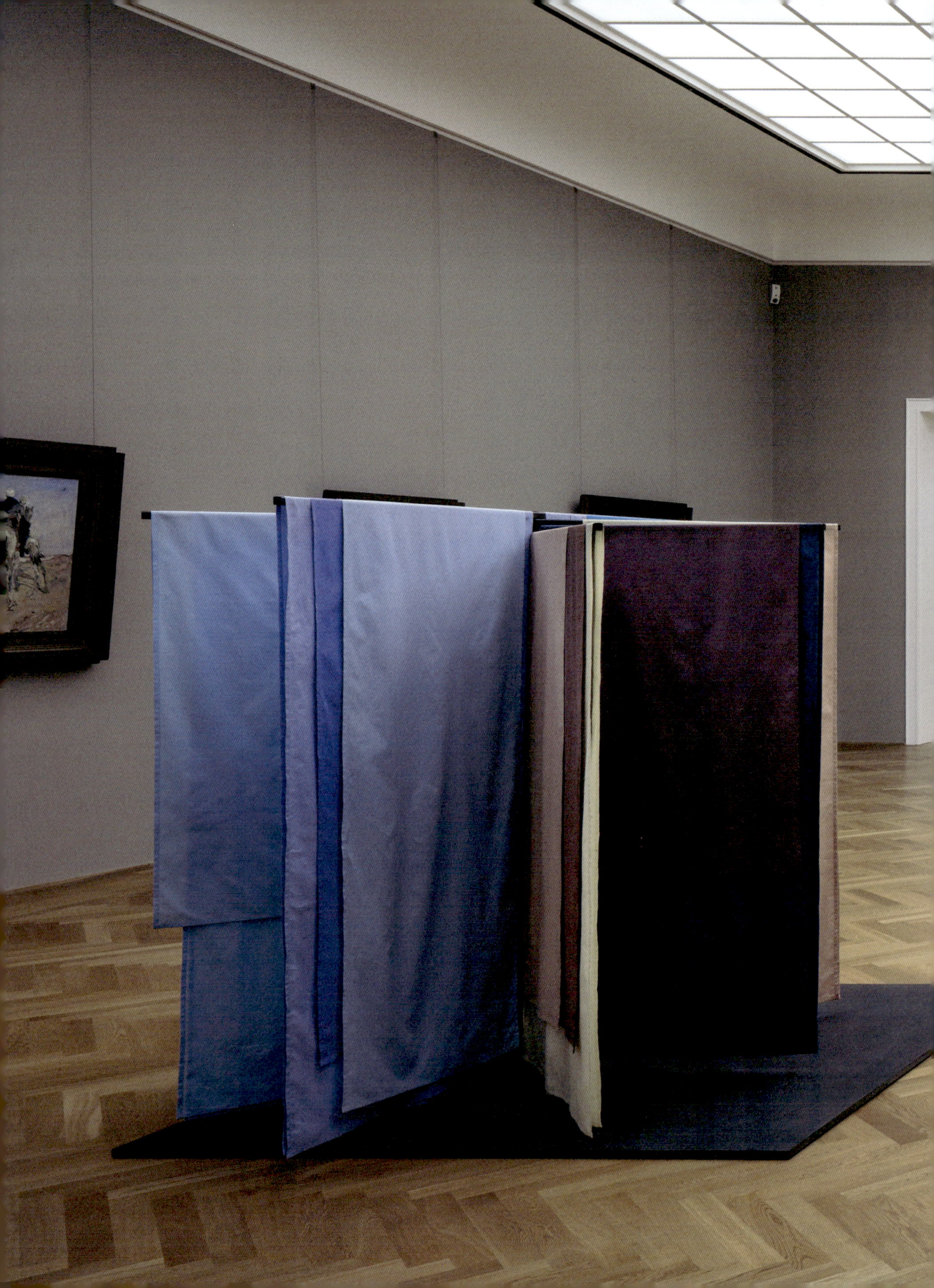

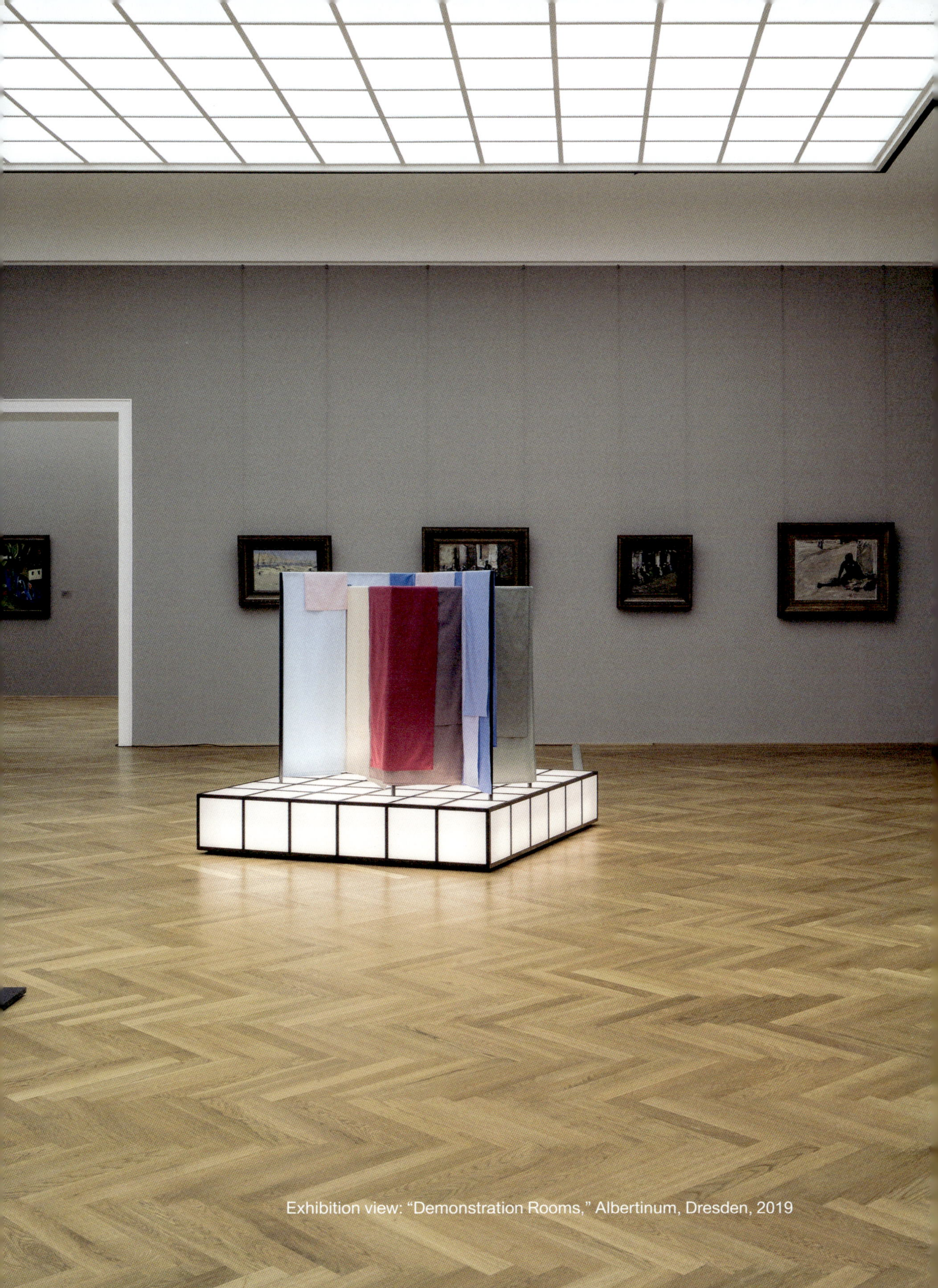

Exhibition view: "Demonstration Rooms," Albertinum, Dresden, 2019

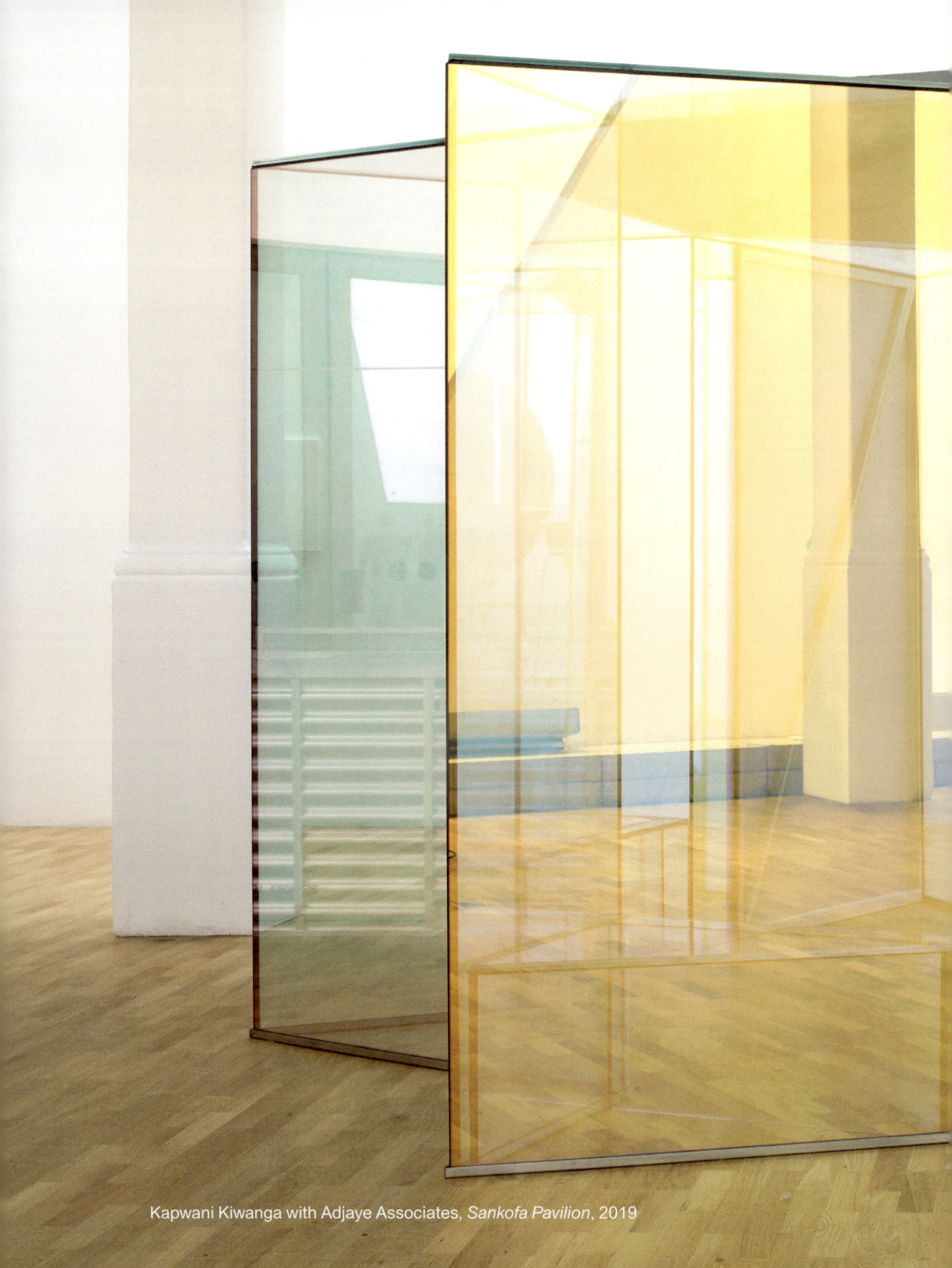

Kapwani Kiwanga with Adjaye Associates, *Sankofa Pavilion*, 2019

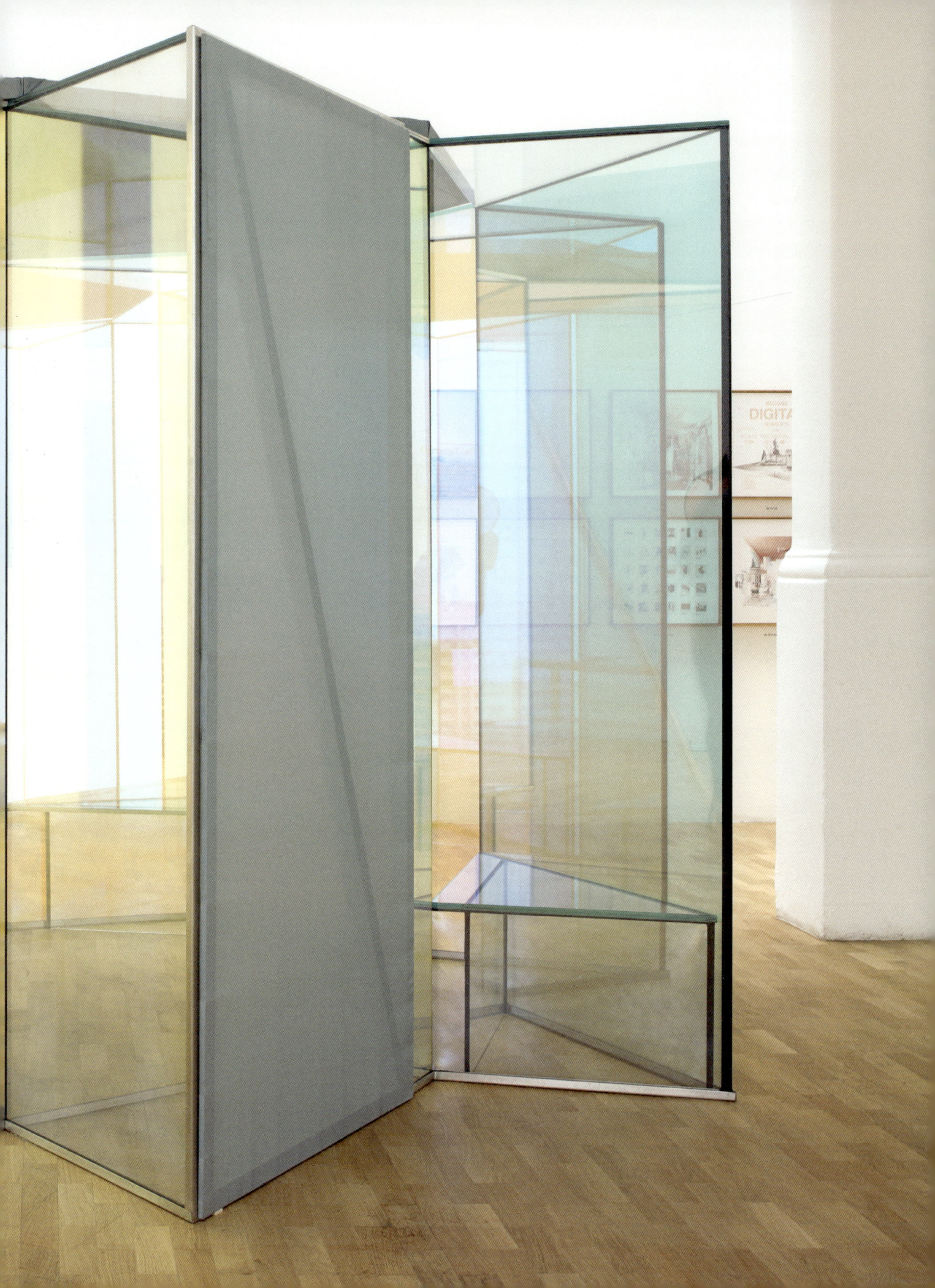

Sankofa Pavilion, 2019 (detail)

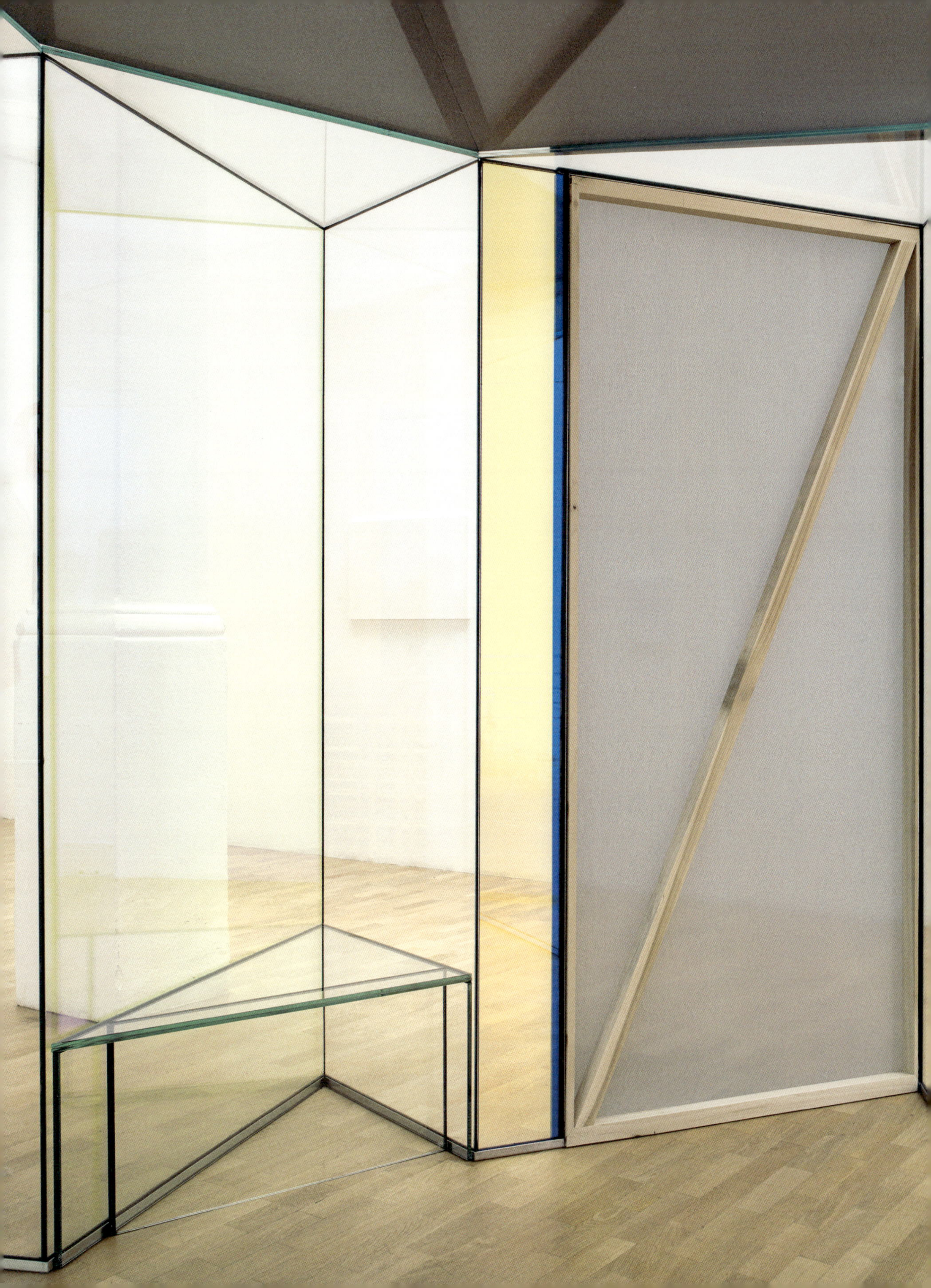

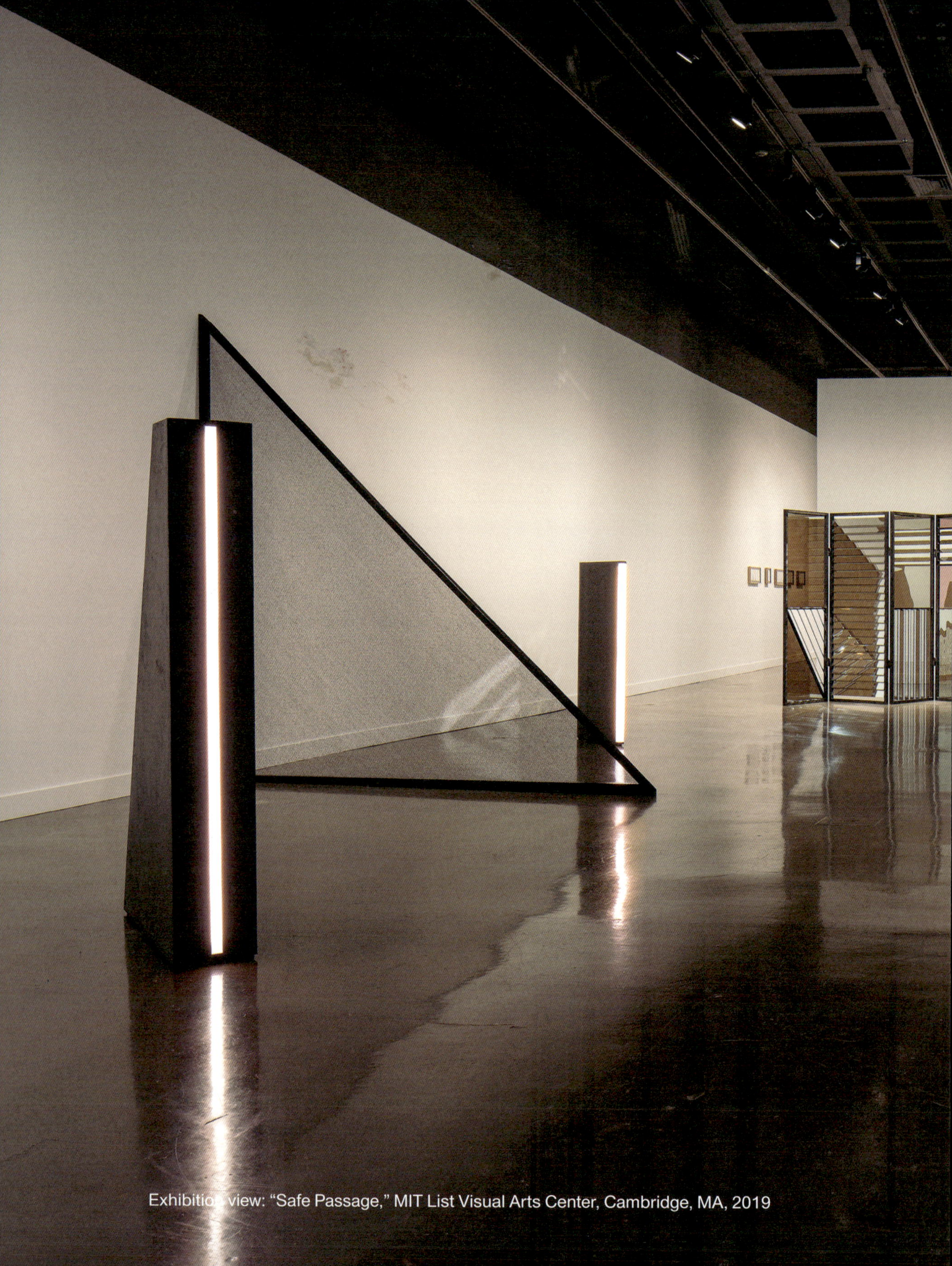

Exhibition view: “Safe Passage,” MIT List Visual Arts Center, Cambridge, MA, 2019

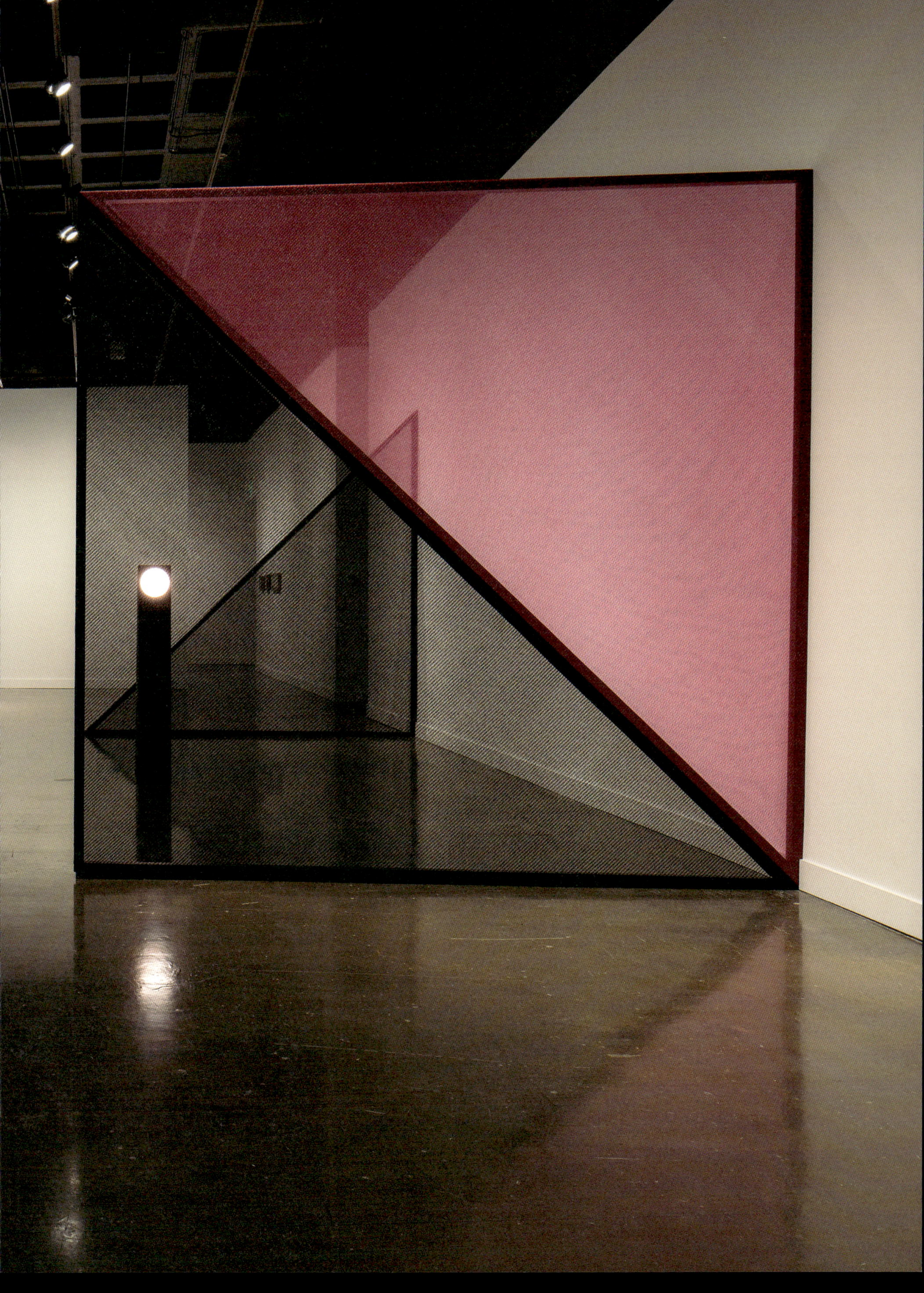

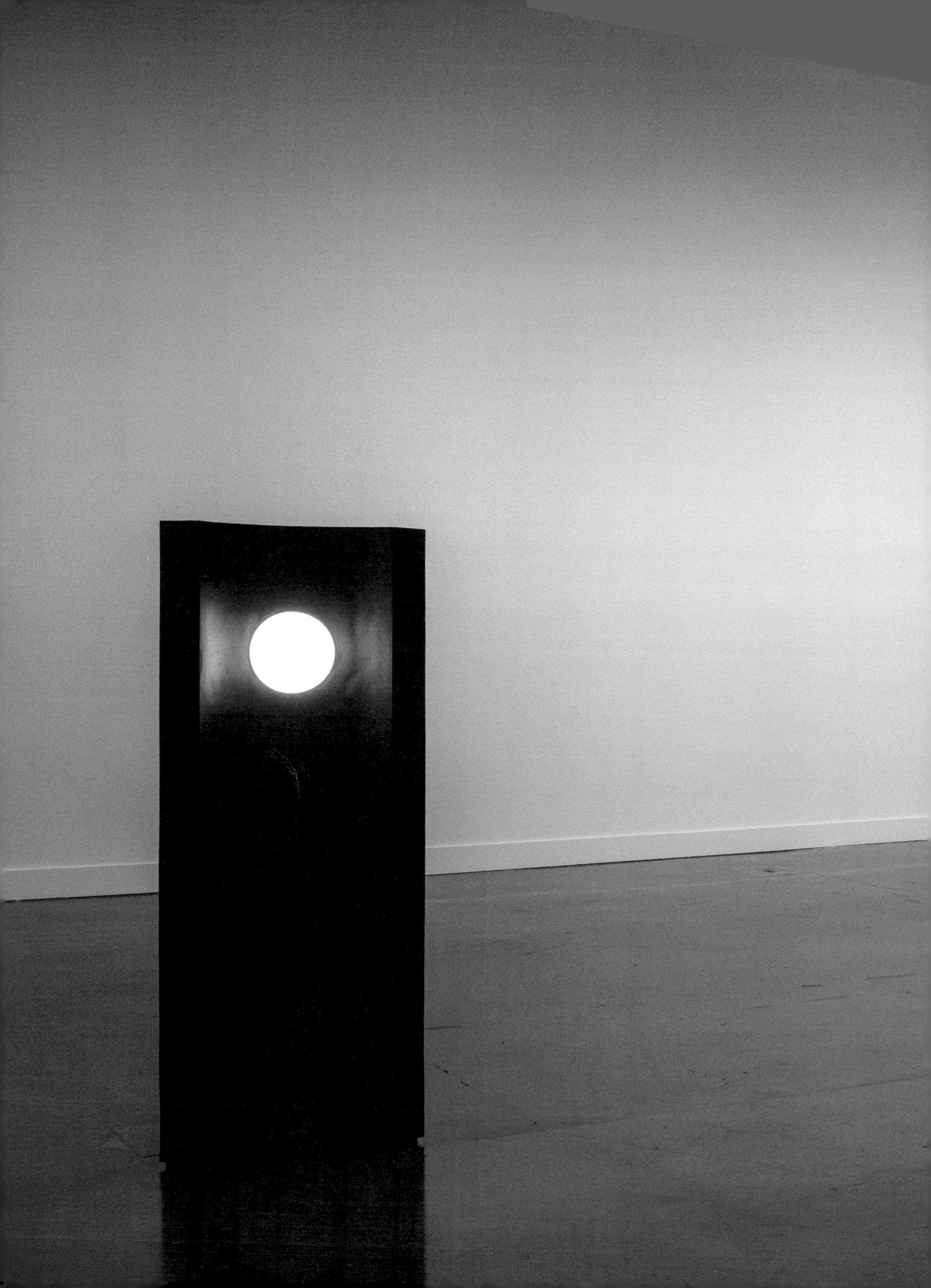

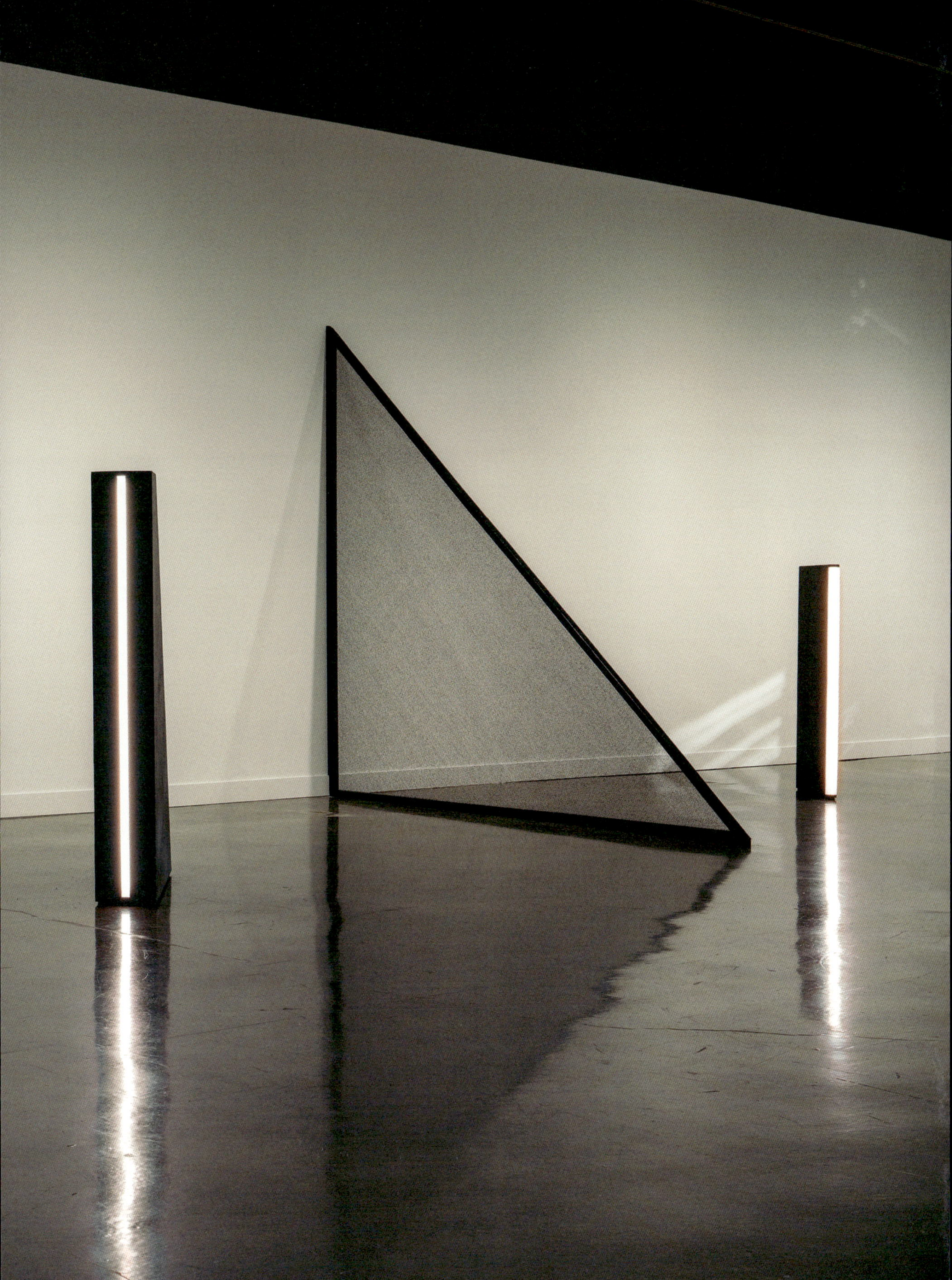

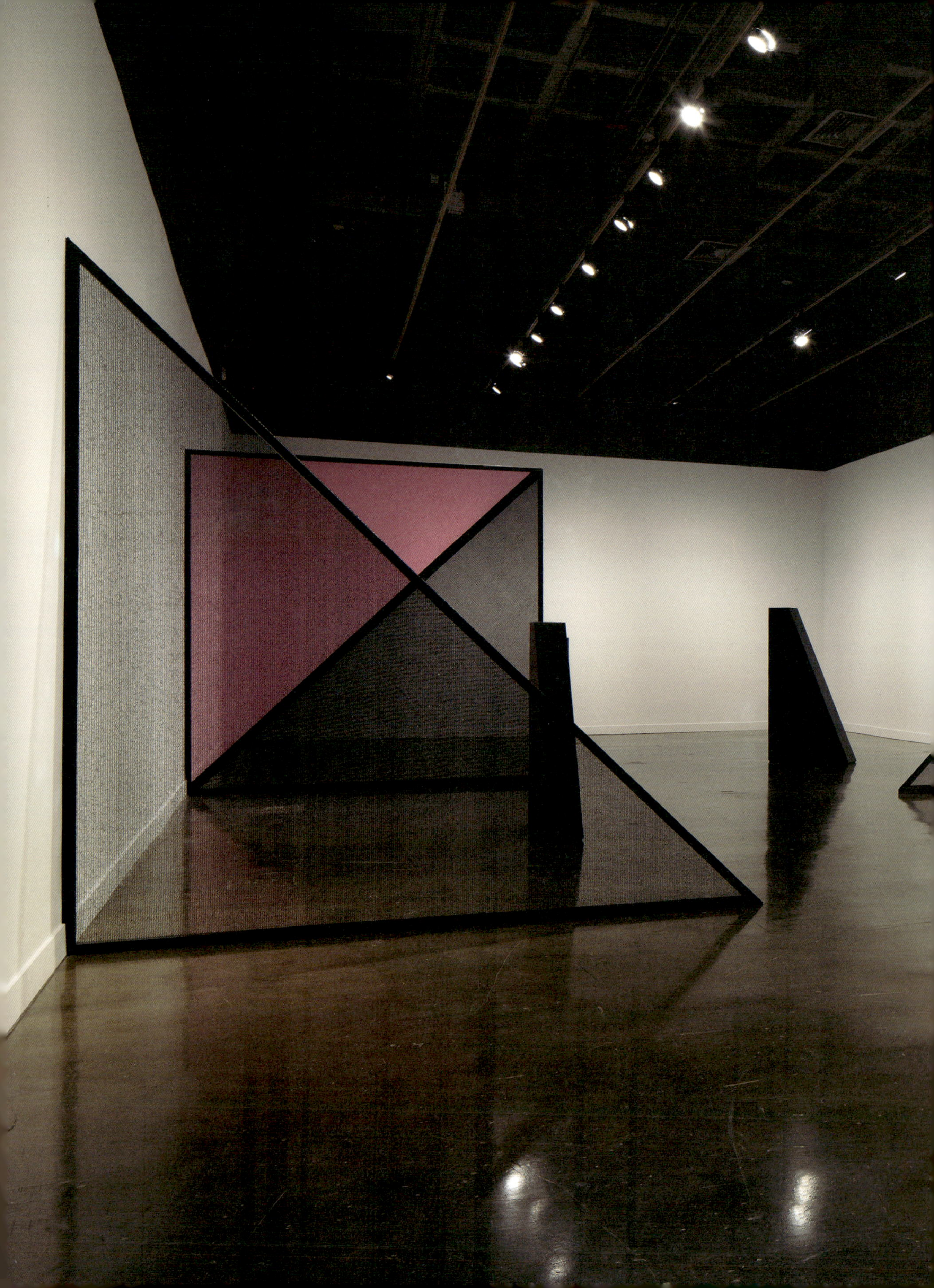

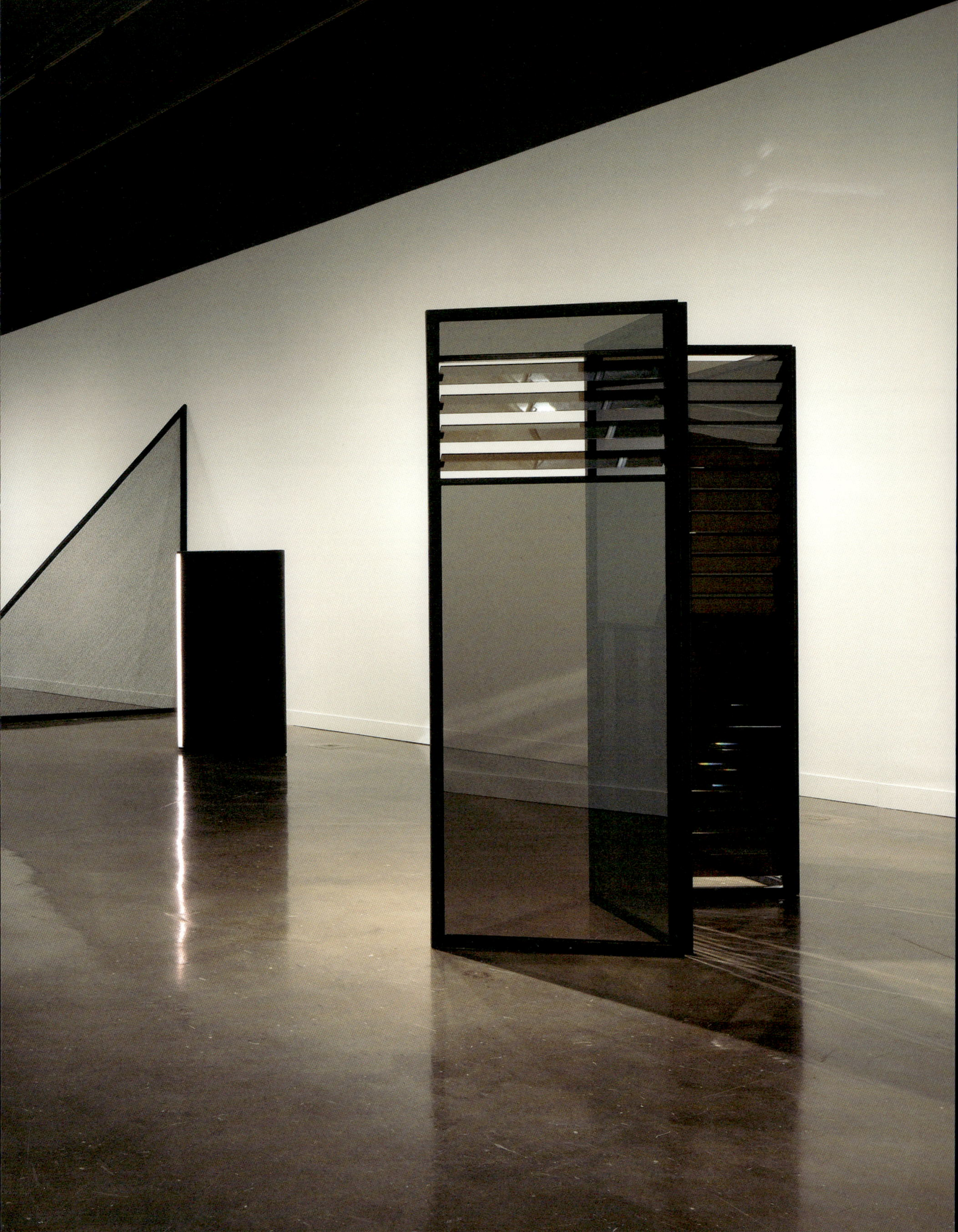

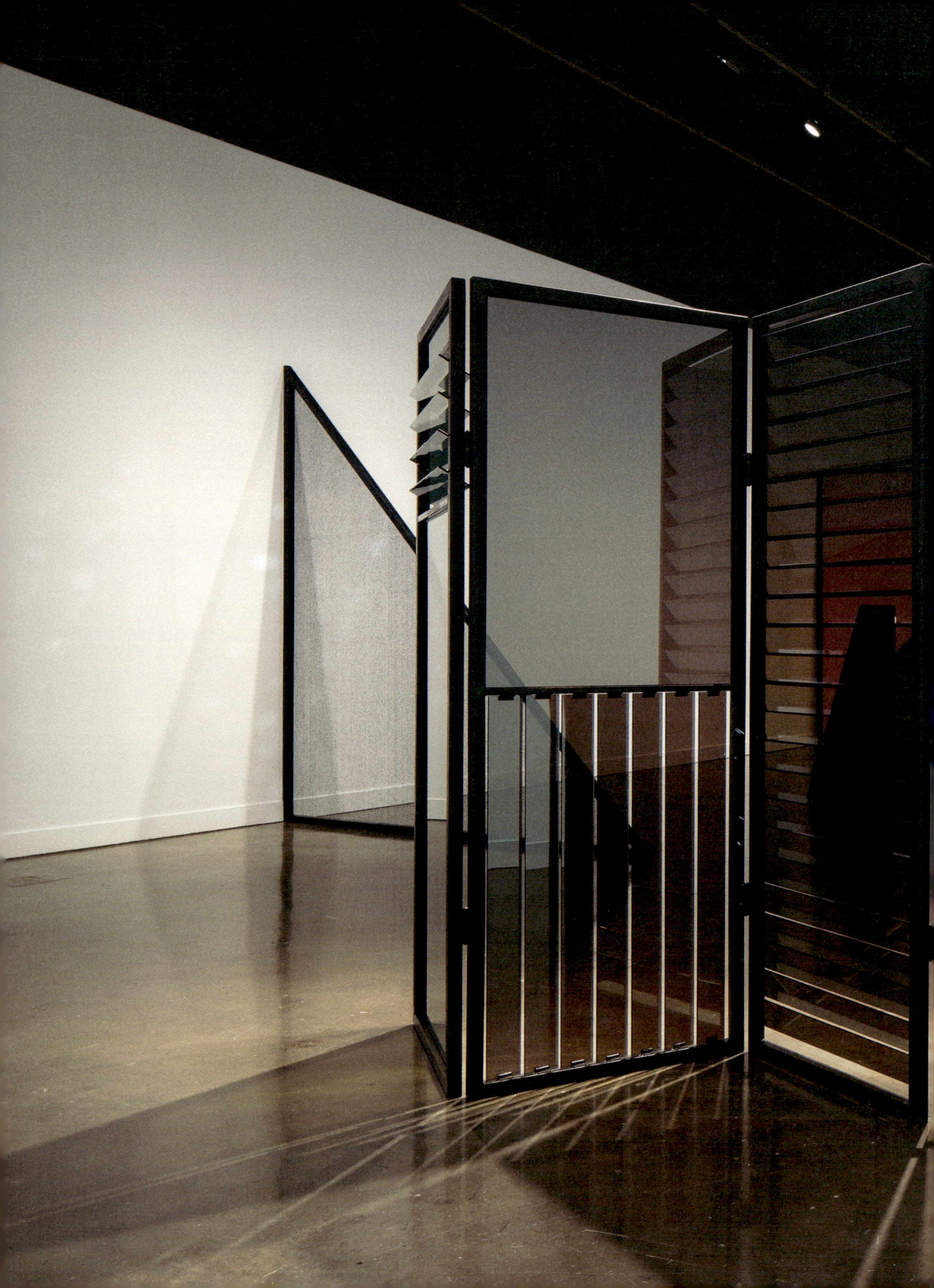

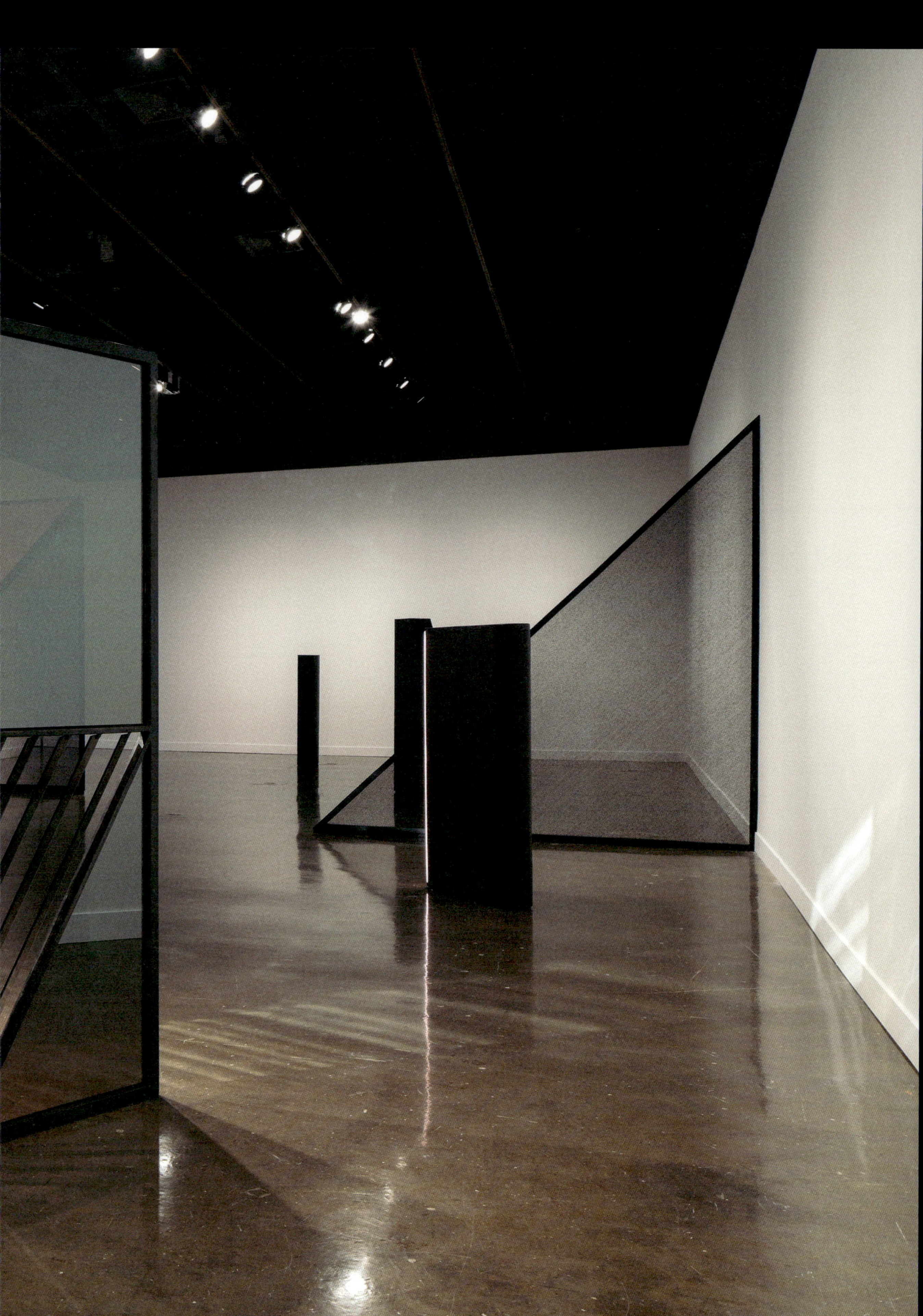

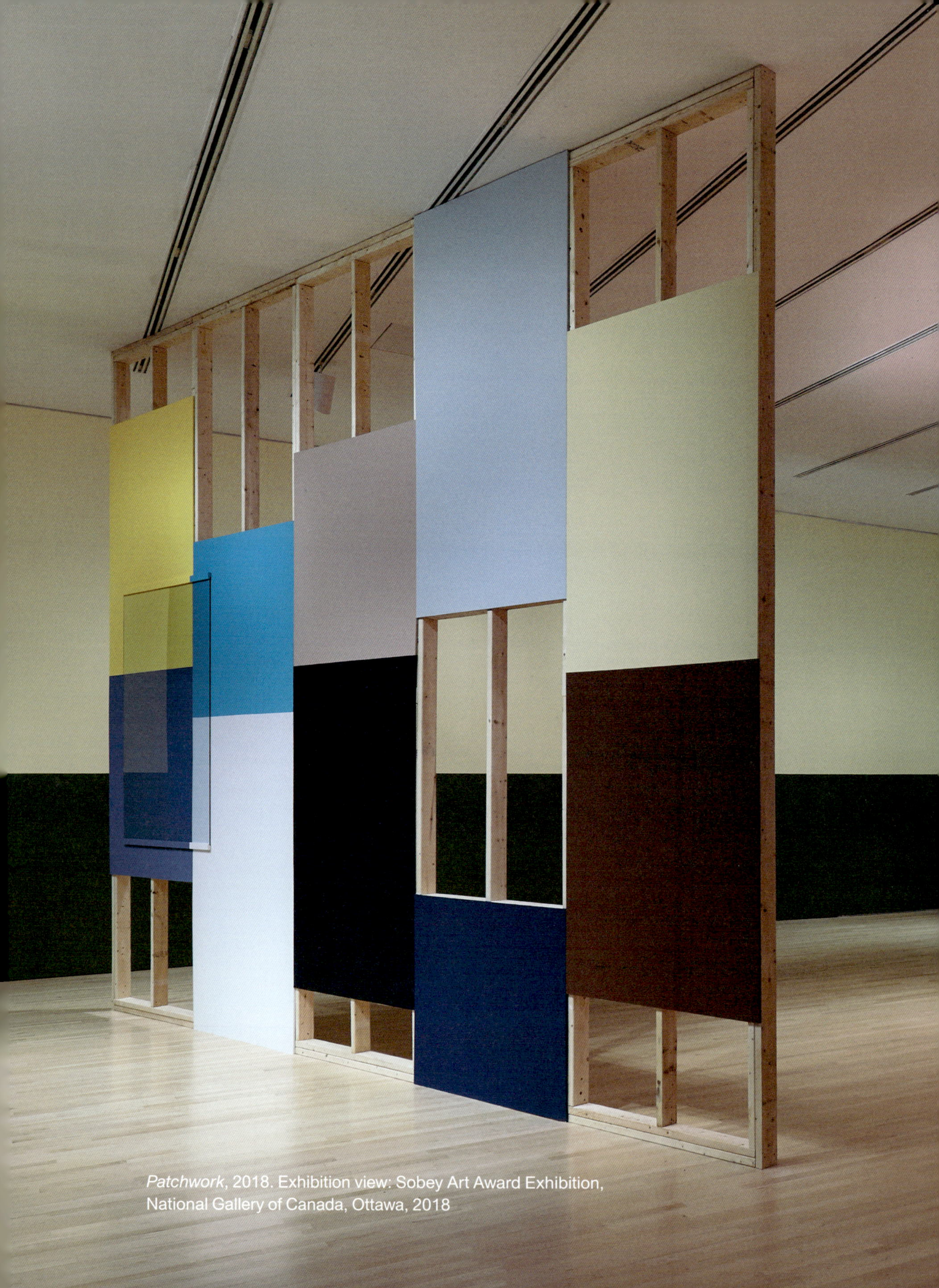

Patchwork, 2018. Exhibition view: Sobey Art Award Exhibition, National Gallery of Canada, Ottawa, 2018

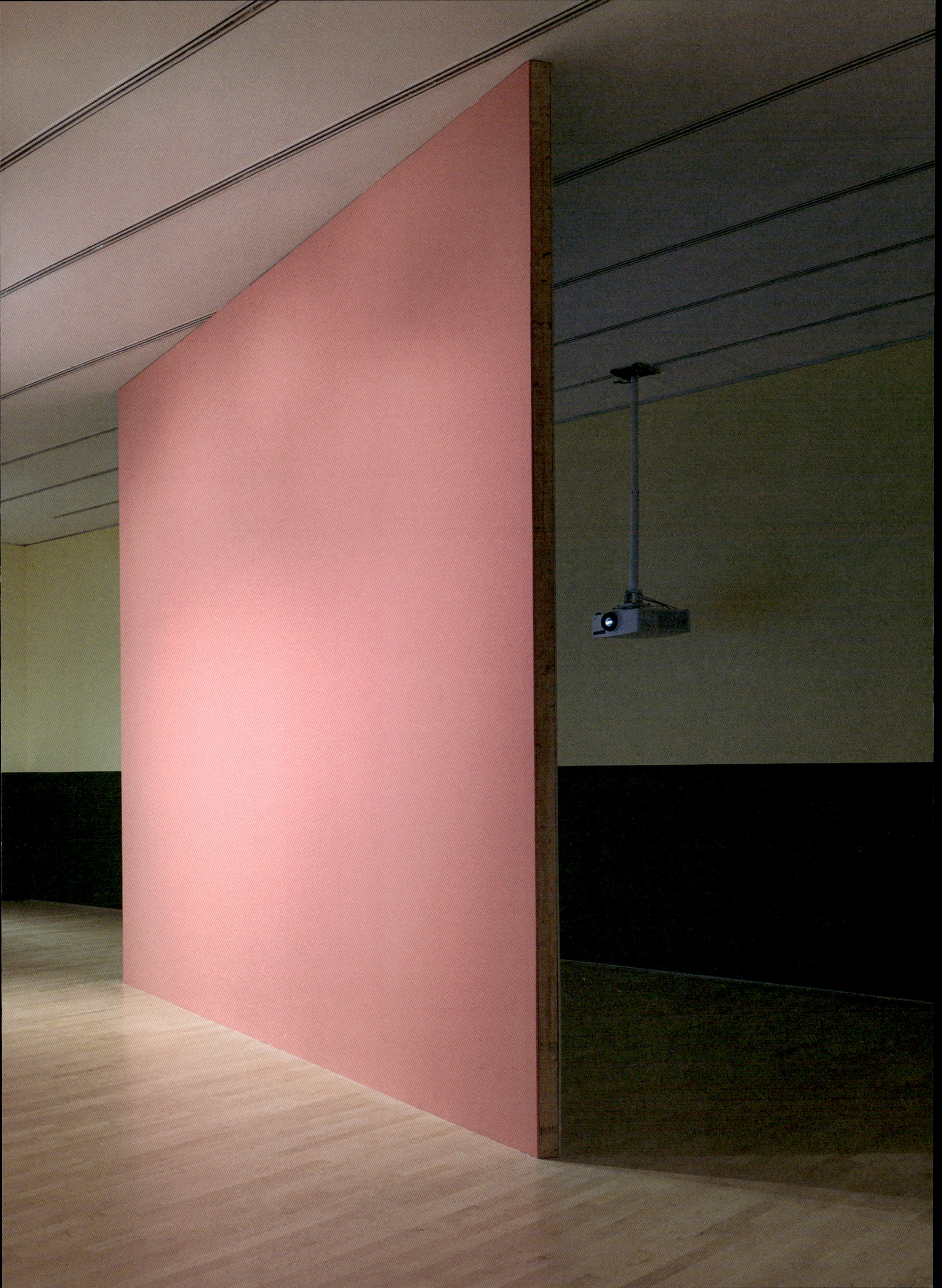

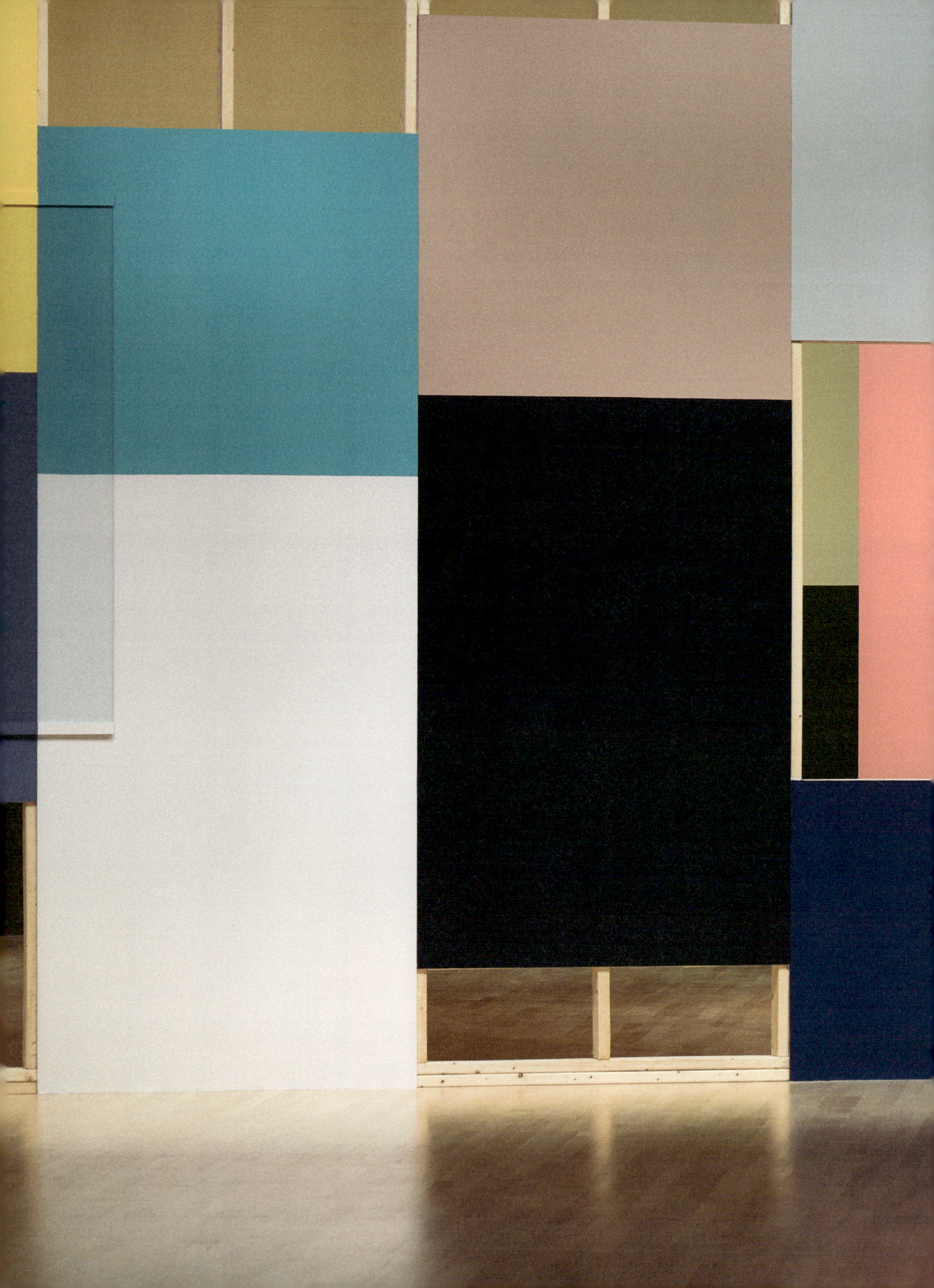

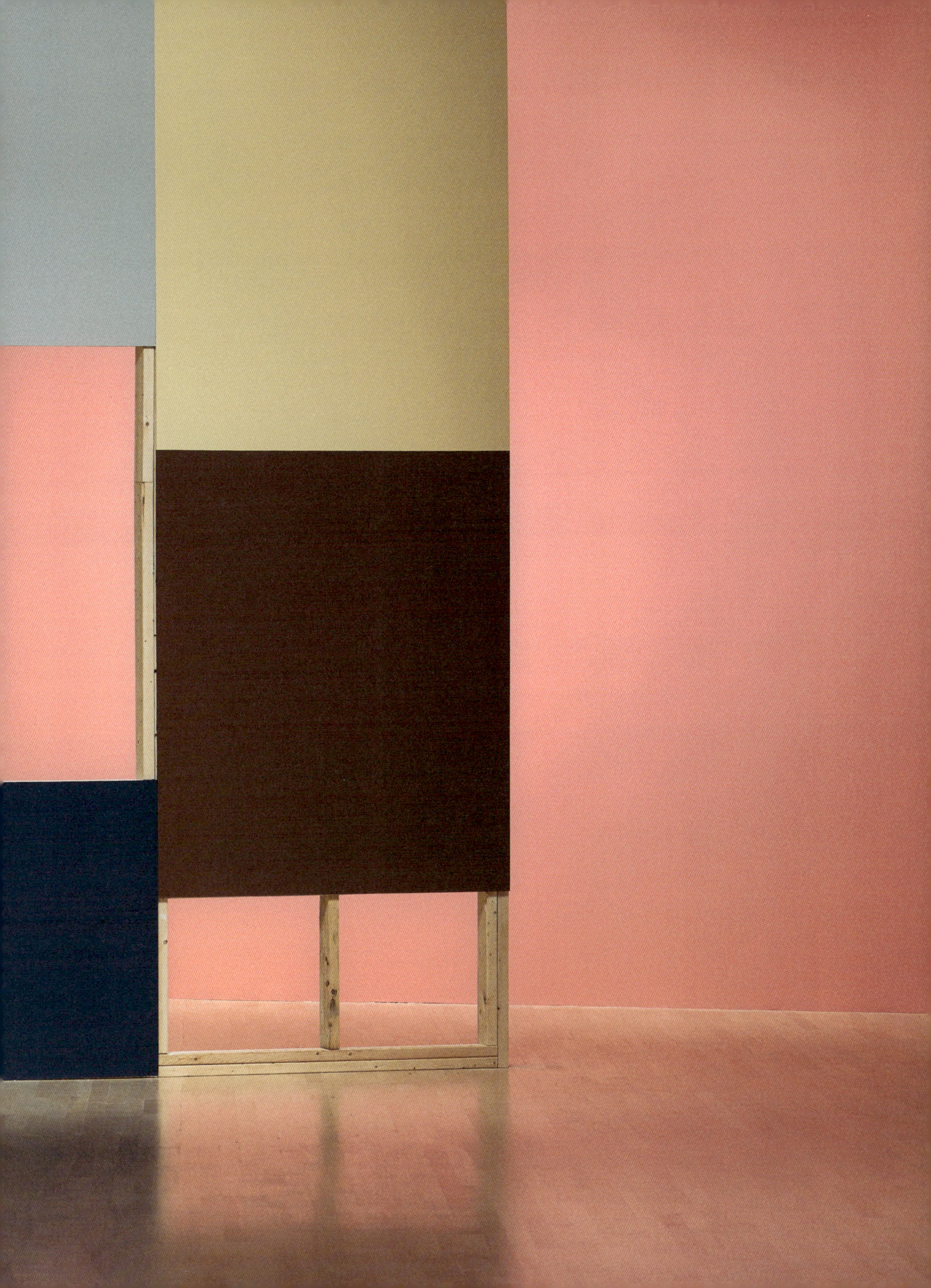

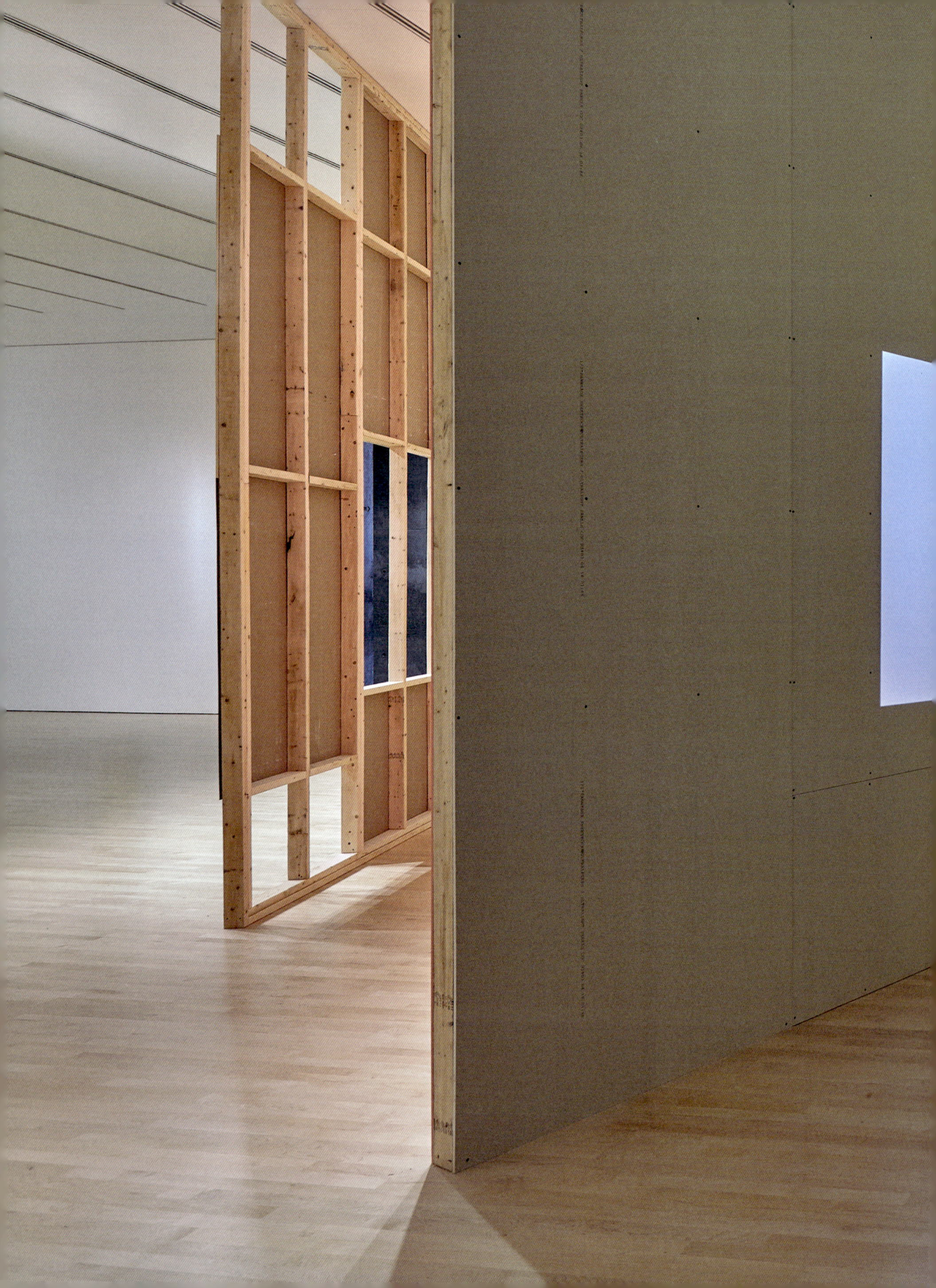

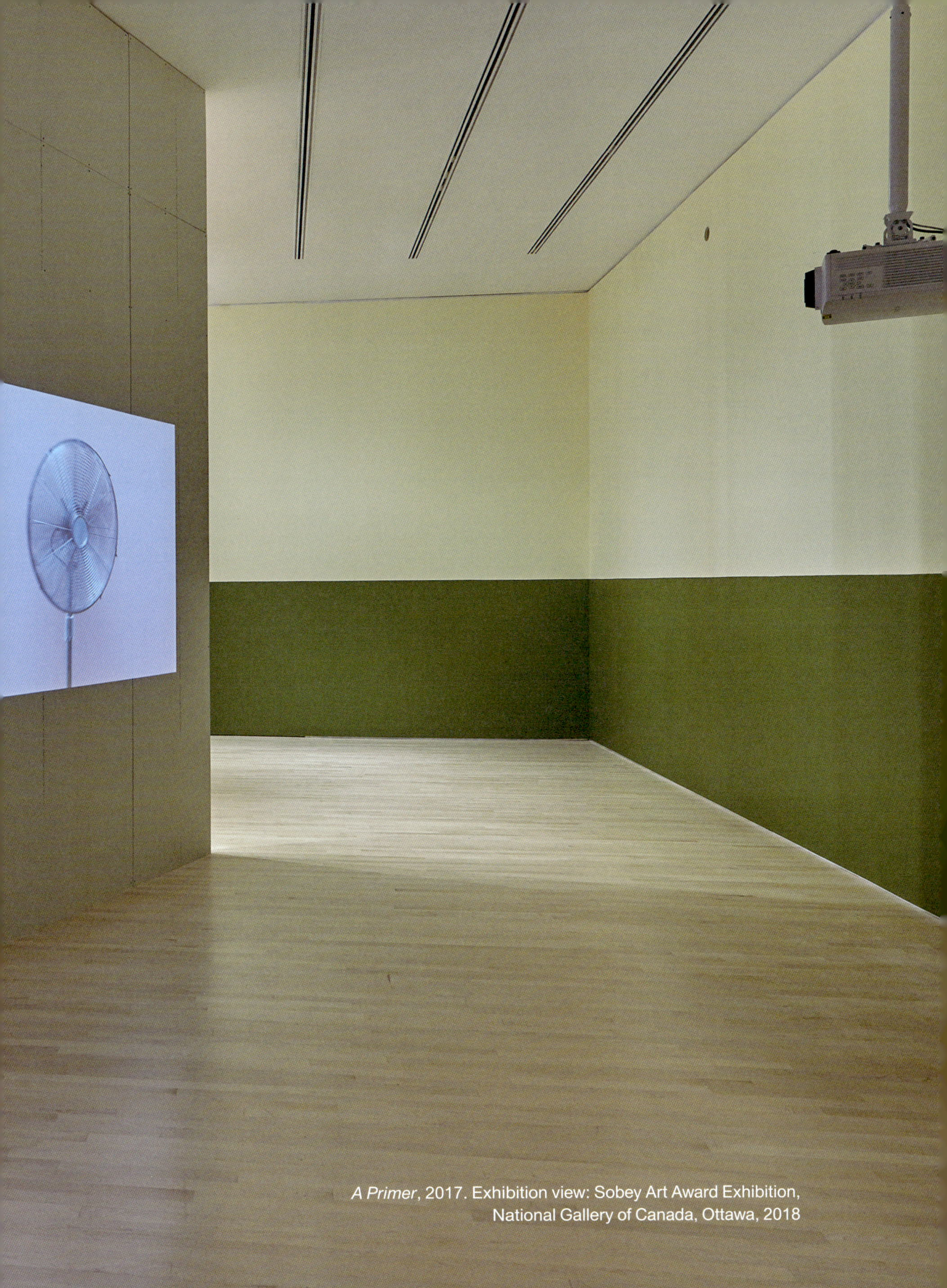

A Primer, 2017. Exhibition view: Sobey Art Award Exhibition, National Gallery of Canada, Ottawa, 2018

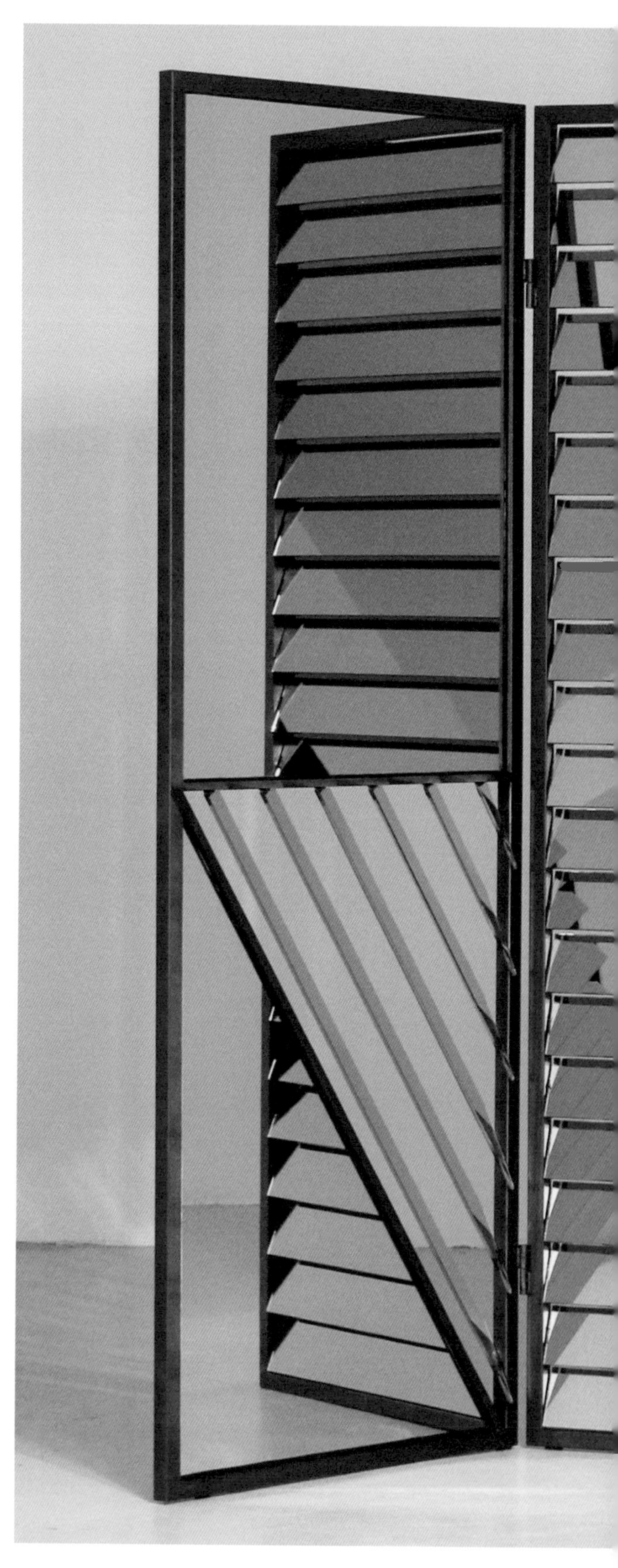

Jalousie, 2018

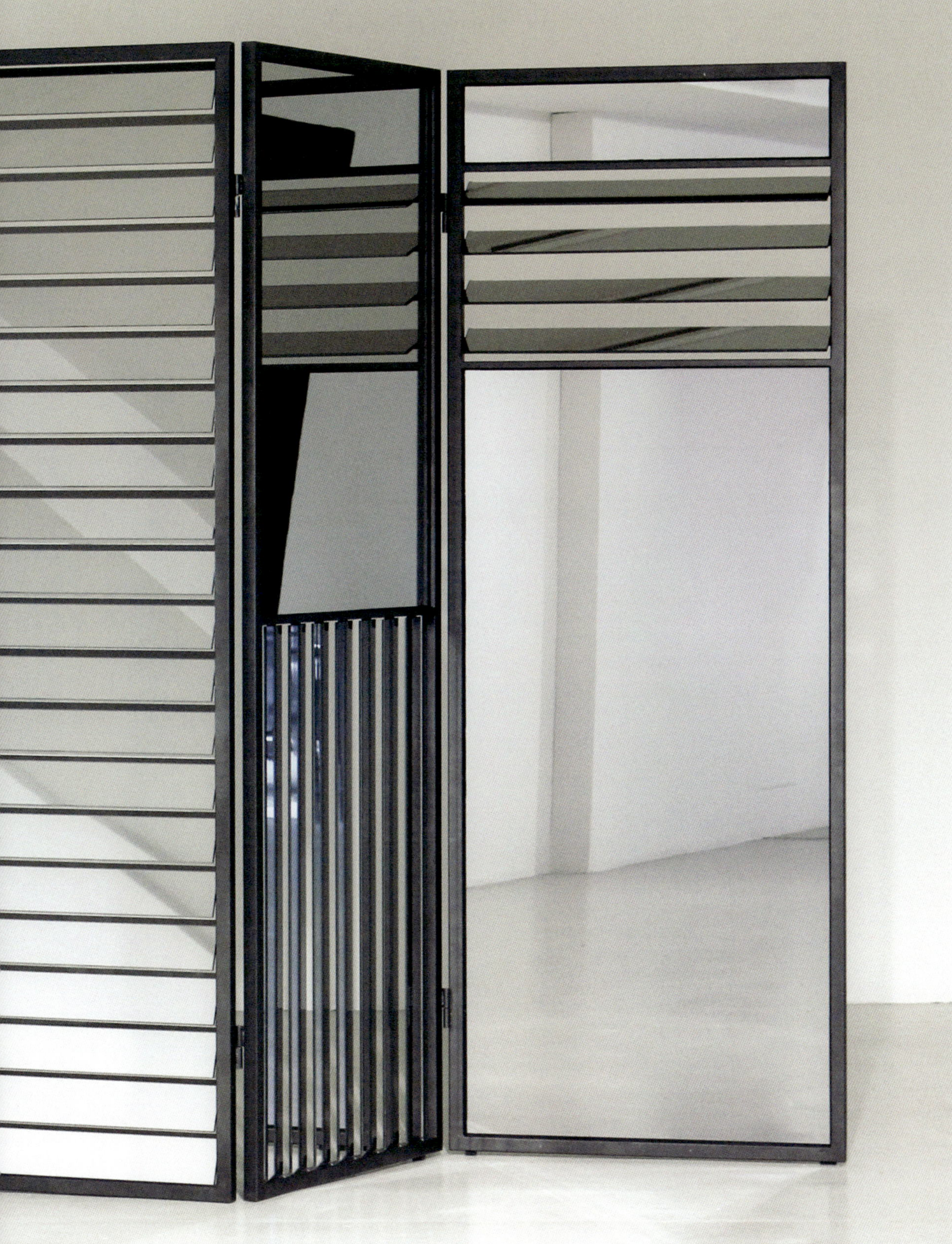

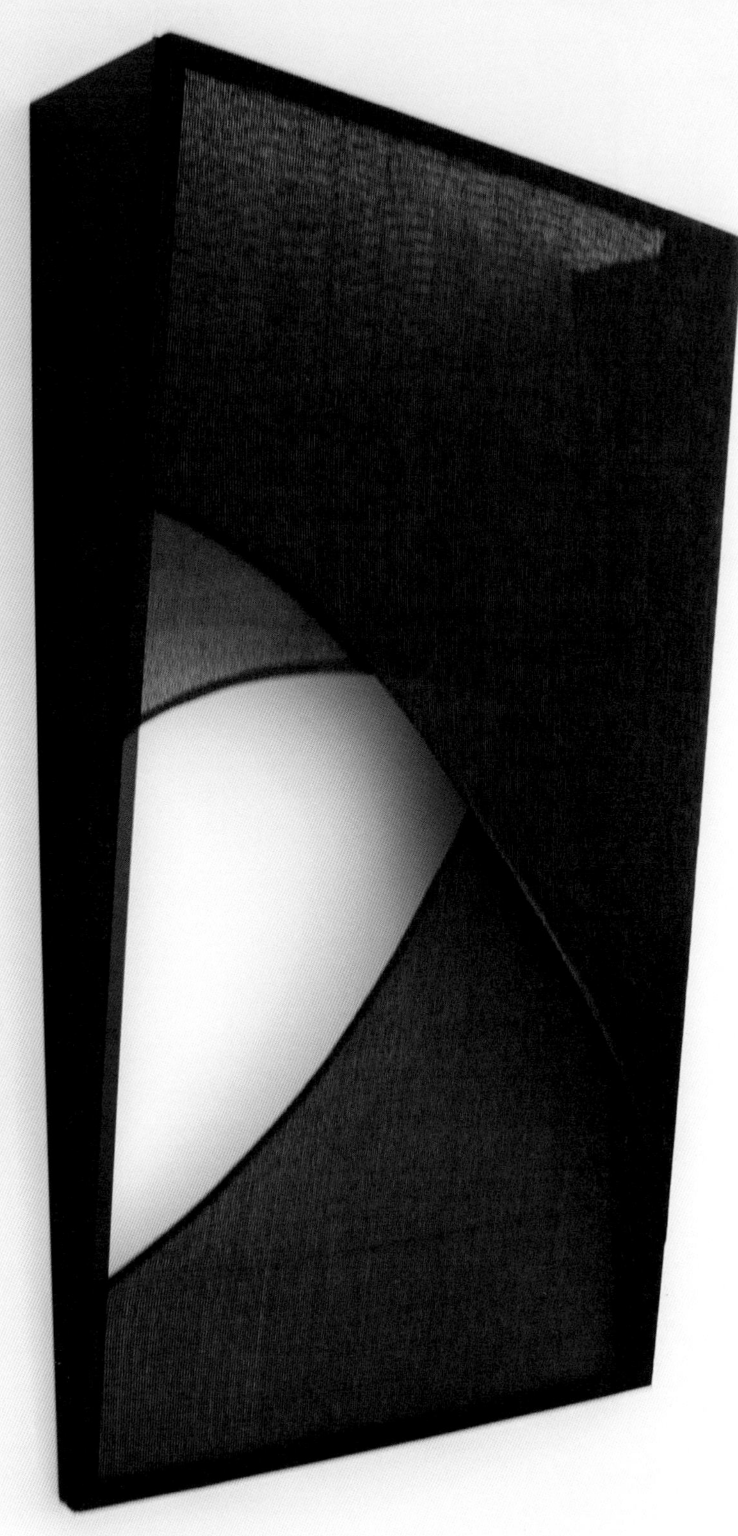

Three Shades, 2018 (detail)

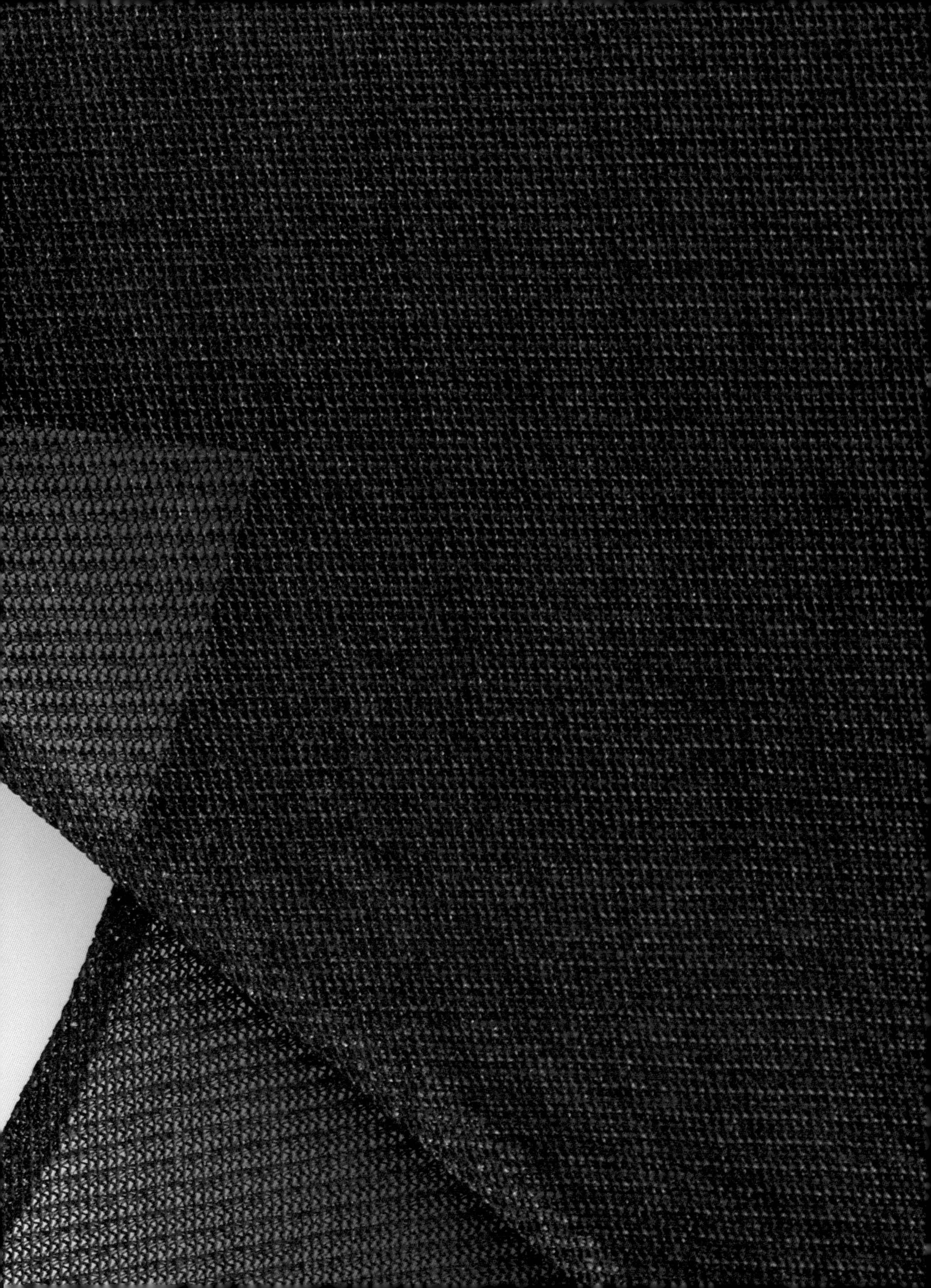

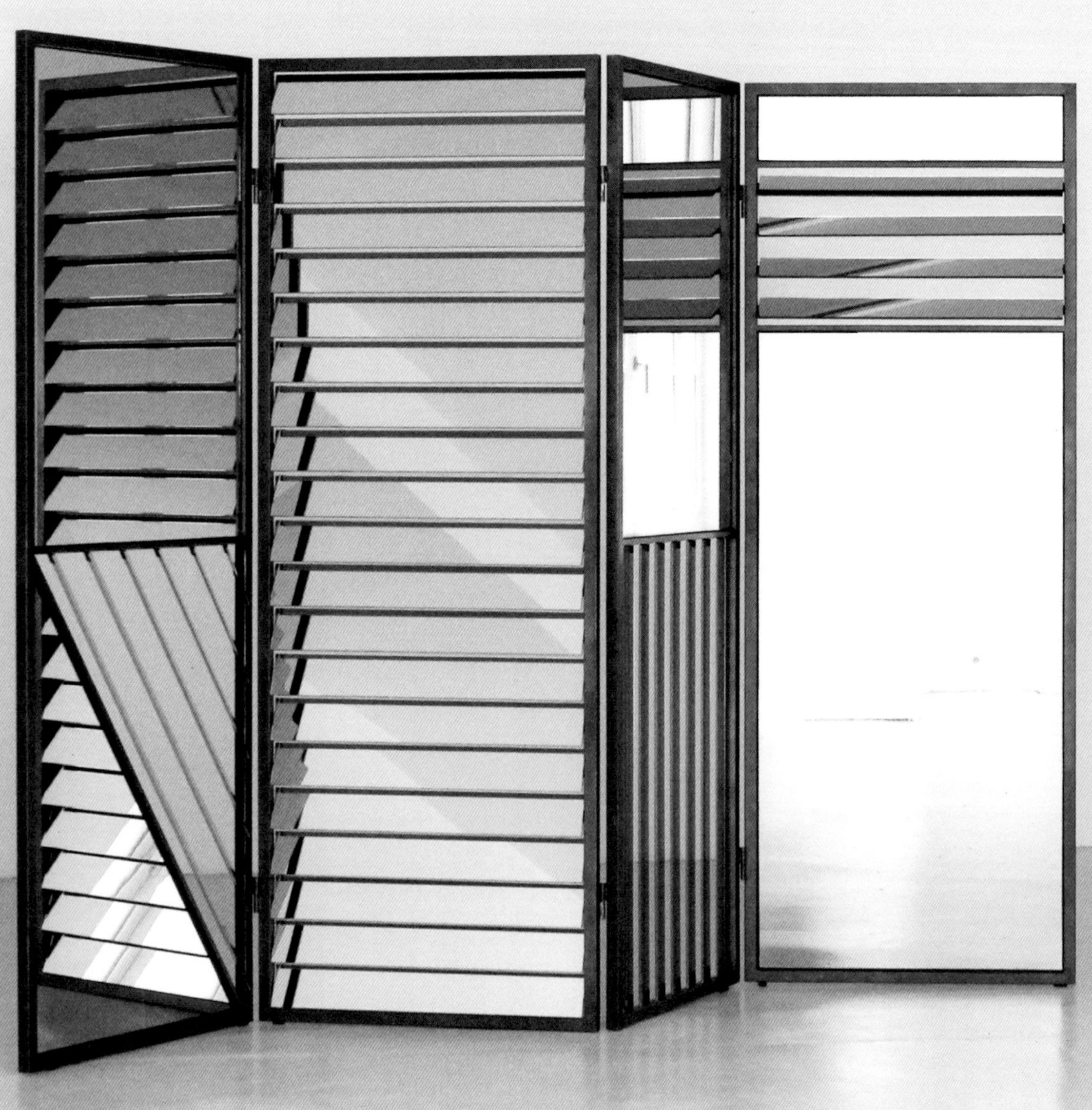

Exhibition view: “Surface Tensions,” Galerie Poggi, Paris, 2018

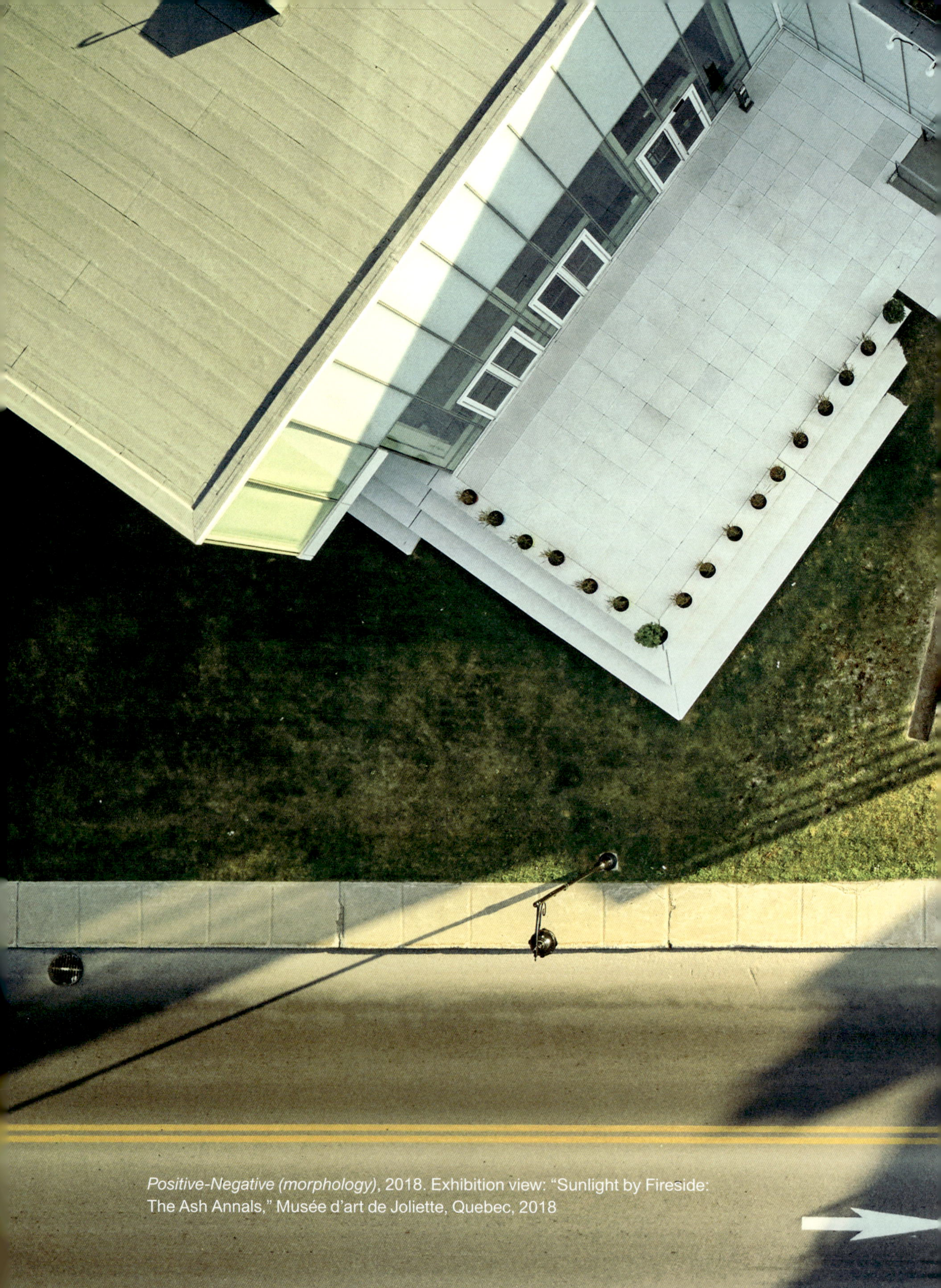

Positive-Negative (morphology), 2018. Exhibition view: "Sunlight by Fireside: The Ash Annals," Musée d'art de Joliette, Quebec, 2018

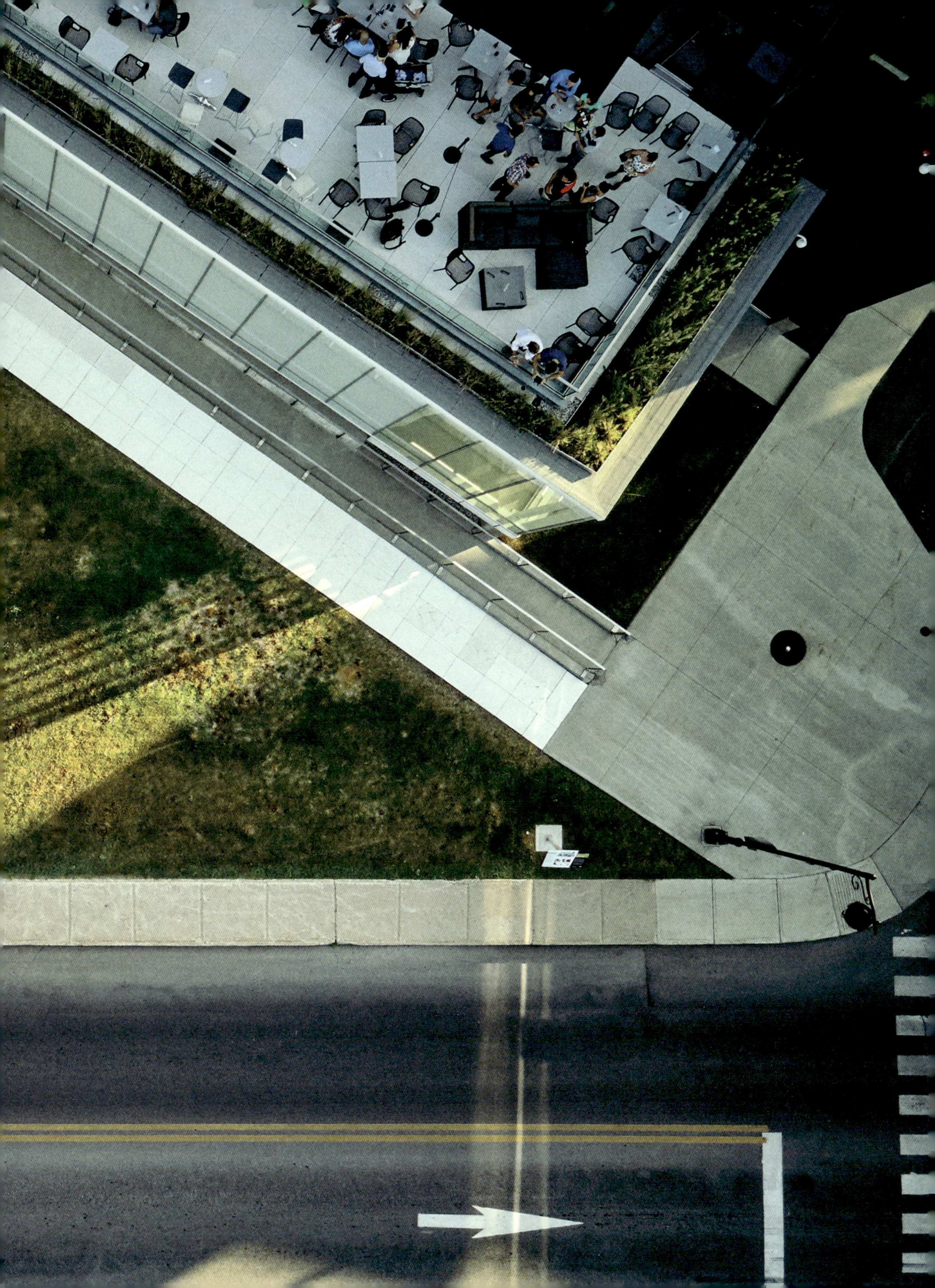

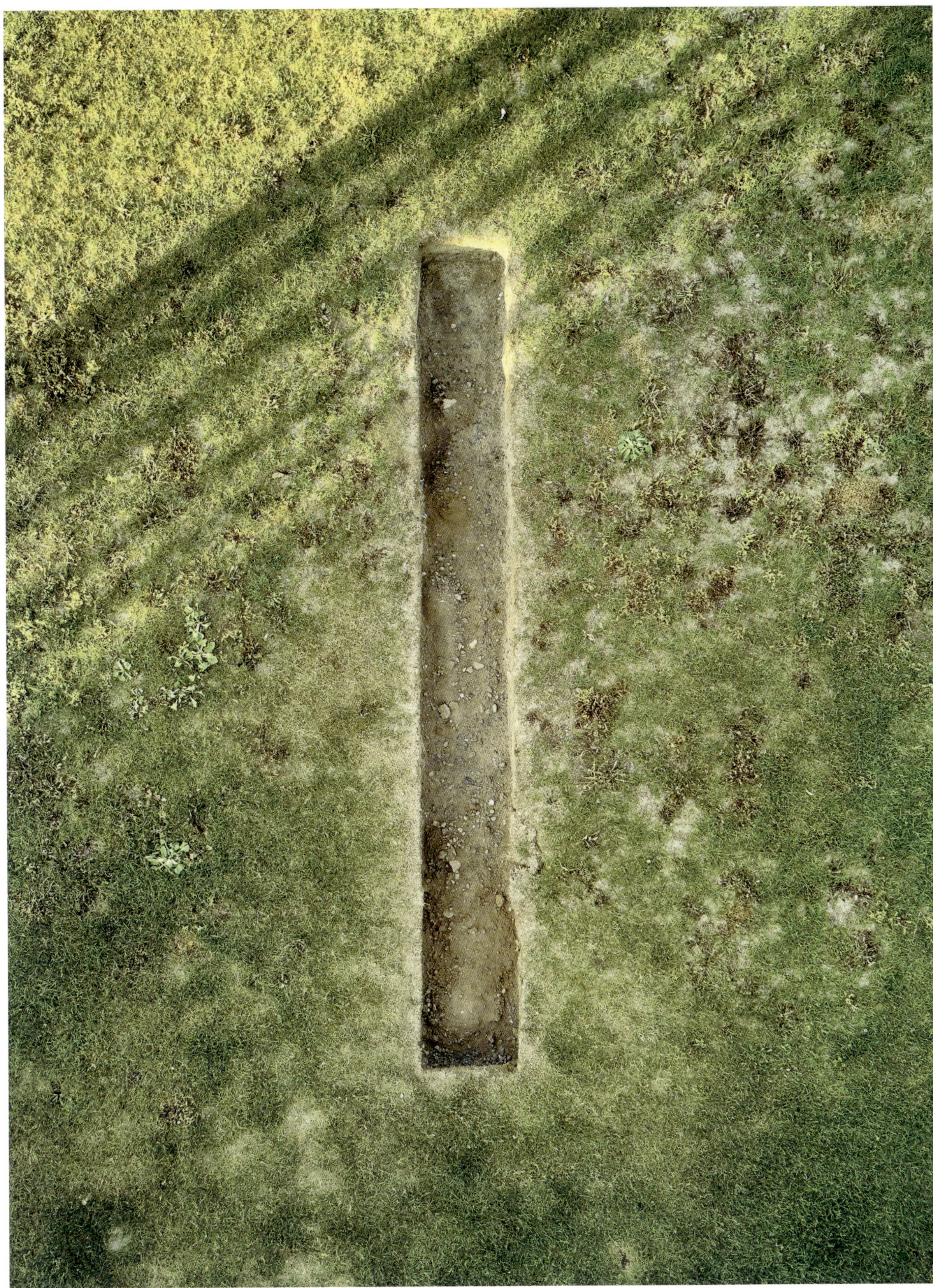

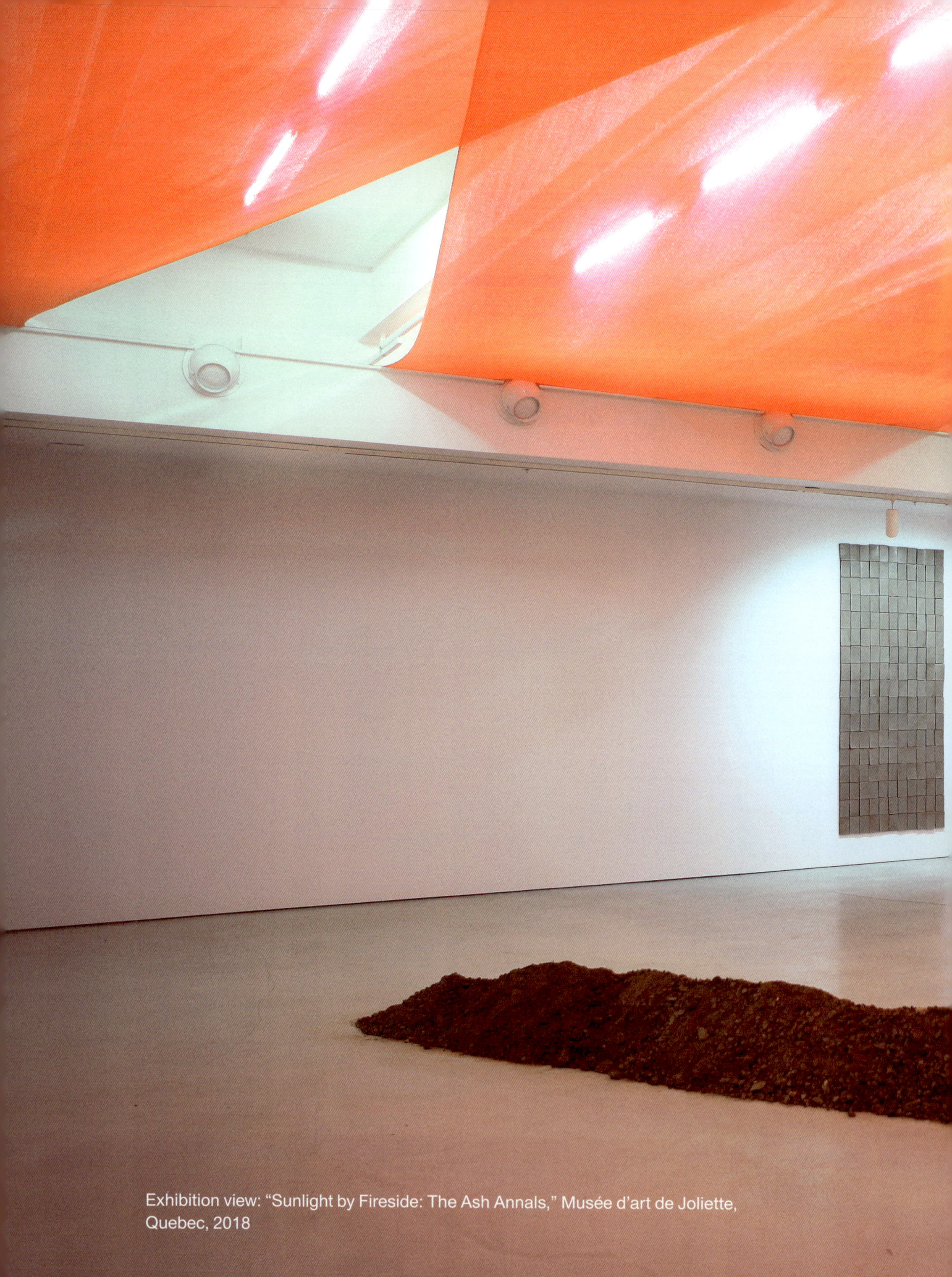

Exhibition view: “Sunlight by Fireside: The Ash Annals,” Musée d’art de Joliette, Quebec, 2018

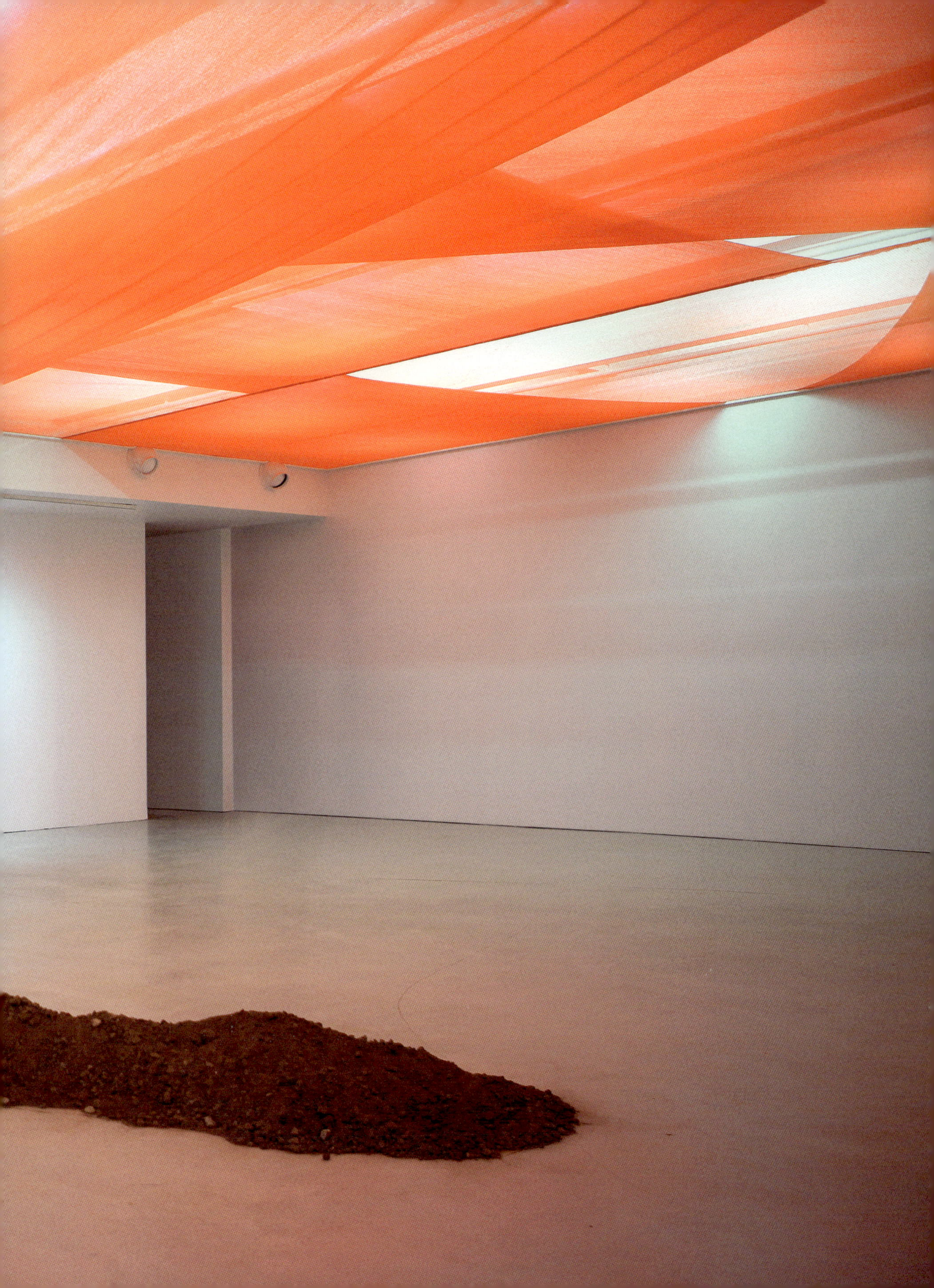

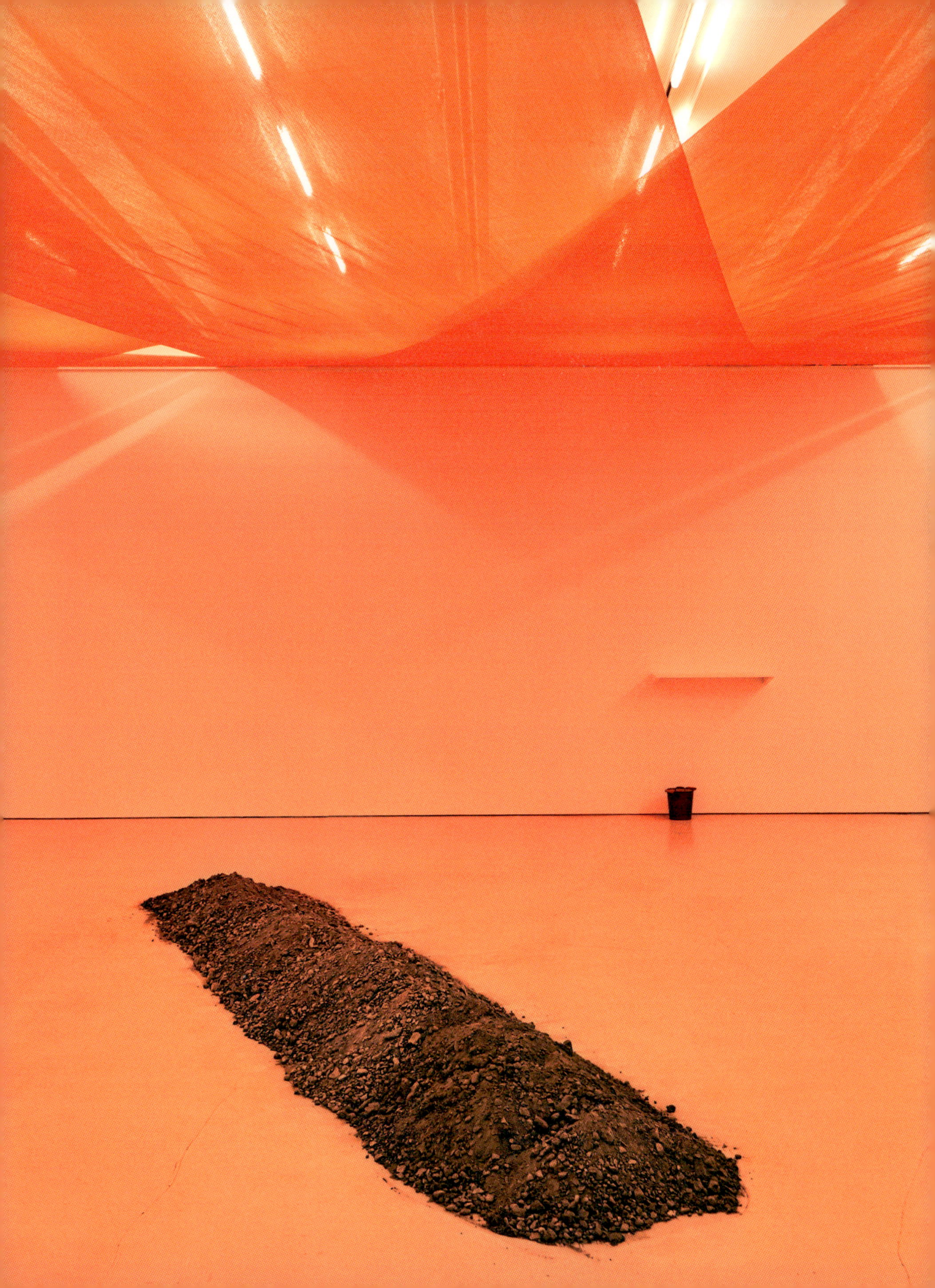

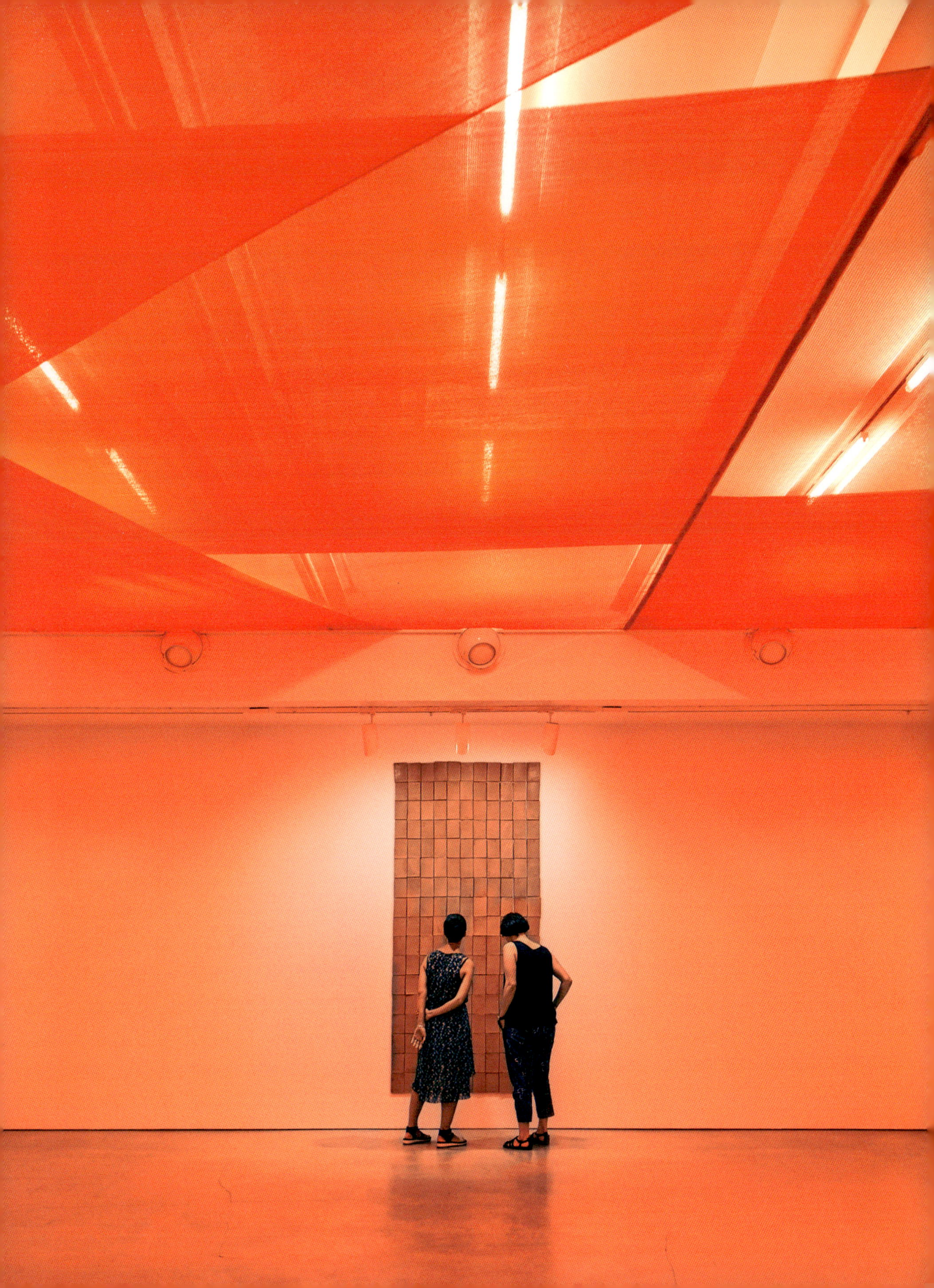

Black and Blue (Spine), 2018

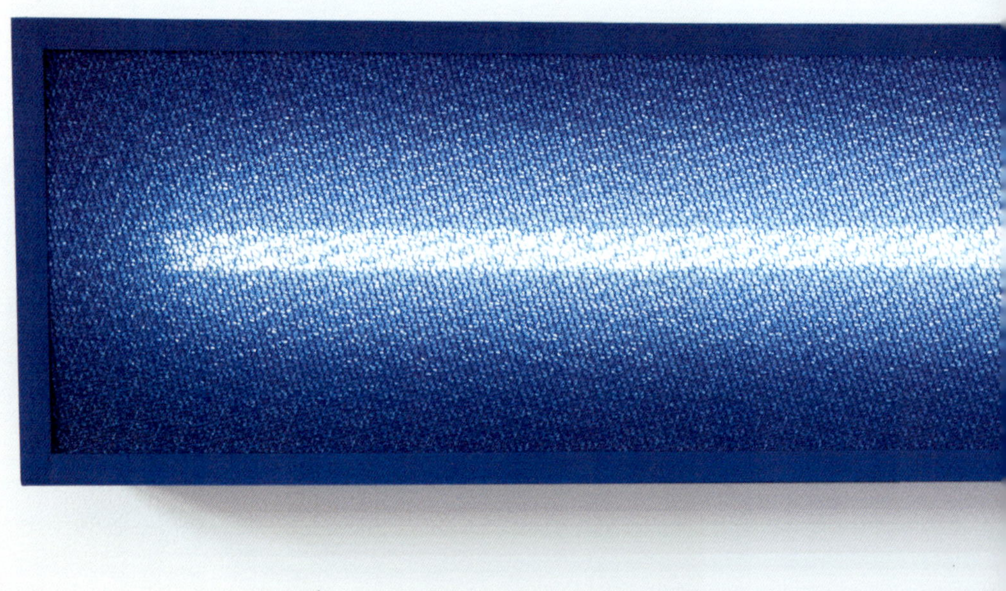

Hazy (Blue), 2018

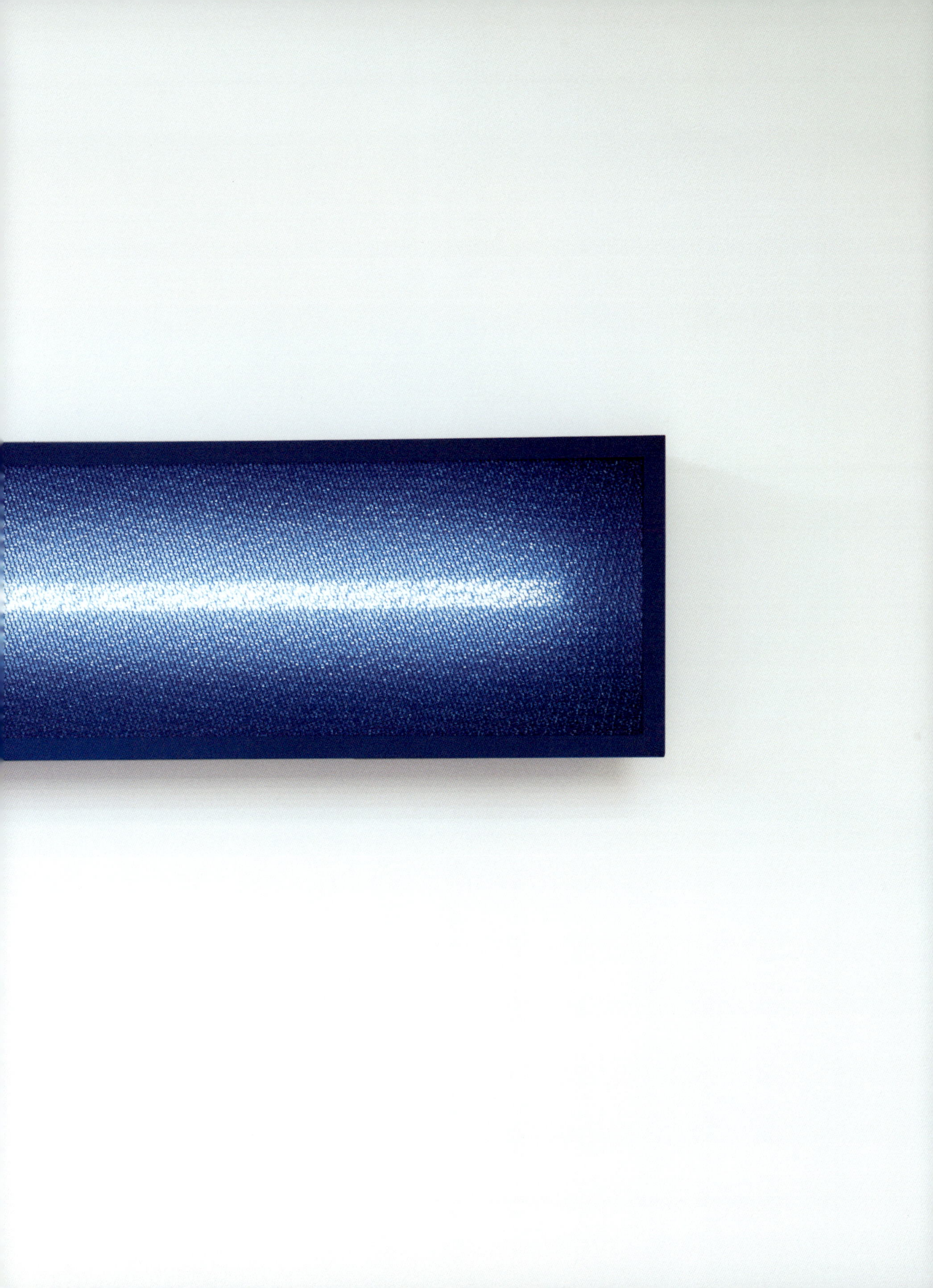

TRI (magenta, black and red), 2019

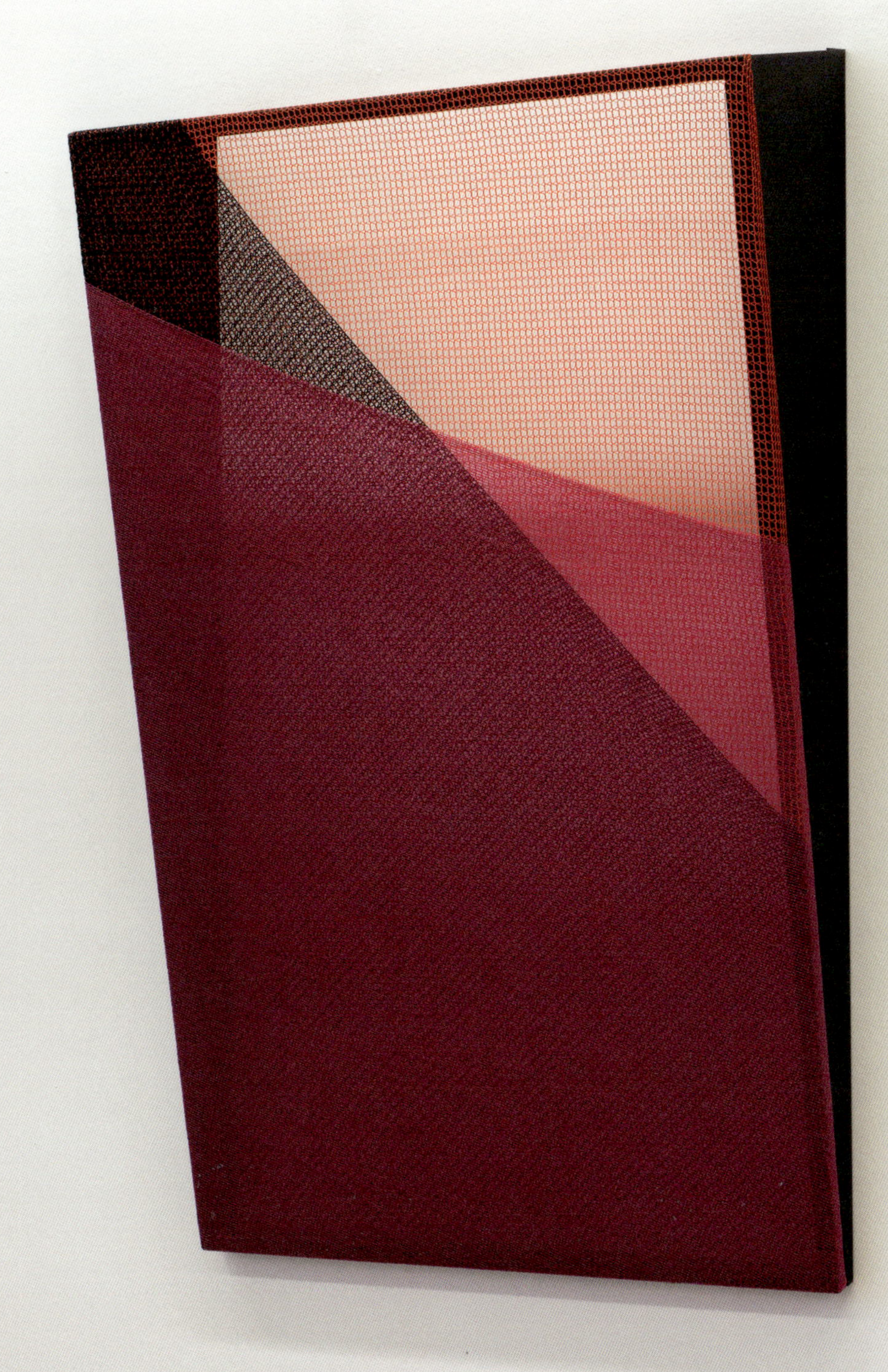

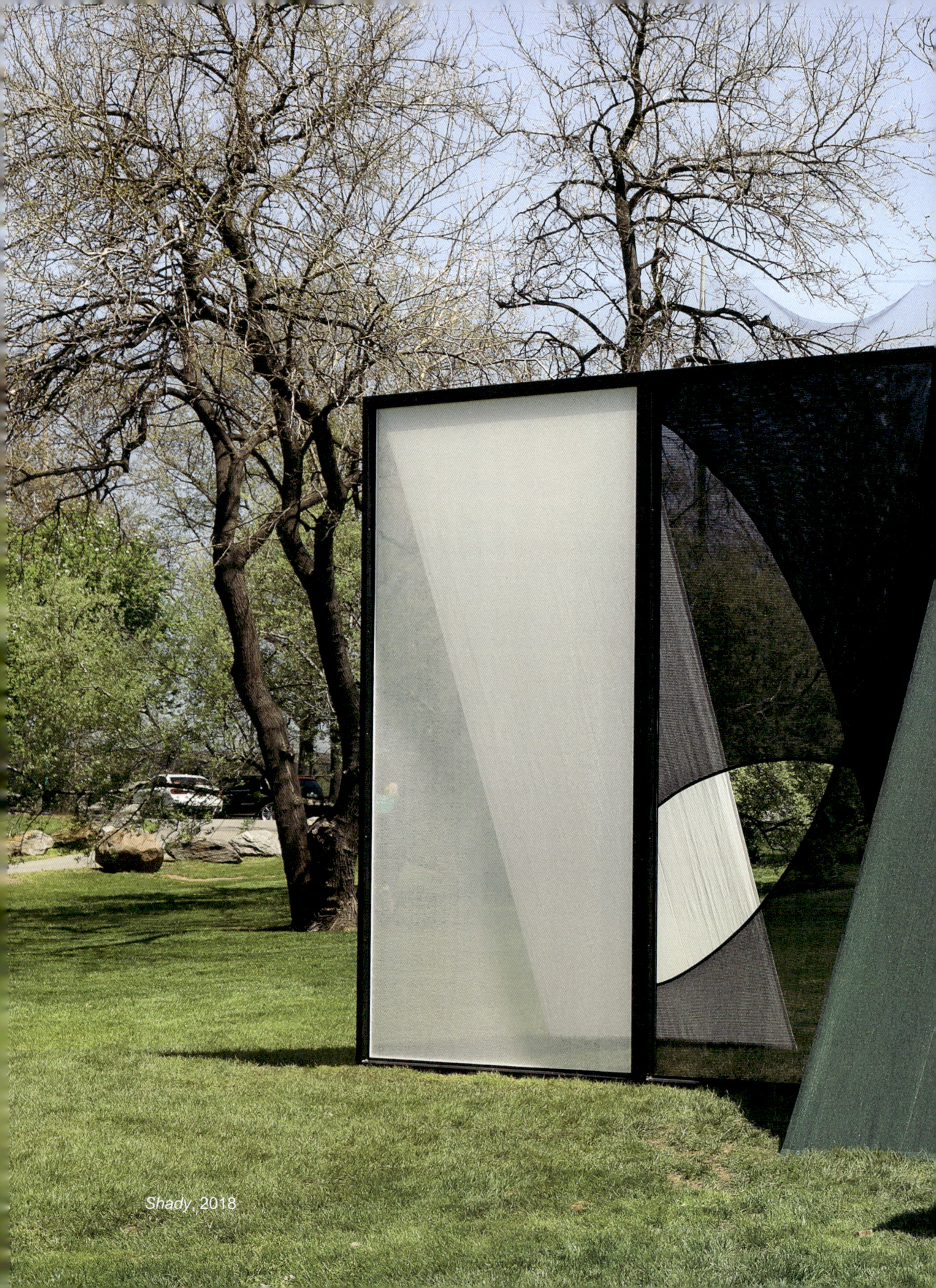

Shady, 2018

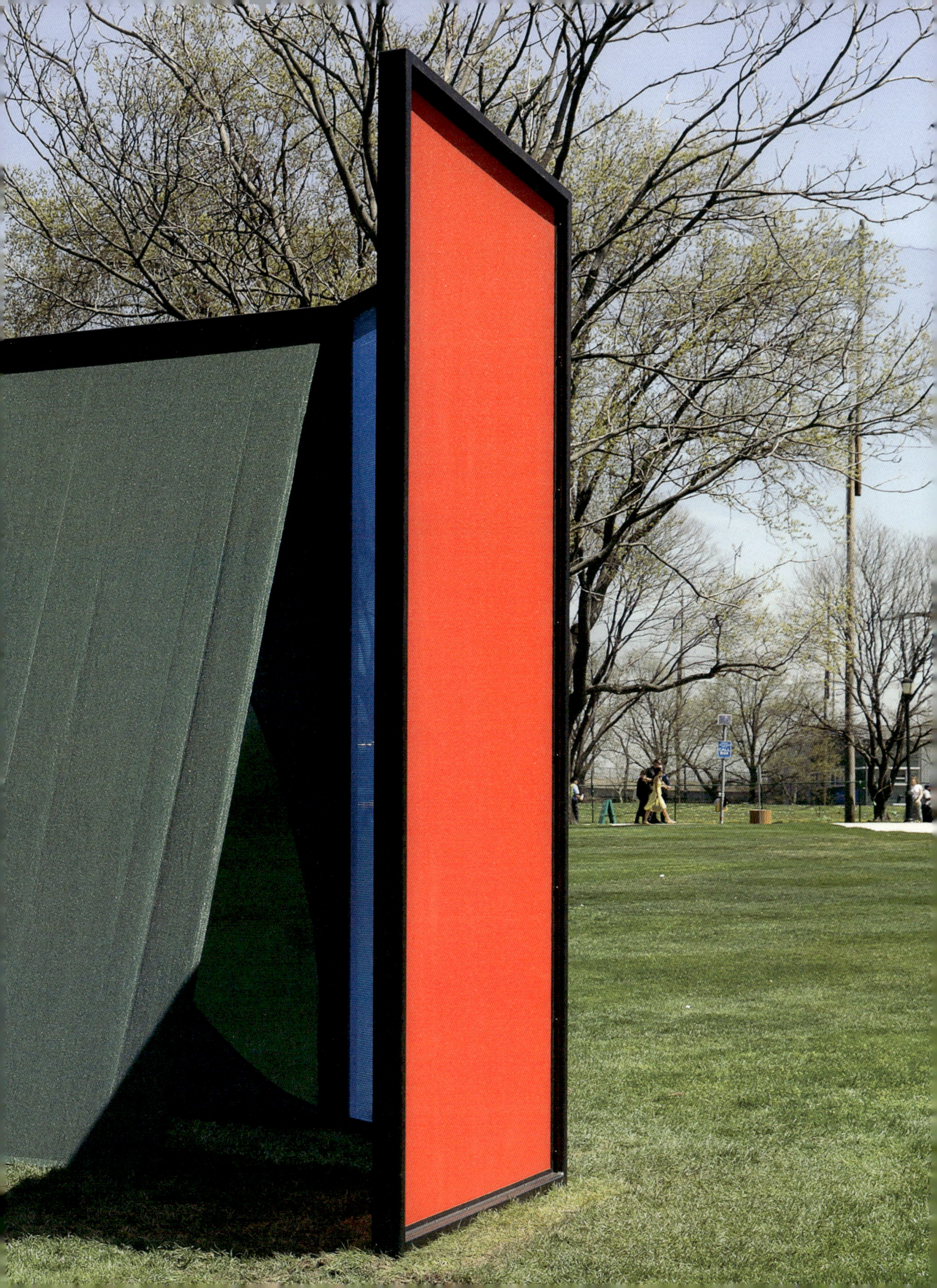

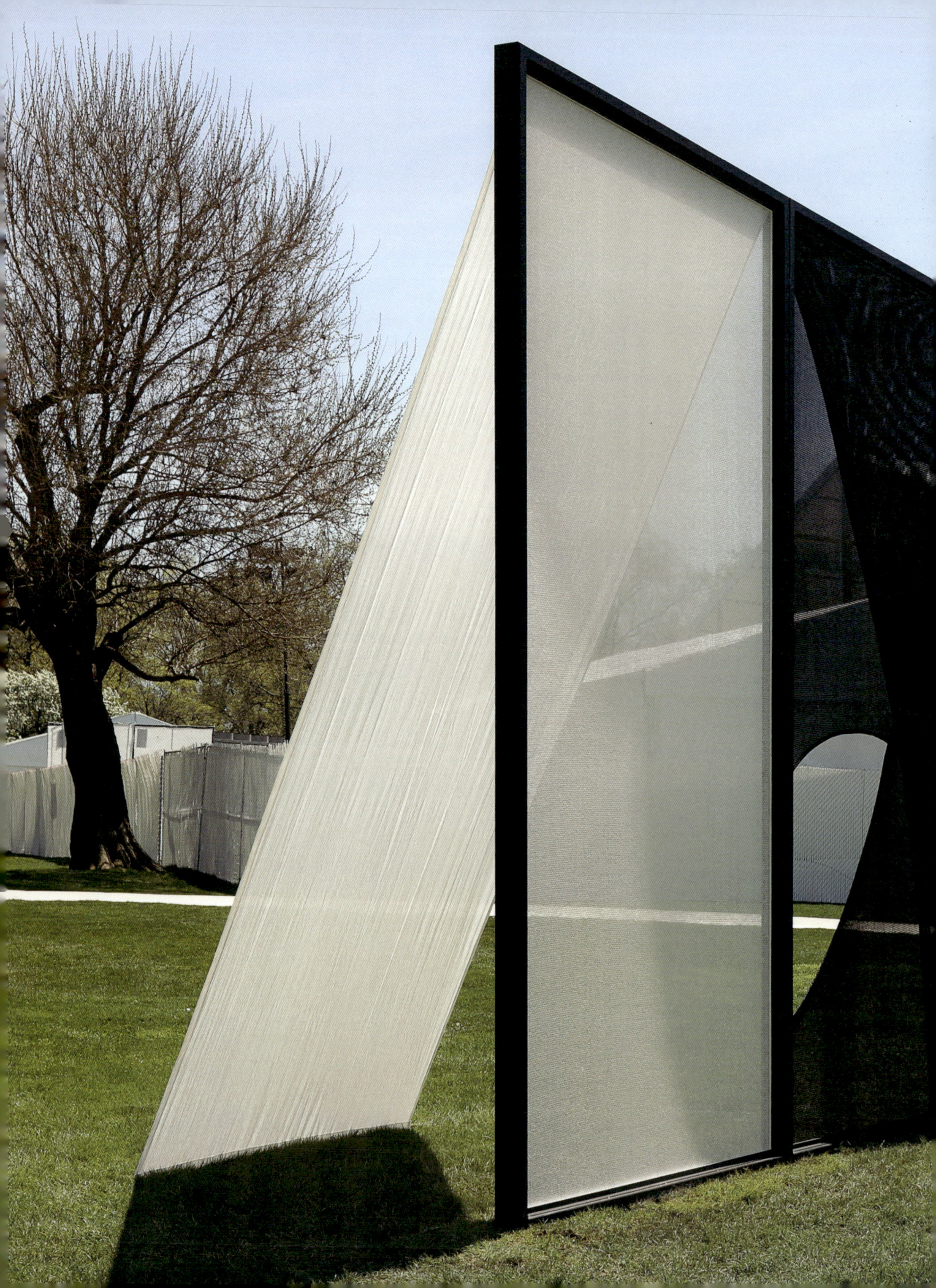

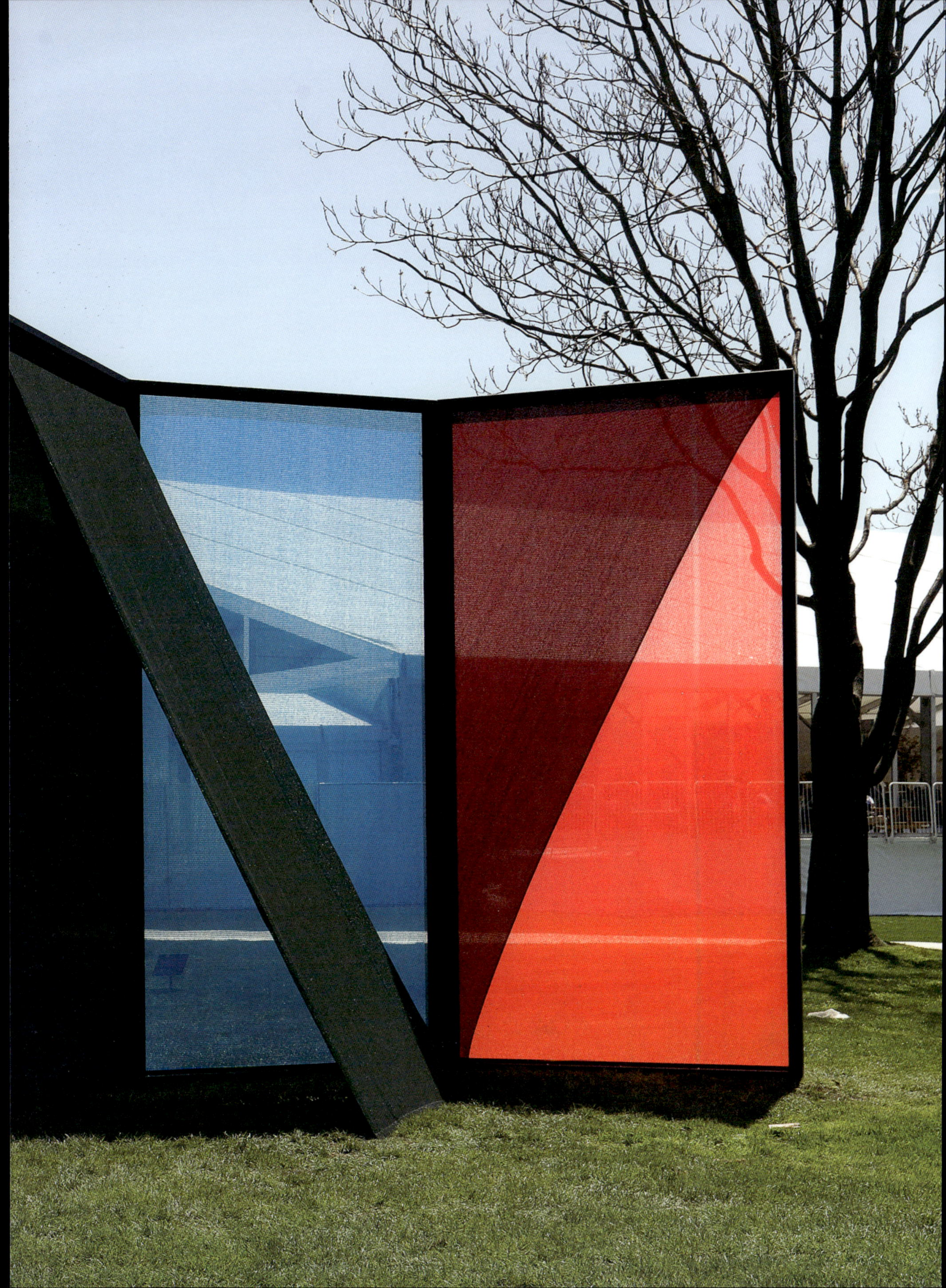

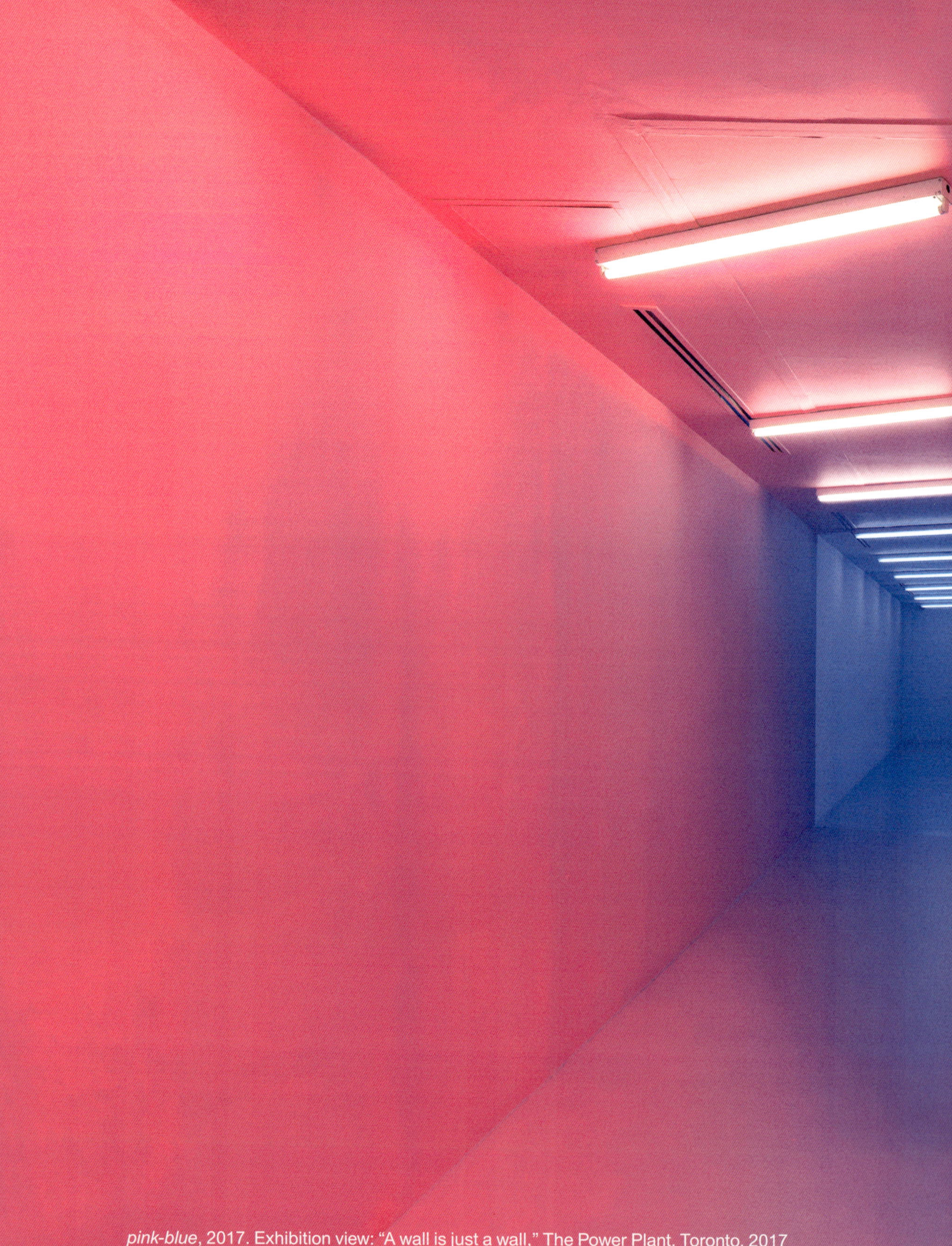

pink-blue, 2017. Exhibition view: "A wall is just a wall," The Power Plant, Toronto, 2017

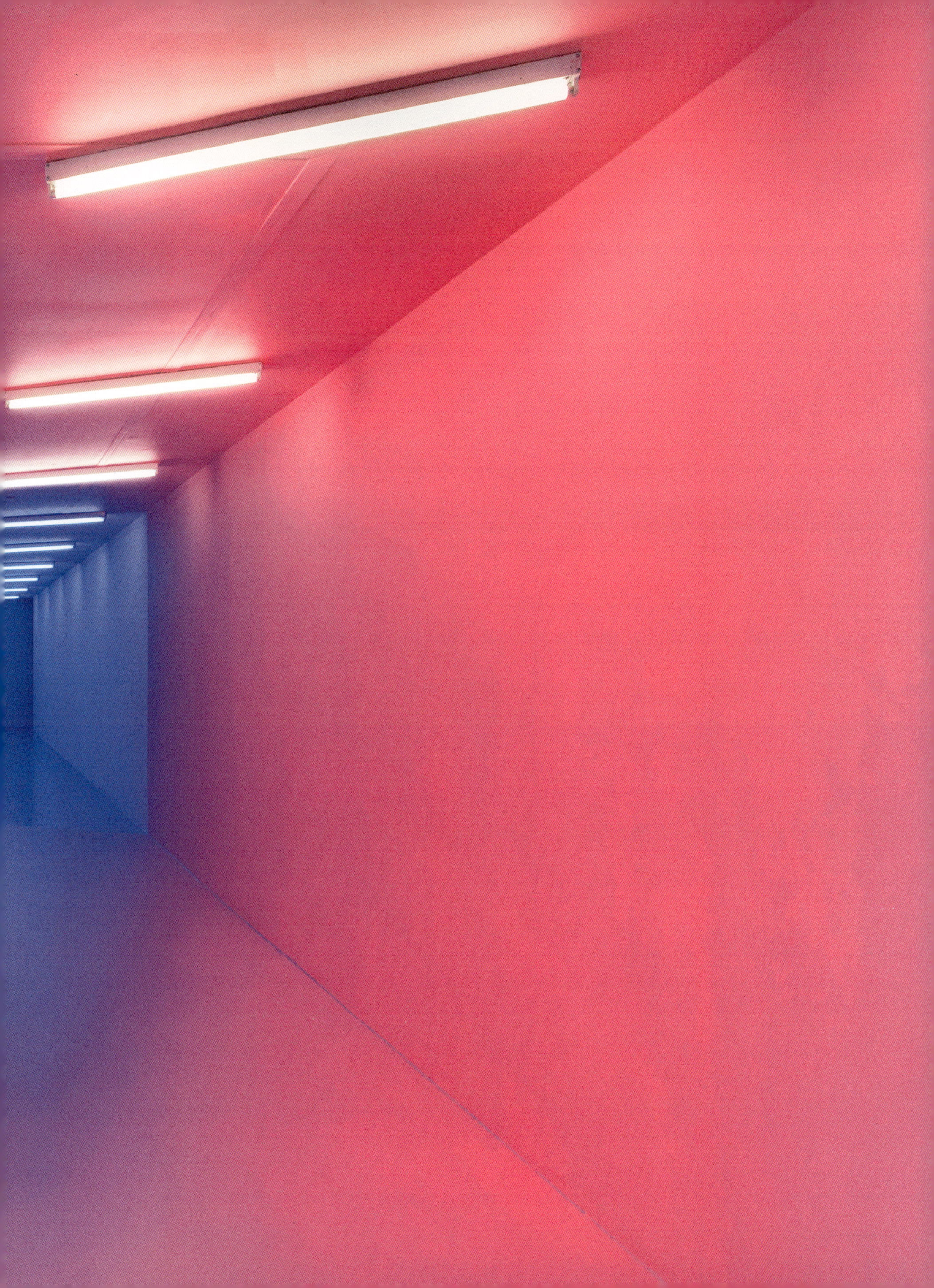

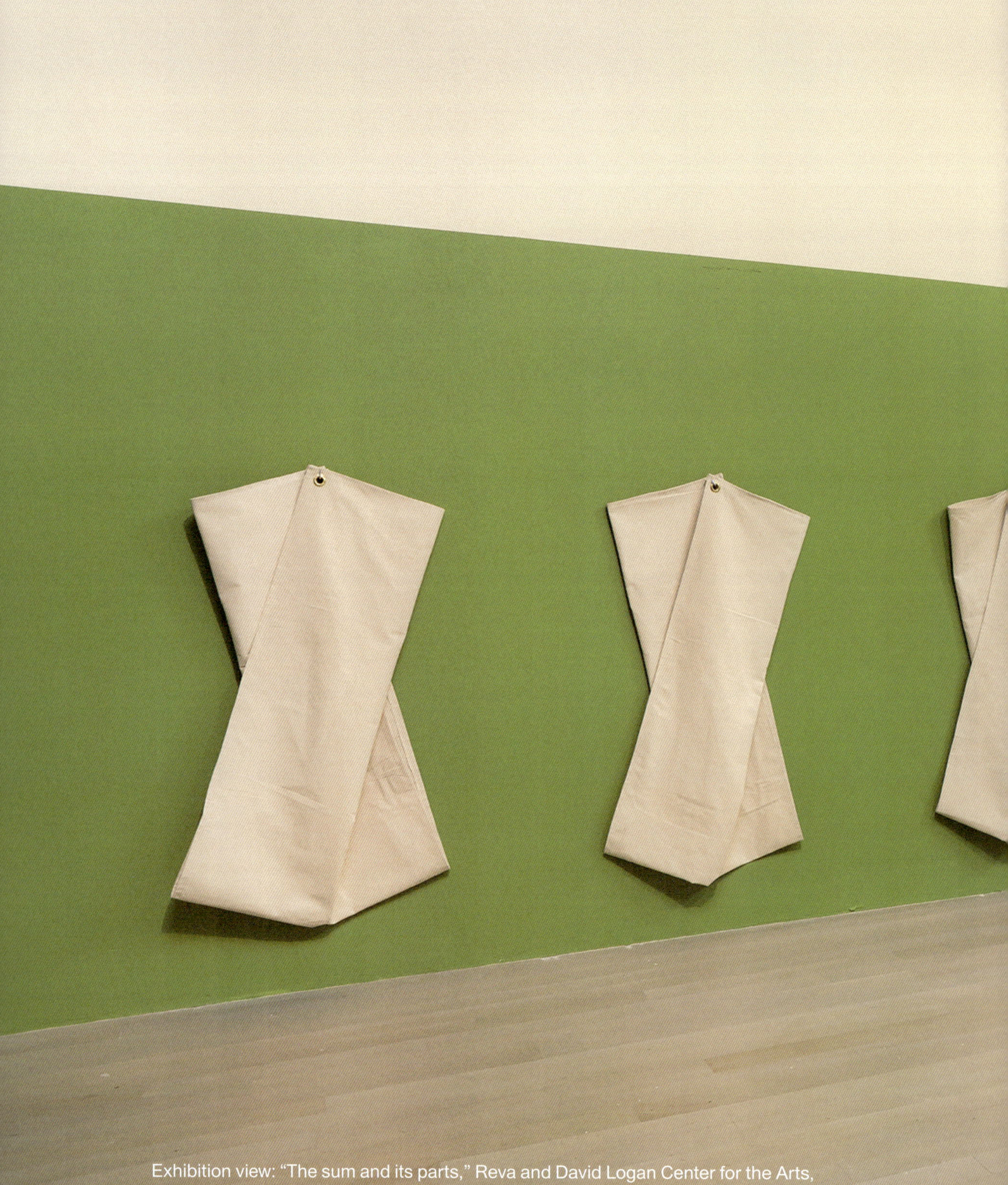

Exhibition view: "The sum and its parts," Reva and David Logan Center for the Arts, University of Chicago, 2017

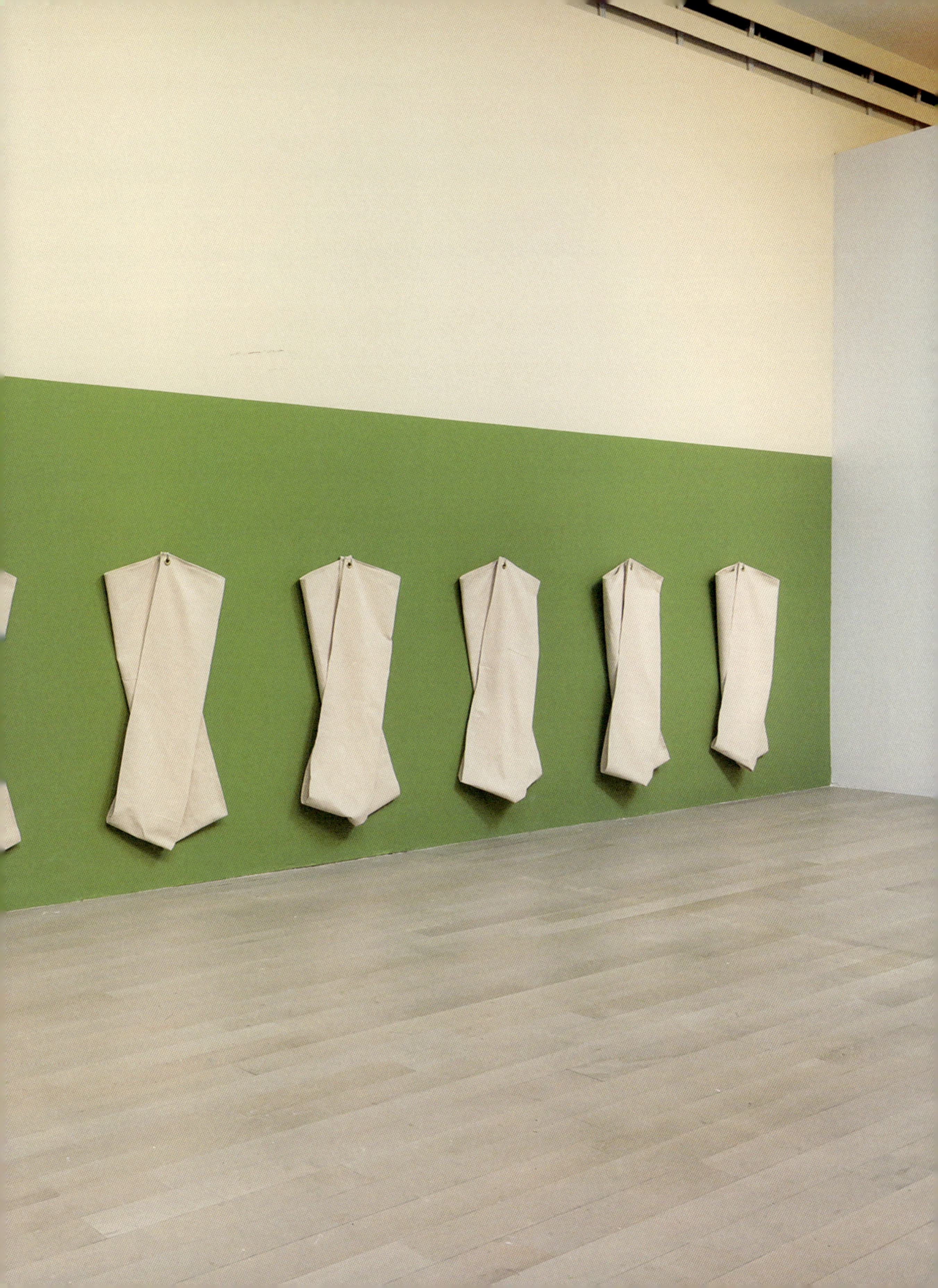

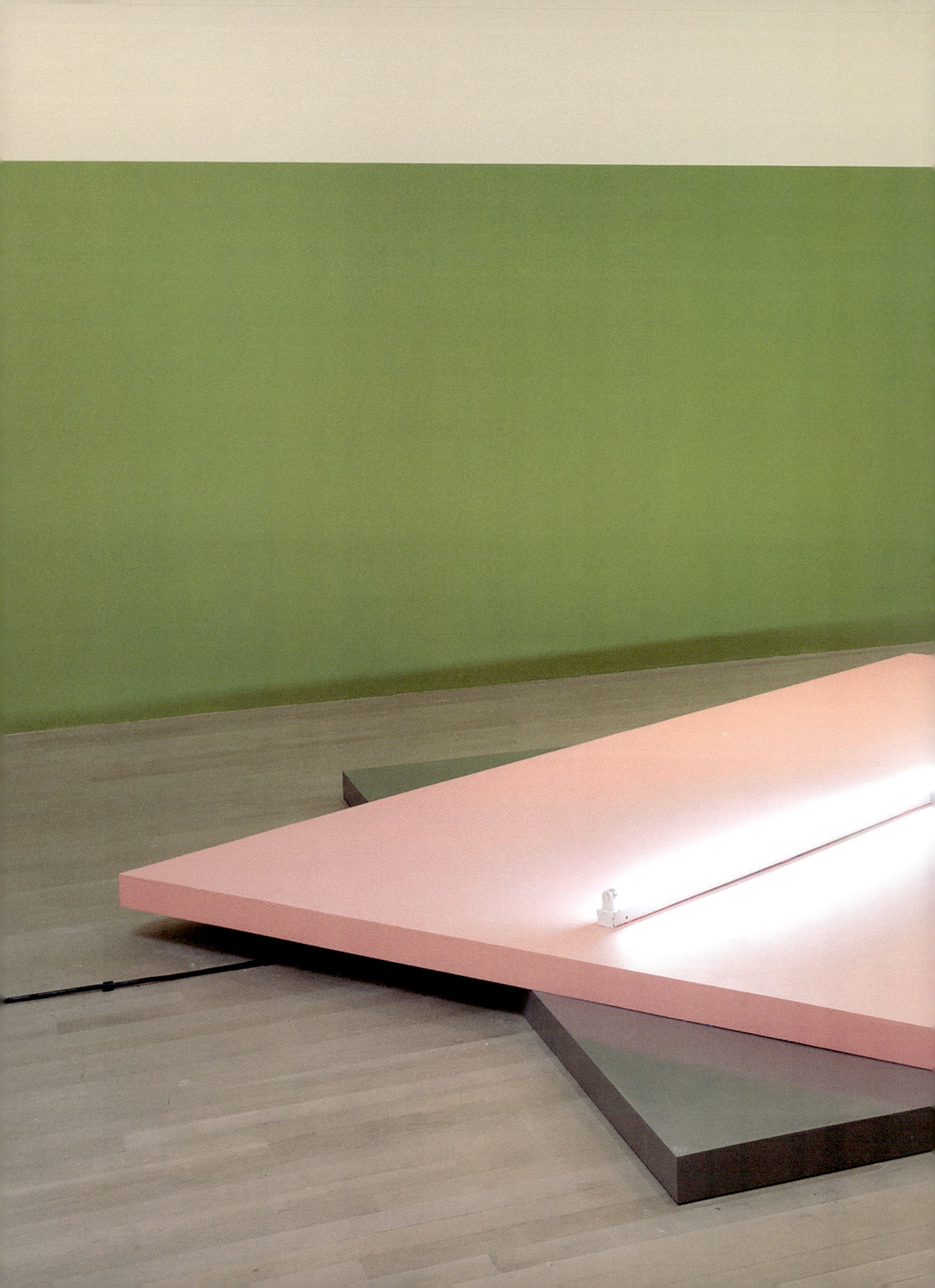

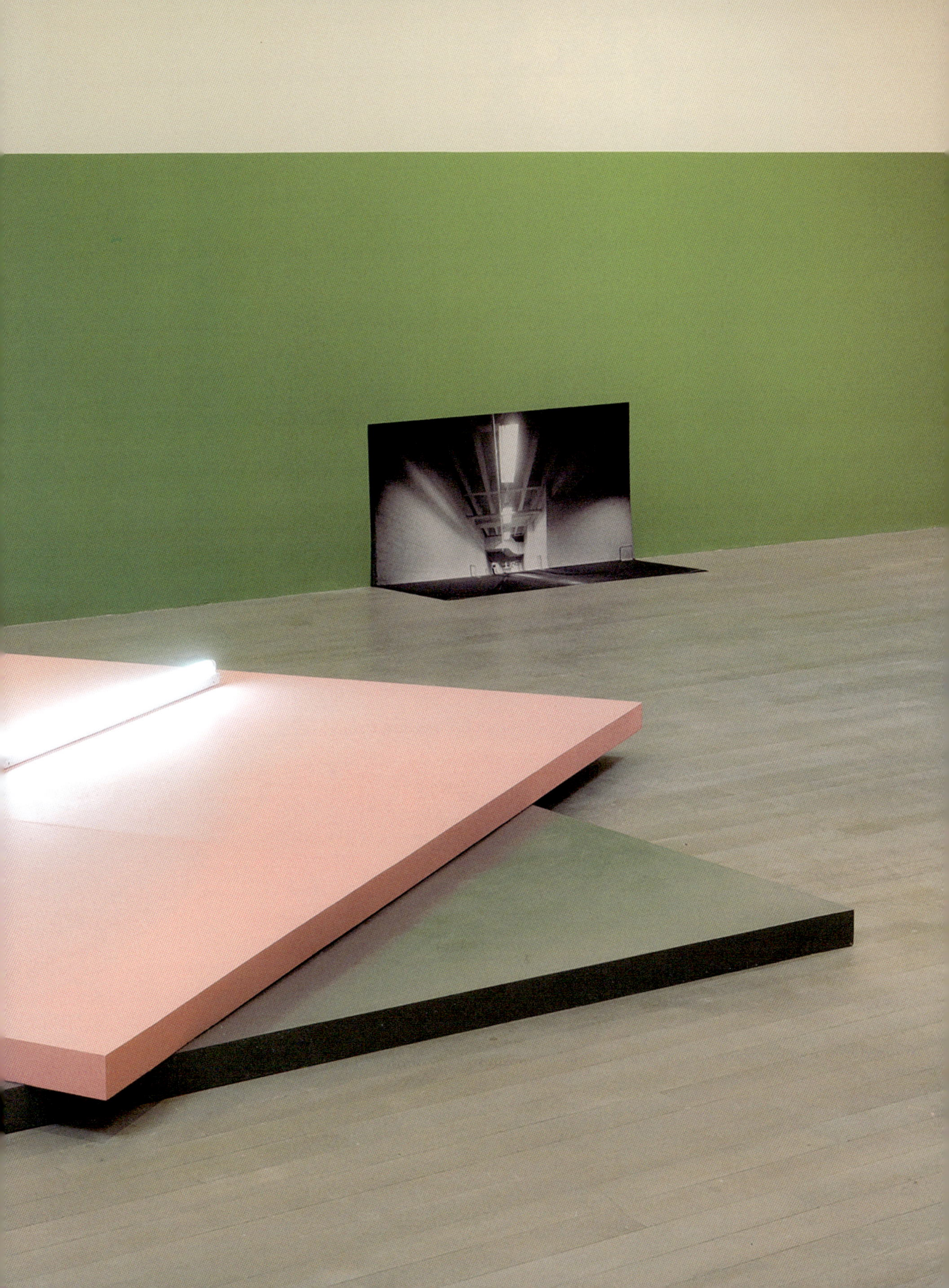

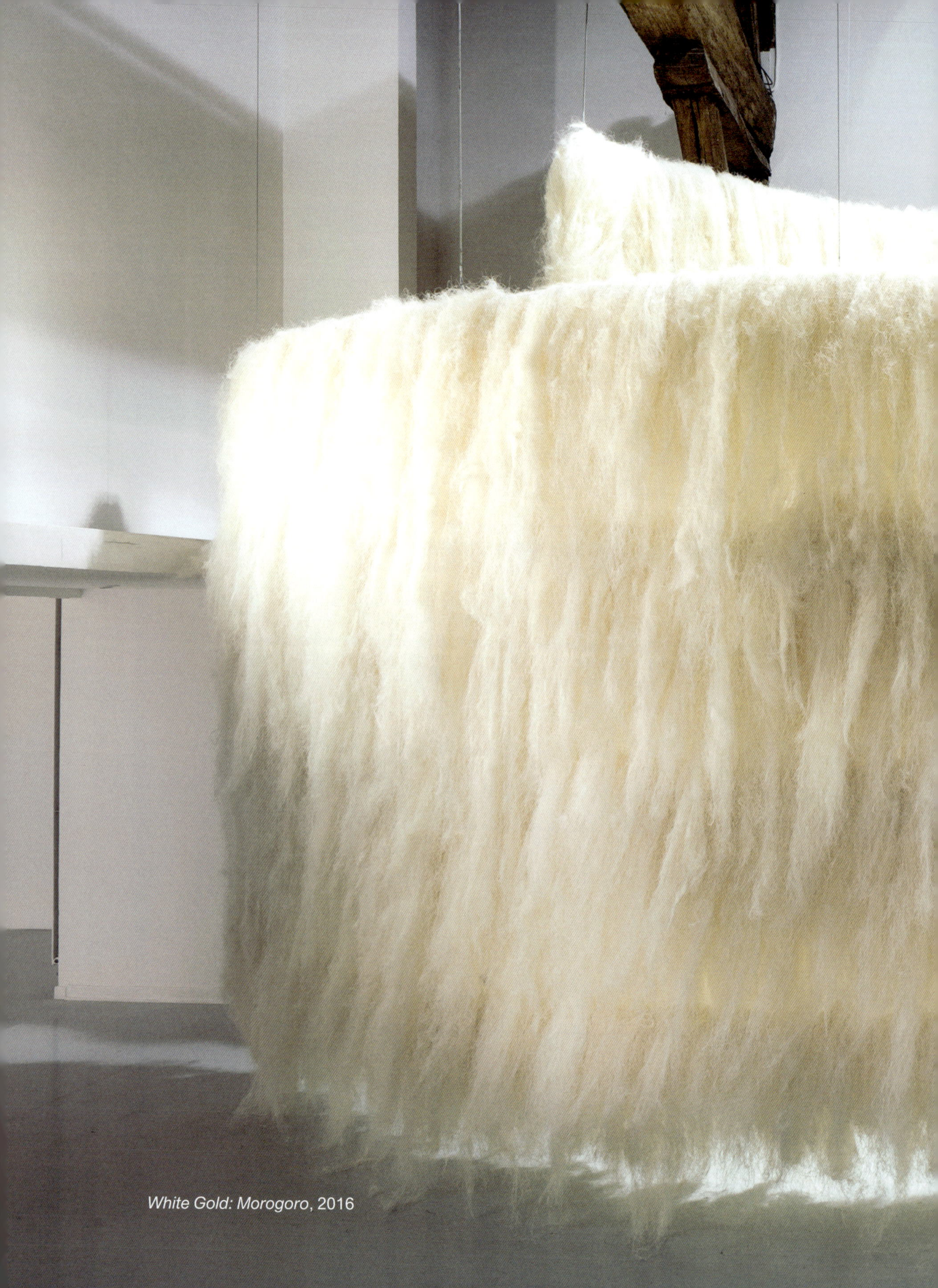

White Gold: Morogoro, 2016

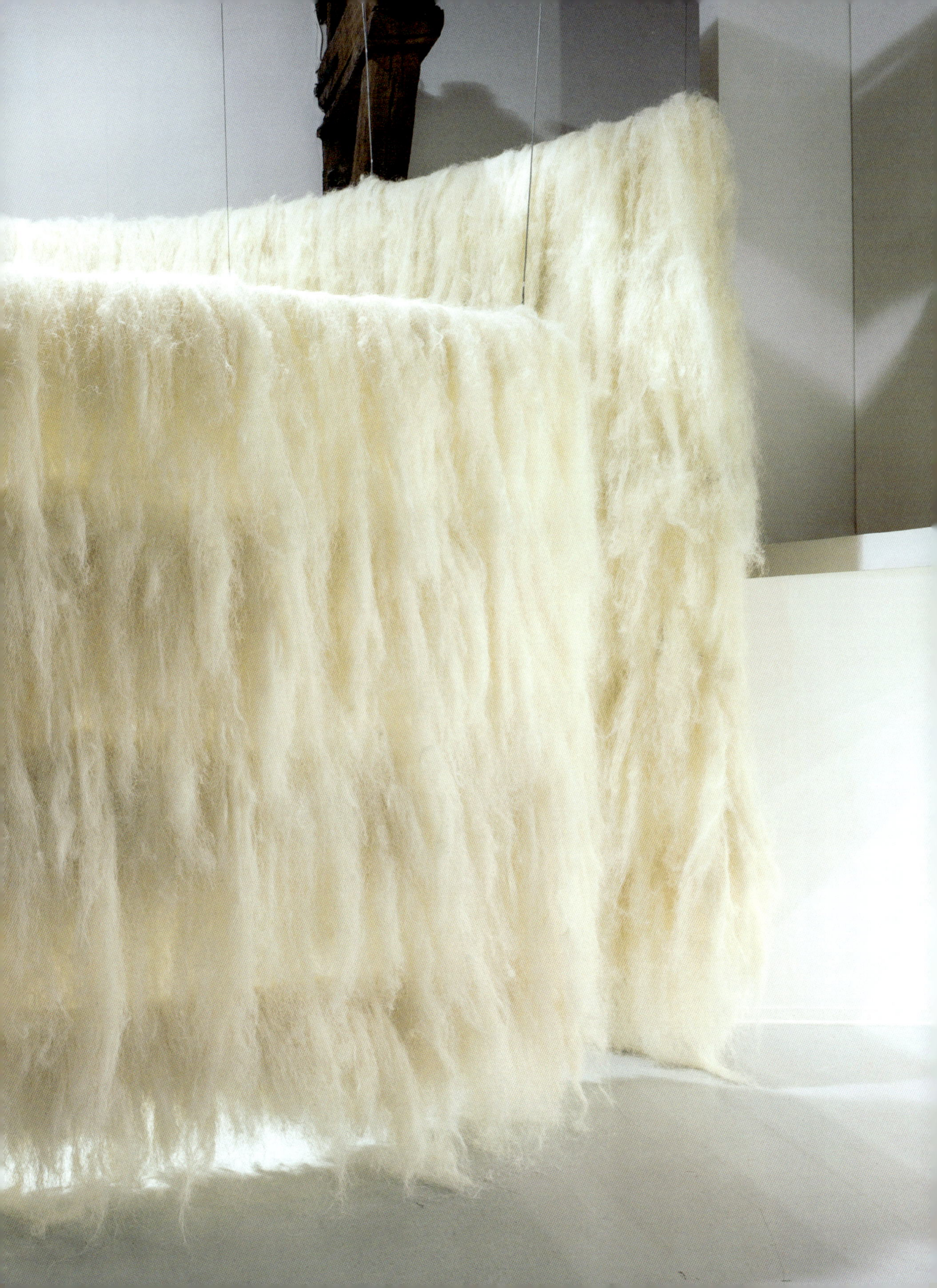

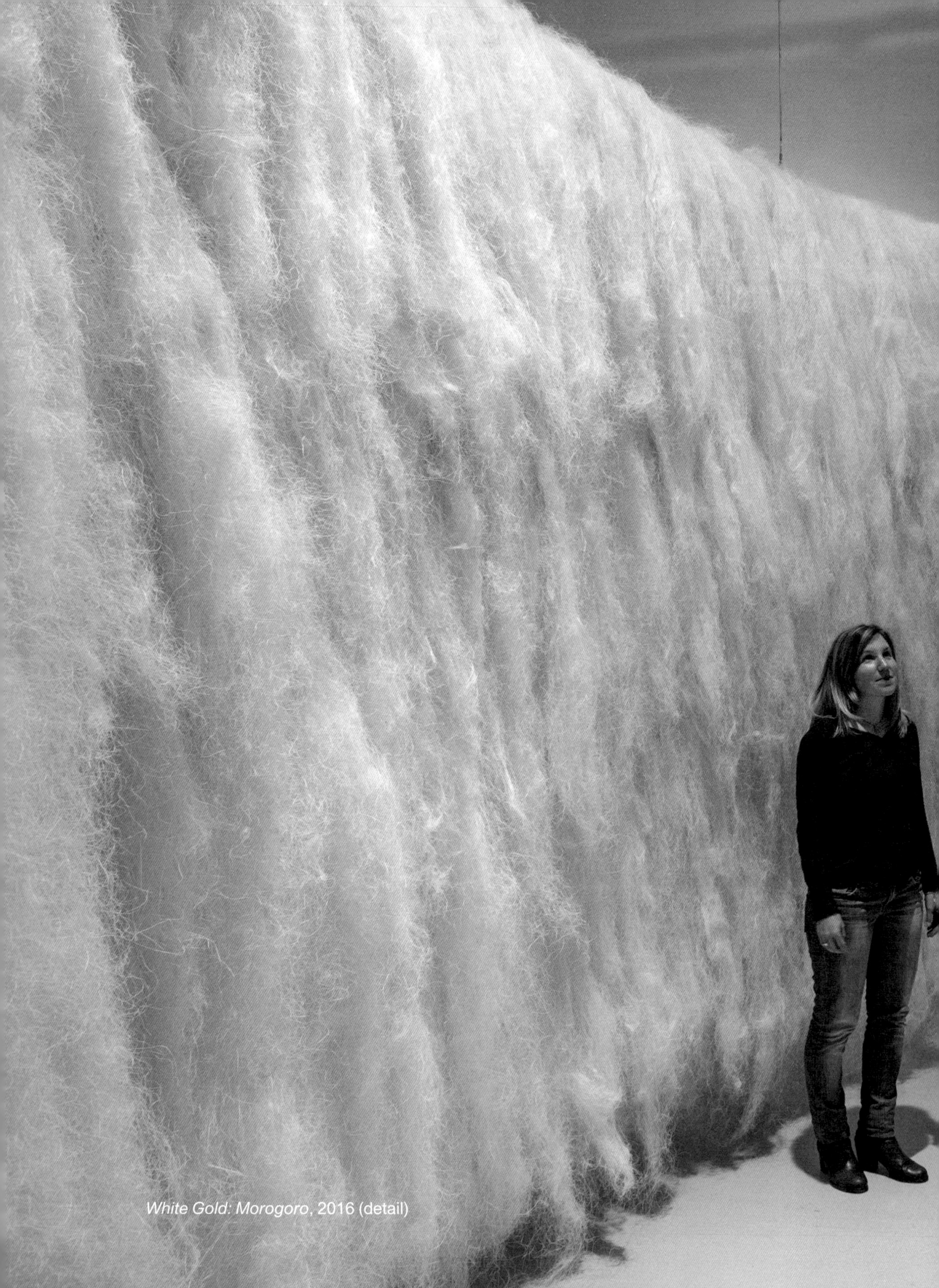

White Gold: Morogoro, 2016 (detail)

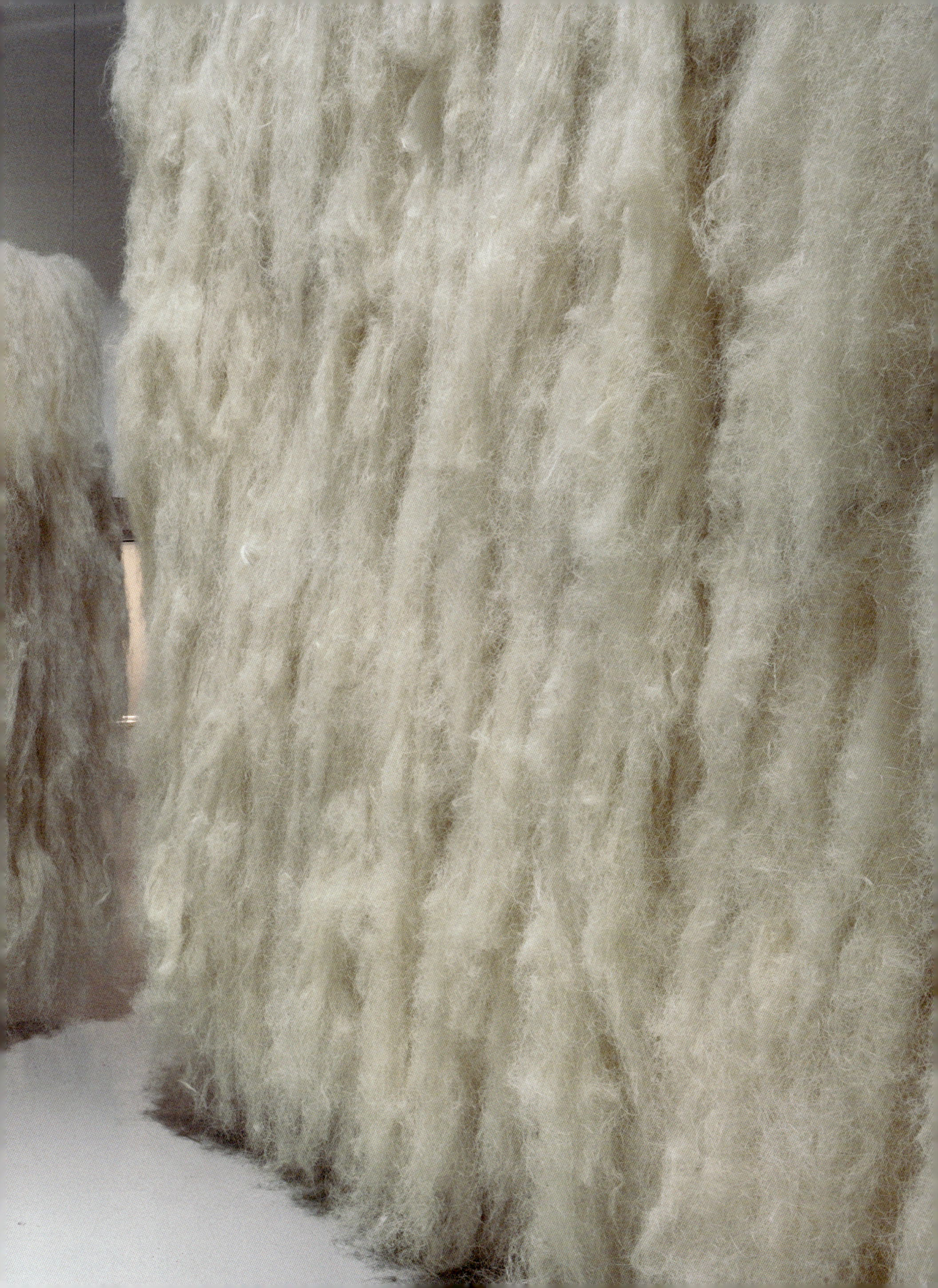

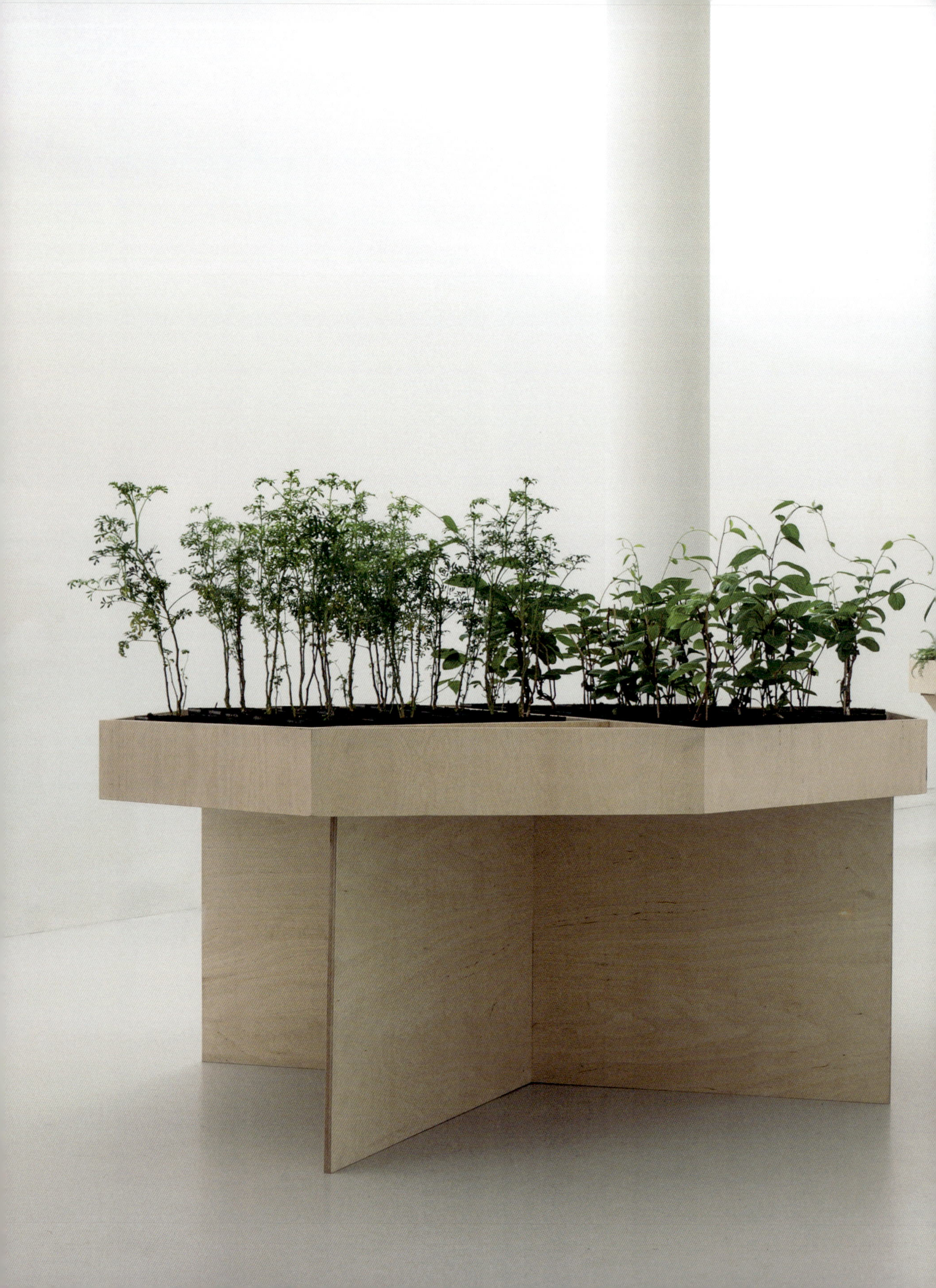

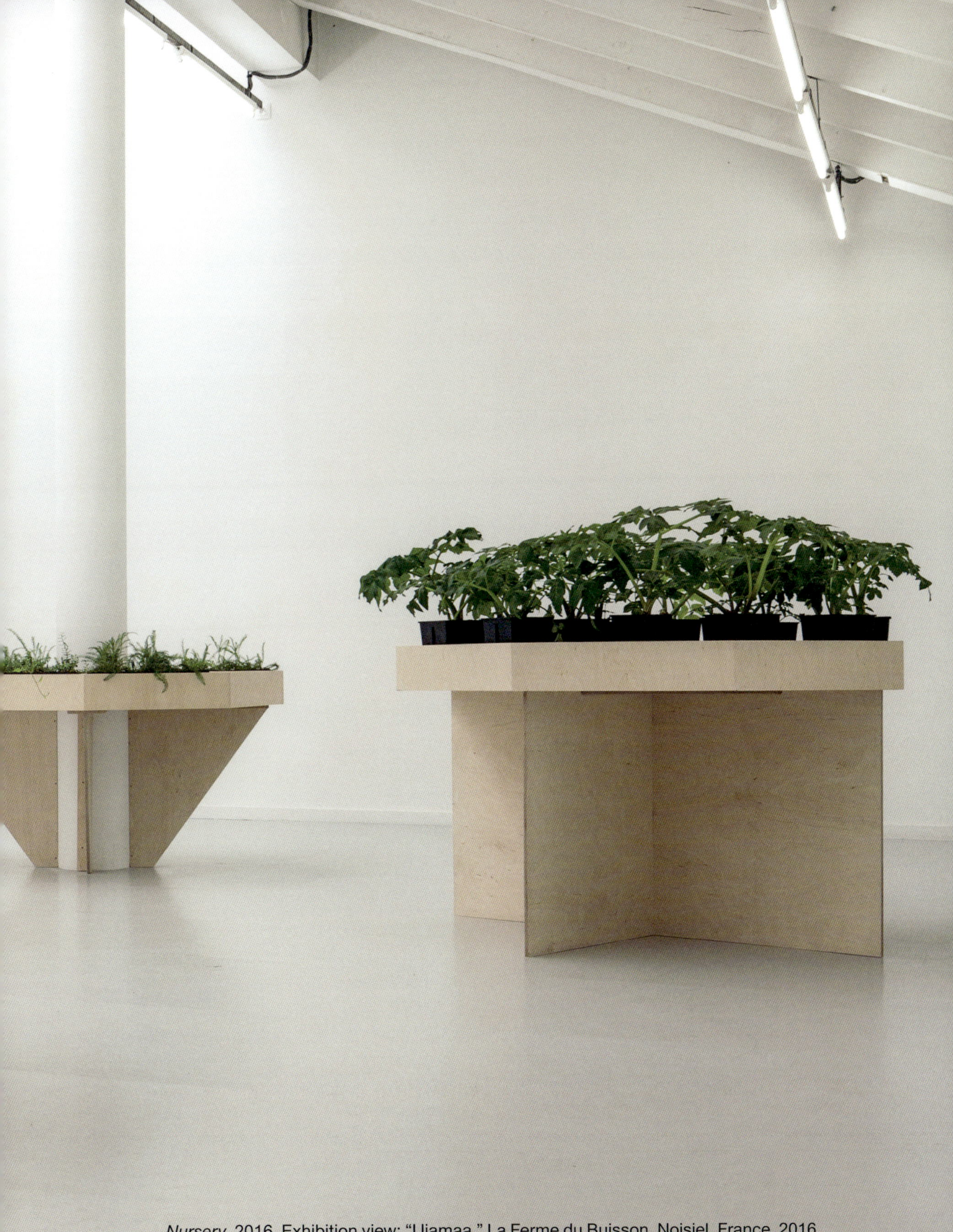

Nursery, 2016. Exhibition view: "Ujamaa," La Ferme du Buisson, Noisiel, France, 2016

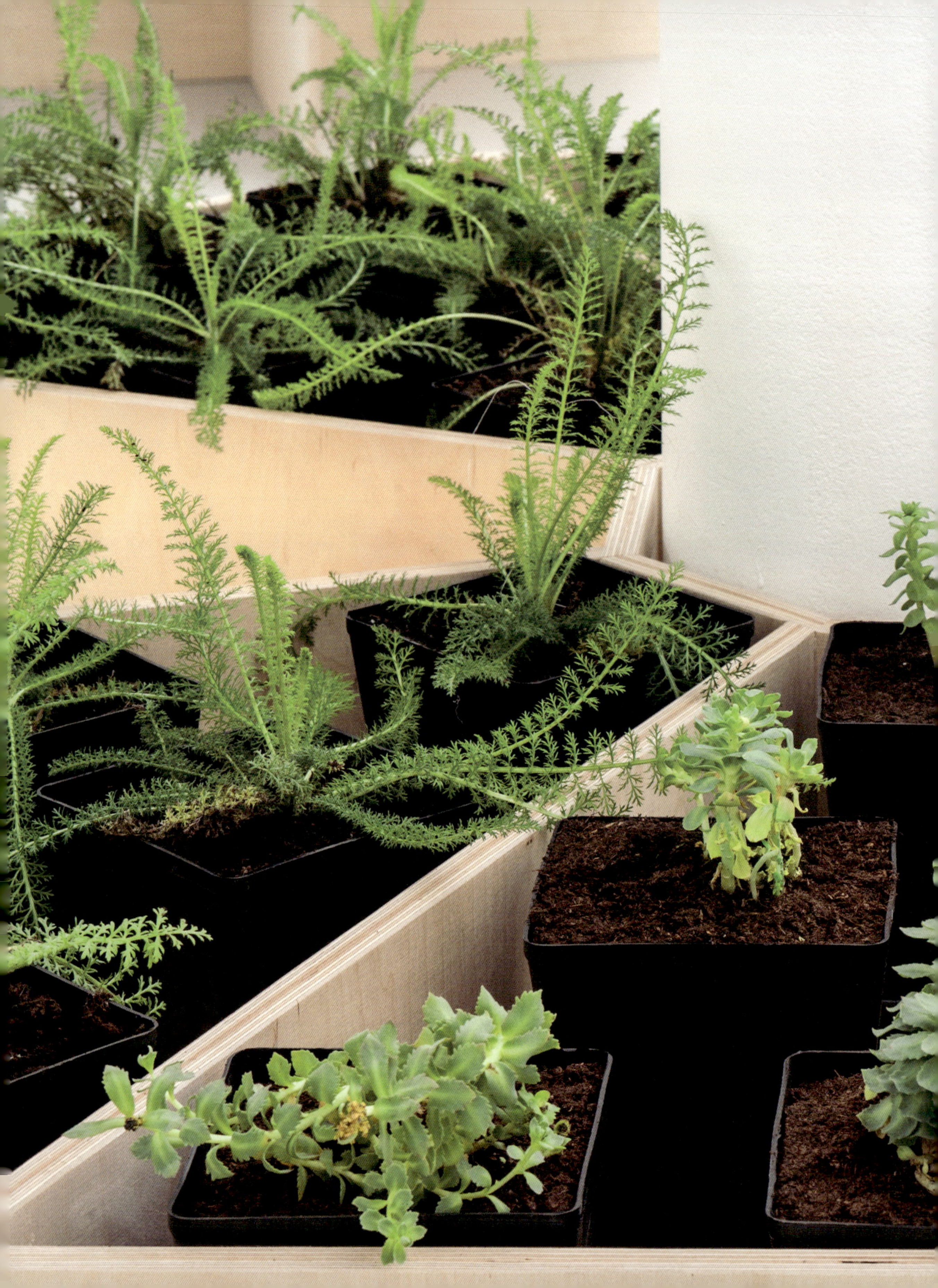

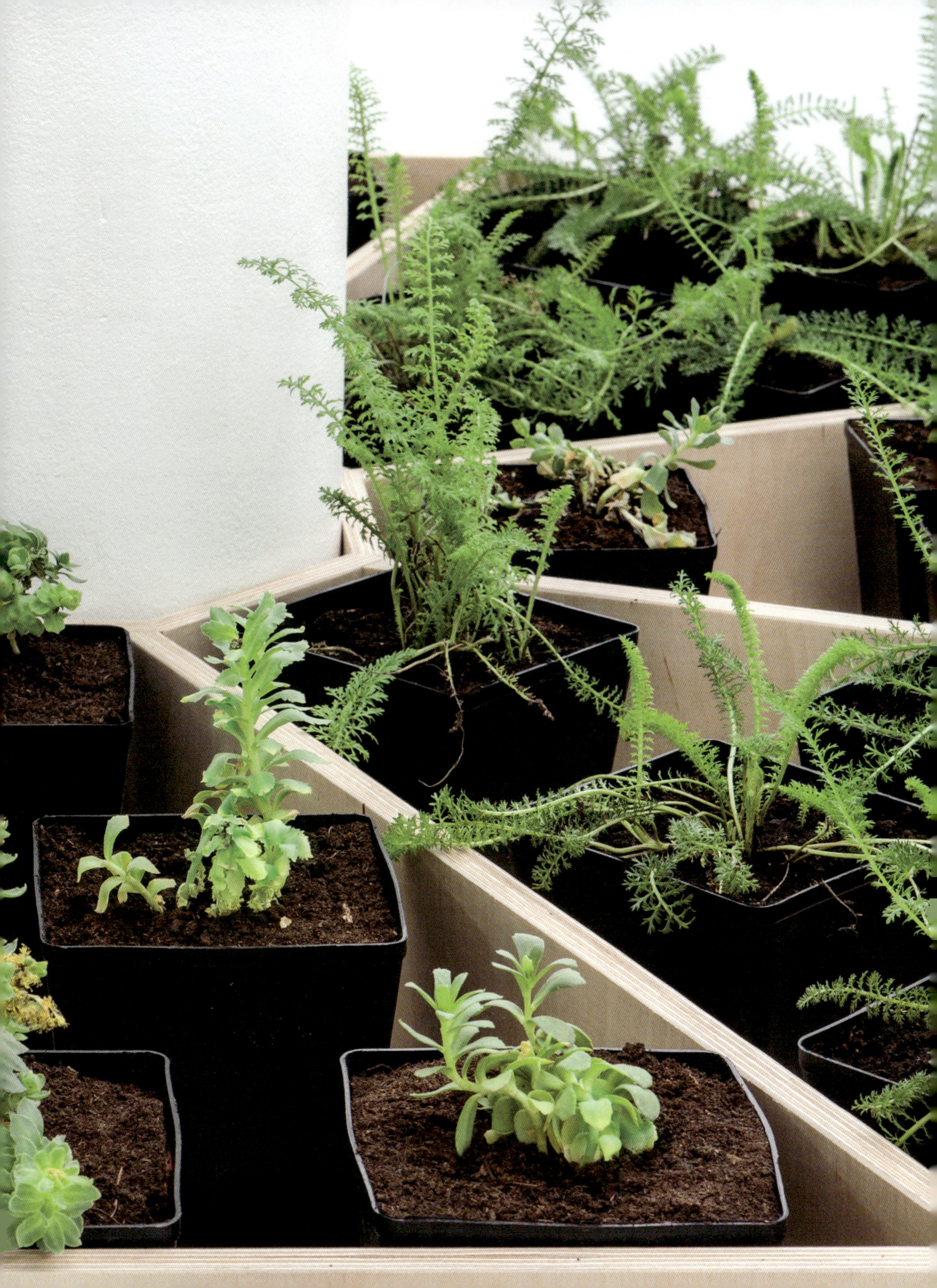

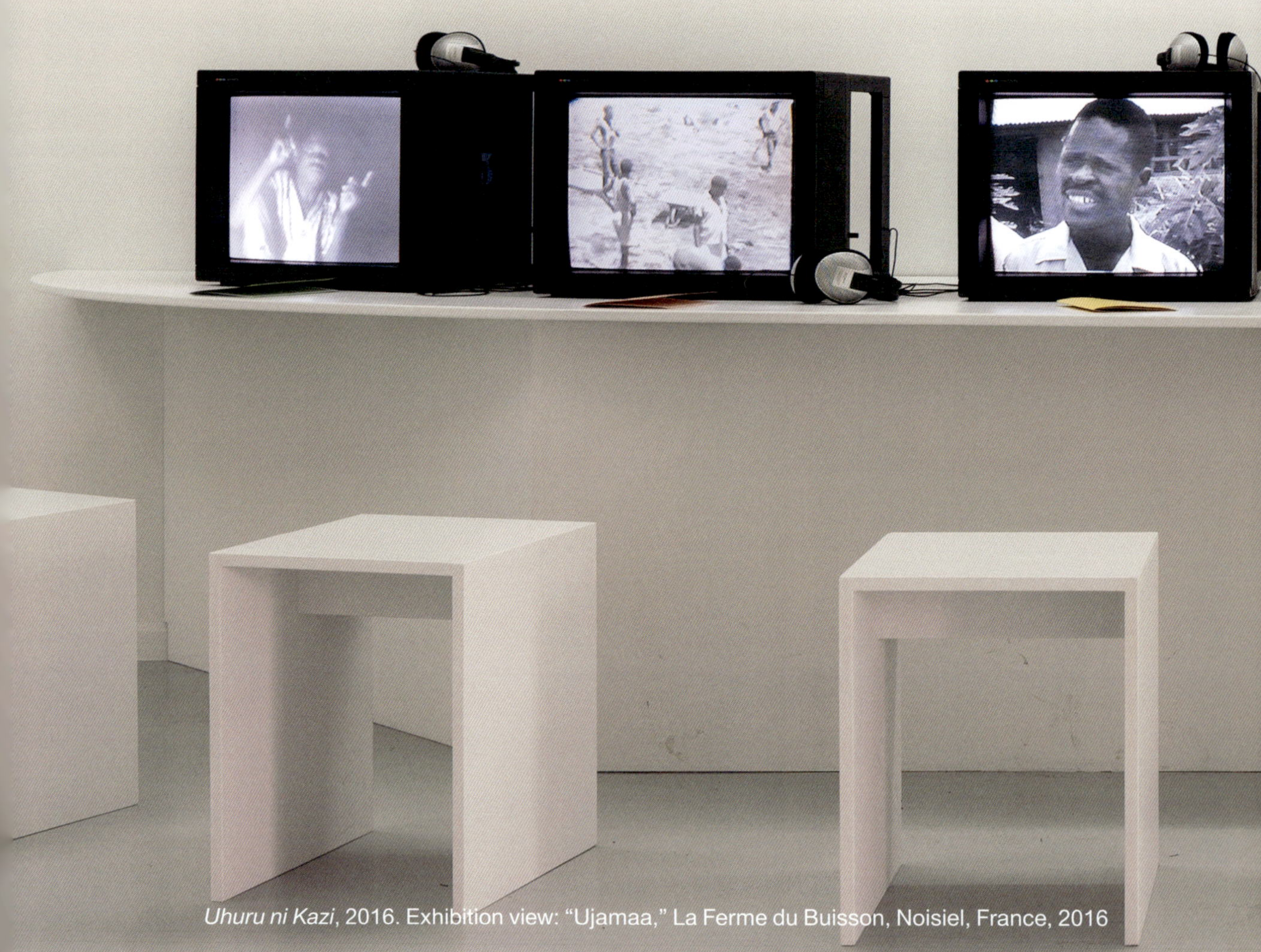

Uhuru ni Kazi, 2016. Exhibition view: “Ujamaa,” La Ferme du Buisson, Noisiel, France, 2016

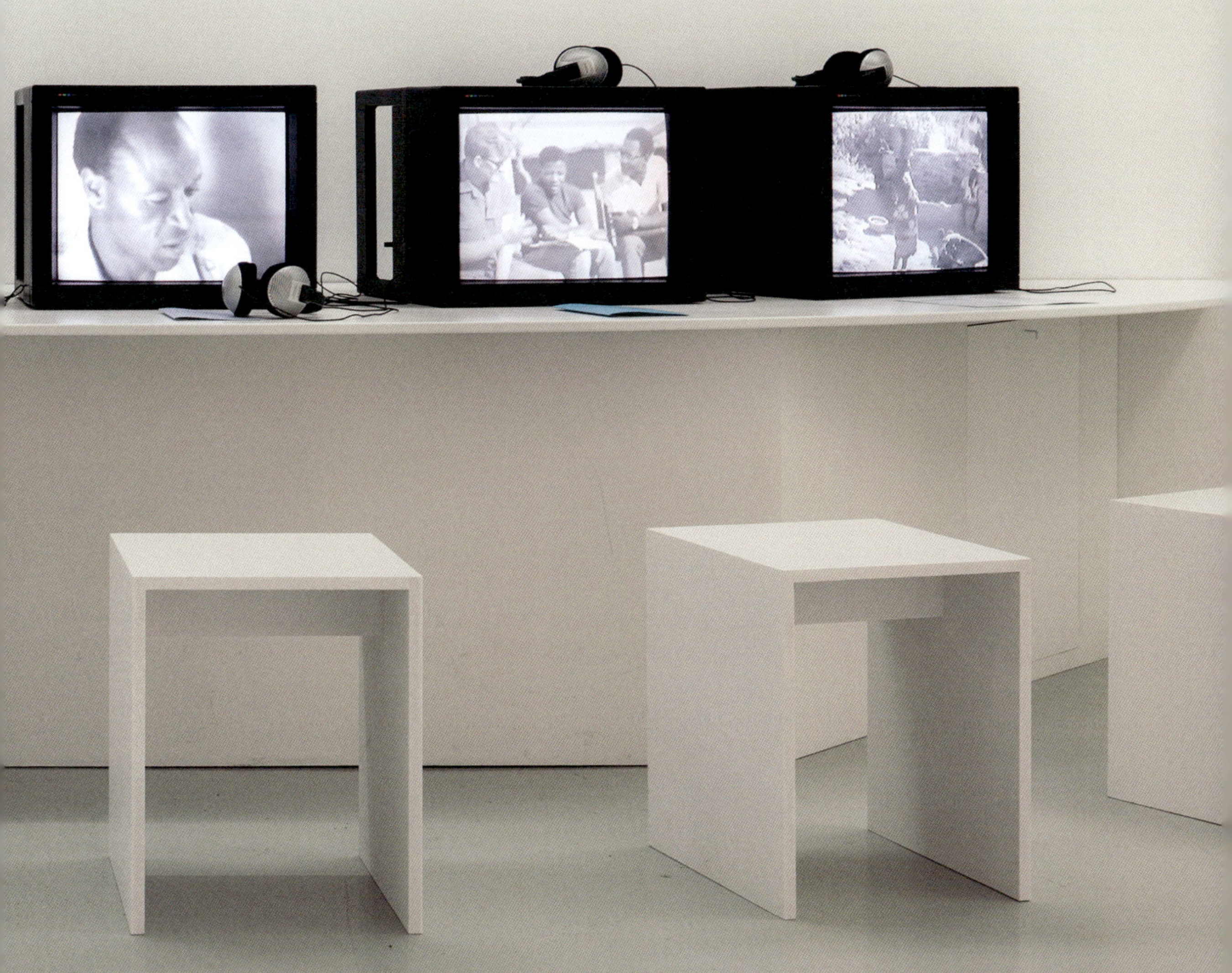
UHURU NI JASHO
UHURU NI KAZI
UHURU NI JASHO
UHURU NI JASHO
UHURU NI JASHO
UHURU NI KAZI
UHURU NI JASHO
UHURU NI KAZI
UHURU NI JASHO
UHURU NI KAZI
UHURU NI KAZI
UHURU NI JASHO
UHURU NI JASHO
UHURU NI KAZI
UHURU NI KAZI
UHURU NI JASHO
UHURU NI JASHO
UHURU NI KAZI
UHURU NI KAZI
UHURU NI JASHO
UHURU NI JASHO
UHURU NI KAZI
UHURU NI JASHO
UHURU NI JASHO
UHURU NI KAZI
UHURU NI KAZI
UHURU NI JASHO
UHURU NI KAZI
UHURU NI JASHO
UHURU NI KAZI
UHURU NI KAZI
UHURU NI JASHO
UHURU NI JASHO

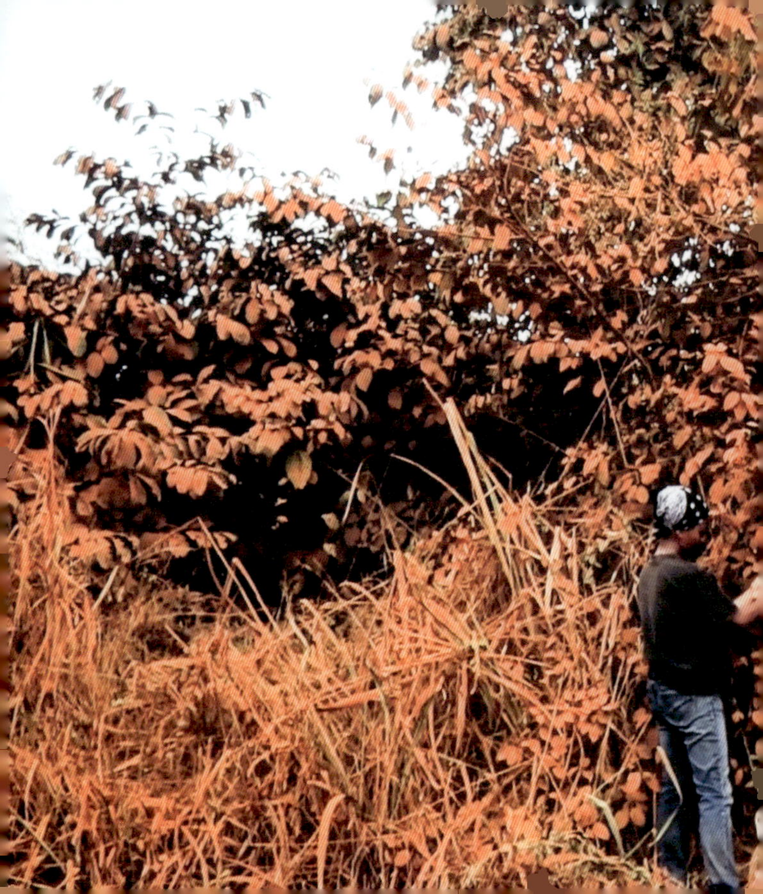

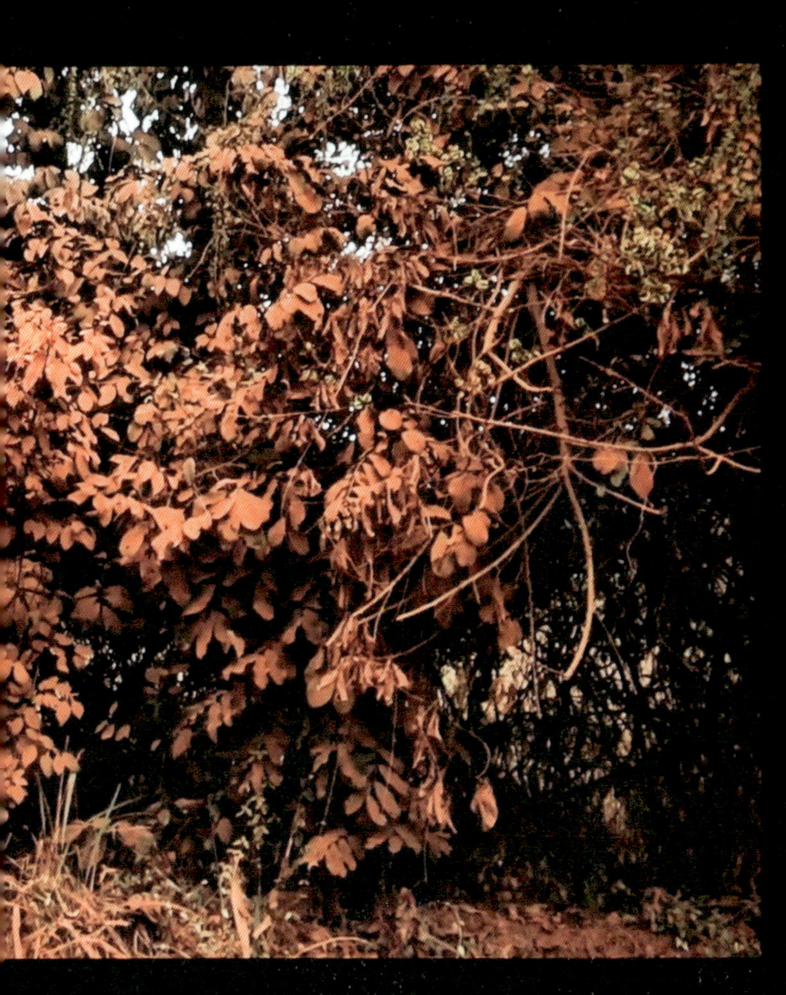

List of Illustrated Works

pp. 74–81
Flowers for Africa, 2012–ongoing
Protocol of assembly and display including archival iconography to guide the reconstruction of a floral arrangement consisting of cut flowers and/or foliage
Dimensions variable
Exhibition view: “Prélude,” La Mécanique Générale, LUMA Arles, France, 2021
Photos: Marc Domage

pp. 82–87
Maya-Bantu, 2019
Sisal fiber, steel
181 1⁄10 × 281 ½ × 133 9⁄10 in.
(460 × 715 × 340 cm)
Exhibition view: “The Sand Recalls the Moon’s Shadow,” Moody Center for the Arts, Houston, 2021
Photos: Nash Baker

pp. 88–97
Dune, 2021
Slumped glass lenses mounted on steel, silica sand, blown glass, plinth
Dimensions variable
Exhibition view: “The Sand Recalls the Moon’s Shadow,” Moody Center for the Arts, Houston, 2021
Photos: Nash Baker

pp. 98–101
Potomitans, 2021
Solid silver chains, handmade solid silver sculptures (*Mimosa pudica* flowers and leaves, *Phytolacca americana* flowers and leaves)
Dimensions variable
Exhibition view: Art Basel, Switzerland, 2021
Photos: Julien Deceroi

pp. 103; 110–11
Vivarium: Apomixis, 2020
PVC, steel, paint
116 1⁄10 × 93 7⁄10 × 118 1⁄10 in.
(295 × 238 × 300 cm)
Exhibition view: “Plot,” Haus der Kunst, Munich, 2020
Photos: Dominik Gigler

pp. 105; 112–13
Vivarium: Cytomixis, 2020
PVC, steel, paint
55 1⁄10 × 84 3⁄5 × 109 4⁄5 × 63 4⁄5 in.
(140 × 215 × 279 × 162 cm)
Exhibition view: “Plot,” Haus der Kunst, Munich, 2020
Photos: Dominik Gigler

pp. 106–09; 114–15
Landscape: Foreground, Middle ground, Background, 2020
Trevira fabric, paint
Dimensions variable
Exhibition view: “Plot,” Haus der Kunst, Munich, 2020
Photos: Dominik Gigler

pp. 117–19
The Marias, 2020
Paper flowers, shaped plinths, paint
Dimensions variable
Remai Modern. Purchased with the support of the Frank and Ellen Remai Foundation, 2021; Institut d’art contemporain, Villeurbanne, France; and Maja Hoffmann/Luma Foundation
Exhibition view: “An apology, a pill, a ritual, a resistance,” Remai Modern, Saskatoon, Canada, 2021
Photos: Blaine Campbell

pp. 121–23
Seed bank, 2020
Wool weave, glazed ceramics
98 ⅖ × 49 ⅕ in. (250 × 125 cm)
Exhibition view: "Kapwani Kiwanga: New Work," Kunstinstituut Melly, Rotterdam, 2020
Photo: Kristien Daem

pp. 125–27
Repository, 2020
Weaving, glass
98 ⅖ × 70 9⁄10 in. (250 × 180 cm)
Exhibition view: "Nine Lives," The Renaissance Society at the University of Chicago, 2020
Photo: Useful Art Services

p. 128
Counter-Illumination #1, 2020
Inkjet print on Hahnemühle paper photo, diasec, oak frame
32 7⁄10 × 48 ⅖ × 1 ⅗ in.
(83 × 123 × 4 cm)
Collection Deutsche Bank; TD Bank Corporate Art

p. 129
Counter-Illumination #2, 2020
Inkjet print on Hahnemühle paper photo, diasec, oak frame
32 7⁄10 × 48 ⅖ × 1 ⅗ in.
(83 × 123 × 4 cm)
Collection Deutsche Bank; TD Bank Corporate Art

pp. 130–31
Counter-Ilumination #1, 2020
Installation view: BC Hydro Dal Grauer Substation for Capture Photography Festival, Vancouver, 2020
Photo: Rachel Topham

p. 133
Glow #1, 2019
Wood, stucco, acrylic, steel, LEDs
59 1⁄10 × 31 ½ × 12 ⅖ in.
(150 × 80 × 31.5 cm)
Photo: Peter Harris Studio

p. 134
Glow #2, 2019
Wood, stucco, acrylic, steel, LEDs
59 1⁄10 × 23 ⅗ × 12 ⅖ in.
(150 × 60 × 20 cm)
Photo: Peter Harris Studio

p. 135
Glow #3, 2019
Wood, stucco, acrylic, steel, LEDs
70 1⁄10 × 39 ⅖ × 9 ⅖ in.
(178 × 100 × 25 cm)
Photo: Peter Harris Studio

p. 137
Glow #4, 2019
Wood, stucco, acrylic, steel, LEDs
59 1⁄10 × 39 ⅖ × 7 9⁄10 in.
(150 × 100 × 20 cm)
Private collection
Photo: Peter Harris Studio

p. 138
Glow #8, 2019
Quartzite stone, LEDs, Plexiglas
70 9⁄10 × 27 ⅗ × 4 7⁄10 in.
(180 × 70 × 12 cm)
Photo: Matthew Bradley

p. 139
Glow #9, 2019
Labradorite stone, LEDs, Plexiglas
70 9⁄10 × 62 9⁄10 × 11 ⅘ in.
(180 × 60 × 30 cm)
Photo: Matthew Bradley

pp. 140–41
Glow, 2019
Installation view: Frieze London, 2019

pp. 142–43
Oriental Studies: Frauen, 2019
Steel, dyed Egyptian cotton, wood, paint
63 ⅕ × 68 9⁄10 × 72 ⅘ in.
(160.5 × 175 × 185 cm)
Exhibition view: "Demonstration Rooms," Albertinum, Dresden, 2019
Photo: Klemens Renner

pp. 144–45
Oriental Studies: Morgen, 2019
Steel, dyed Egyptian cotton, Plexiglas, LEDs
63 1/5 × 64 3/5 × 64 3/5 in.
(160.5 × 164 × 164 cm)
On permanent loan to the Albertinum, Dresden by Gesellschaft für Moderne Kunst, Dresden
Exhibition view: "Demonstration Rooms," Albertinum, Dresden, 2019
Photo: Klemens Renner

pp. 146–47
Exhibition view: "Demonstration Rooms," Albertinum, Dresden, 2019
Photo: Klemens Renner

pp. 148–51
Kapwani Kiwanga with Adjaye Associates
Sankofa Pavilion, 2019
Dichroic and toughened glass, metal, acoustic fabric, wood
78 7/10 × 149 3/5 × 149 3/5 in.
(200 × 380 × 380 cm)
Exhibition view: "Is This Tomorrow?," Whitechapel Gallery, London, 2019
Photos: Stephen White

pp. 152–59
Exhibition view: "Safe Passage," MIT List Visual Arts Center, Cambridge, MA, 2019
Photos: Peter Harris Studio

pp. 160–63
Patchwork, 2018
Drywall, paint, wood, glass
Dimensions variable
Exhibition view: Sobey Art Award Exhibition, National Gallery of Canada, Ottawa, 2018
Photos: NGC

pp. 164–65
A Primer, 2017
Video, color; 7:43 min.
RBC Art Collection
Exhibition view: Sobey Art Award Exhibition, National Gallery of Canada, Ottawa, 2018
Photo: NGC

pp. 166–67
Jalousie, 2018
Steel, two-way mirror
86 3/5 × 126 × 3 9/10 in.
(220 × 320 × 10 cm)
Collection Musée d'art contemporain de Montréal; Private collection, Lyon
Exhibition view: "Surface Tensions," Galerie Poggi, Paris, 2018

pp. 169–71
Three Shades, 2018
Steel, wood, shade cloth, epoxy paint
82 7/10 × 47 1/5 × 15 7/10 in.
(210 × 120 × 40 cm)
Collection Maribel Unanue

pp. 172–73
Exhibition view: "Surface Tensions," Galerie Poggi, Paris, 2018

pp. 174–83
Positive-Negative (morphology), 2018
Protocol, soil from hole dug outside of the museum
11 4/5 × 19 7/10 × 181 1/10 in.
(30 × 50 × 460 cm)
Exhibition view: "Sunlight by Fireside: The Ash Annals," Musée d'art de Joliette, 2018
Photos: Romain Guilbault

p. 185
Black and Blue (Spine), 2018
Steel, wood, shade cloth, epoxy paint
56 3/10 × 28 3/10 × 11 4/5 in.
(143 × 72 × 30 cm)
Private collection

pp. 186–87
Hazy (Blue), 2018
Shade cloth, wood, fluorescent light, paint
12 1⁄5 × 52 × 8 3⁄10 in. (31 × 132 × 21 cm)
Photo: Charlie Kitchen

p. 189
TRI (magenta, black and red), 2019
Shade cloth, wood, fluorescent light, paint
70 9⁄10 × 43 3⁄10 × 15 7⁄10 in.
(180 × 110 × 40 cm)
Collection Poggi
Photo: Stefan Rohner

pp. 190–93
Shady, 2018
Steel, wood, shade cloth, epoxy paint
157 1⁄2 × 318 9⁄10 × 161 2⁄5 in.
(400 × 810 × 410 cm)
Installation view: Frieze New York, 2018
Photo: Mark Blower

pp. 194–95
pink-blue, 2017
Baker-Miller Pink paint, white paint, white fluorescent lights, blue fluorescent lights
Dimensions variable
Giverny Capital Collection, Montreal
Exhibition view: "A wall is just a wall," The Power Plant, Toronto, 2017
Photos: Toni Hafkenscheid

pp. 196–99
Exhibition view: "The sum and its parts," Reva and David Logan Center for the Arts, University of Chicago, 2017
Photos: RCH-EKH

pp. 200–03
White Gold: Morogoro, 2016
Sisal fiber, metal bars, wire rope
157 1⁄2 × 196 9⁄10 × 236 1⁄5 in.
(400 × 500 × 600 cm)
Collection Centre national des arts plastiques, Paris
Exhibition view: "Ujamaa," La Ferme du Buisson, Noisiel, France, 2016
Photos: Emile Ouroumov

pp. 204–07
Nursery, 2016
Plants, wood, oral transmissions
Dimensions variable
Exhibition view: "Ujamaa," La Ferme du Buisson, Noisiel, France, 2016
Photos: Emile Ouroumov

pp. 208–09
Uhuru ni Kazi, 2016
Six films by Gerald Belkin, black and white, sound; six translation booklets
Dimensions variable
Exhibition view: "Ujamaa," La Ferme du Buisson, Noisiel, France, 2016
Photo: Emile Ouroumov
Courtesy the artist. Films courtesy Belkin Estate

pp. 210–11
Vumbi, 2012
Video, color, sound; 31 min.
Collection Frac Provence-Alpes-Côte d'Azur; The Wedge; Private collection
Exhibition view: "Ujamaa," La Ferme du Buisson, Noisiel, France, 2016
Photo: Emile Ouroumov

About the Artist

Kapwani Kiwanga (b. 1978, Hamilton, Canada) is a Franco-Canadian artist living and working in Paris. Kiwanga studied anthropology and comparative religion at McGill University in Montreal and art at L'école des Beaux-Arts de Paris. She is the winner of the 2022 Zurich Art Prize, 2020 Marcel Duchamp Prize, 2018 Sobey Art Award, and 2018 Frieze Award. Kiwanga has had solo exhibitions at the Moody Center for the Arts, Rice University, Houston, TX (2021); Haus der Kunst, Munich, Germany (2020); Kunstinstituut Melly, Rotterdam, Netherlands (2020); Albertinum, Dresden, Germany (2020); MIT List Visual Arts Center, Cambridge, MA (2019); Esker Foundation, Calgary, Canada (2018); Artpace, San Antonio, TX (2018); Tramway, Glasgow, UK (2018); The Power Plant, Toronto, Canada (2017); Logan Center for the Arts, Chicago, IL (2017); South London Gallery, UK (2015); and Jeu de Paume, Paris, France (2014); among others. Her work was included in the 59th Venice Biennale (2022). Kiwanga's work has also been featured in numerous group exhibitions at institutions including the Museum of Contemporary Art Tokyo, Japan (2020); Museum für Moderne Kunst, Frankfurt, Germany (2020); Museum of African Contemporary Art Al Maaden, Marrakech, Morocco (2020); Whitechapel Gallery, London, UK (2019); Serpentine Galleries, London, UK (2019); MACBA, Barcelona, Spain (2019); Yuz Museum, Shanghai, China (2018); National Gallery of Canada, Ottawa (2018); Contemporary Arts Museum Houston, TX (2018); Hammer Museum, Los Angeles, CA (2018); and Centre Pompidou, Paris, France (2017).

Board of Trustees

Photography Credits

Except:

Courtesy the artist; Galerie Poggi, Paris; Goodman Gallery, Johannesburg, Cape Town, London; and Galerie Tanja Wagner, Berlin. Photo: Andy Keate: p. 16

Courtesy the artist; Galerie Poggi, Paris; Goodman Gallery, Johannesburg, Cape Town, London; and Galerie Tanja Wagner, Berlin. Photo: Mick Bello: p. 20

Courtesy PhotoStock-Israel / Alamy Stock Photo: p. 32

Courtesy the artist and Galerie Poggi, Paris: pp. 32, 98–101, 125–29, 133–37, 166–73, 185, 189

Courtesy the artist; Galerie Poggi, Paris; Goodman Gallery, Johannesburg, Cape Town, London; and Galerie Tanja Wagner, Berlin. Photo: Emile Ouroumov: p. 45

Courtesy Robin Rhode and Lehmann Maupin, New York, Hong Kong, Seoul, London: p. 62

Courtesy the artist and Goodman Gallery, Johannesburg, Cape Town, London: pp. 82–97, 138–39, 148–51, 186–87, 190–93

Courtesy the artist and Galerie Tanja Wagner, Berlin: pp. 103–15, 121–23, 140–47

Courtesy the artist and Galerie Karima Célestin, Marseille; Galerie Poggi, Paris; Goodman Gallery, Johannesburg, Cape Town, London; and Galerie Tanja Wagner, Berlin: pp. 210–11

Published by
New Museum
235 Bowery
New York, NY 10002

On the occasion of the exhibition
"Kapwani Kiwanga: Off-Grid"
June 30–October 16, 2022

Curators: Massimiliano Gioni, *Edlis Neeson Artistic Director*, and Madeline Weisburg, Curatorial Assistant

Contributors:
Glenn Adamson
Simone Browne
Massimiliano Gioni
Rashid Johnson
Kathleen Ritter
Yesomi Umolu
Madeline Weisburg

Copy Editor: Sarah Stephenson
Design Template: An Art Service
Design Production: Nicholas Weltyk
Printing: SPC, Poland

Front cover: Kapwani Kiwanga, *Vivarium: Apomixis,* 2020. PVC, steel, paint; 116 1⁄10 × 93 7⁄10 × 118 1⁄10 in (295 × 238 × 300 cm). Exhibition view: "Plot," Haus der Kunst, Munich, 2020. Photo: Dominik Gigler

Back cover: Kapwani Kiwanga, *Landscape: Foreground, Middle ground, Background,* 2020. Trevira fabric, paint; Dimensions variable. Exhibition view: "Plot," Haus der Kunst, Munich, 2020. Photo: Dominik Gigler

ISBN: 978-0-915557-99-8

This exhibition is part of a three-year initiative, launched in collaboration with Kvadrat, to premiere ambitious new productions by emerging artists.

kvadrat

Major support for this exhibition is provided by the International Leadership Council of the New Museum.

Support for this exhibition is provided by the Toby Devan Lewis Emerging Artists Exhibitions Fund.

Artist commissions are generously supported by the Neeson / Edlis Artist Commissions Fund.

Generous support is provided by:
Shelley Fox Aarons and Phil Aarons
Kaleta A. Doolin Foundation

Special thanks to the Artemis Council of the New Museum.

Thanks to Liza Mauer and Andrew Sheiner, and Nicoletta Fiorucci.

Education and community programs are supported, in part by the American Chai Trust.

Support for the publication has been provided by the J. McSweeney and G. Mills Publications Fund at the New Museum.

NEW MUSEUM